TRACING EXPRESSION IN MERLEAU-PONTY

Northwestern University
Studies in Phenomenology
and
Existential Philosophy

Founding Editor †James M. Edie

General Editor Anthony J. Steinbock

Associate Editor John McCumber

TRACING EXPRESSION IN MERLEAU-PONTY

Aesthetics, Philosophy of Biology, and Ontology

Véronique M. Fóti

Northwestern University Press
Evanston, Illinois

Northwestern University Press
www.nupress.northwestern.edu

Copyright © 2013 by Véronique M. Fóti. Published 2013 by Northwestern University Press. All rights reserved.

Printed in the United States of America

10 9 8 7 6 5 4 3 2 1

Library of Congress Cataloging-in-Publication Data

Fóti, Véronique Marion.
   Tracing expression in Merleau-Ponty: aesthetics, philosophy of biology, and ontology / Véronique M. Fóti.
      p. cm.—(Northwestern University studies in phenomenology and existential philosophy)
   Includes bibliographical references and index.
   ISBN 978-0-8101-2900-9 (pbk.: alk. paper)—ISBN 978-0-8101-2901-6 (cloth: alk. paper)
   1. Merleau-Ponty, Maurice, 1908–1961. 2. Expression (Philosophy) 3. Merleau-Ponty, Maurice, 1908–1961—Aesthetics. 4. Animals (Philosophy) 5. Ontology. I. Title. II. Series: Northwestern University studies in phenomenology & existential philosophy.
   B2430.M3764F68 2013
   194—dc23

                                                          2012036251

♾ The paper used in this publication meets the minimum requirements of the American National Standard for Information Sciences—Permanence of Paper for Printed Library Materials, ANSI Z39.48–1992.

This book is dedicated to the persons, or the memory, of my
treasured teachers in both art and philosophy.
Important among the former are Walter Roshardt and
Karl Schmid-Ambach, and among the latter, Jacques Taminiaux and
Hans-Georg Gadamer.

Contents

Acknowledgments

I owe special thanks to Deniz Durmus, currently a doctoral candidate in philosophy and women's studies here at Pennsylvania State University, who freely offered me any assistance I might need with the preparation of the manuscript of this book. Since its chapters were written, in the margins of teaching and other academic duties, over a span of three years, the notes needed to be collated, so as to achieve uniformity of citation and eliminate repetition. Deniz expertly accomplished this task; and she also provided proofreading and assistance with resolving some questions of biological identification or of correct citation. I deeply appreciate her generosity as well as her professionalism.

I also thank Dr. Michael Vicario for painstakingly proofreading several chapters of the manuscript and for checking my Spinoza citations, thus allowing me to benefit from his scholarly expertise with regard to the Spinozan texts and the secondary literature. Also, I am very grateful to David Agler, currently a doctoral candidate in philosophy here at Penn State, for electronically assembling the manuscript and making sure it conformed typographically with the requirements of the press. Finally, I thank Jessica Landis, who holds a B.A. in classics from Penn State and is planning on graduate study in philosophy, for helping with converting parts of the manuscript to the required font.

TRACING EXPRESSION IN MERLEAU-PONTY

Introduction

> But there is a "good ambiguity" in the phenomenon of expression, a spontaneity which accomplishes what appeared to be impossible when one observed only the separate elements, a spontaneity which gathers together the plurality of monads, the past and the present, nature and culture, into a single whole. To establish this wonder would be metaphysics and would at the same time give us the principle of an ethics.
> —Maurice Merleau-Ponty, "An Unpublished Text by Maurice Merleau-Ponty," translated by Arleen B. Dallery (1964)

In the "Prospectus of His Work" submitted to the Collège de France in 1952–53, on the occasion of his candidacy for the chair in philosophy, Merleau-Ponty outlines the guiding problems of his work from *The Structure of Behavior* of 1942 and *Phenomenology of Perception* of 1945 on to his future projects in what he then envisaged as *The Prose of the World* and *L'origine de la vérité* (The Origin of the Truth).[1] He characterizes his philosophical work as "studies on expression and truth" and explains that these studies epistemologically approach the general problem of human interrelations in a manner involving (through the study of language, including literary language) "the more general order of symbolic relations and of institutions."[2]

Claude Lefort, in his "Preface" to Merleau-Ponty's 1954–55 lecture courses at the Collège de France on institution and passivity,[3] argues that pursuing these themes led Merleau-Ponty to realize that his earlier effort to develop his analyses of perception into a philosophy of expression still left him beholden to a philosophy of consciousness. Therefore, Lefort argues, the problematic of institution superseded, for him, that of "the sensible world and the world of expression" which was still the focus of his early lecture courses at the Collège.[4] There is, however, no real evidence that Merleau-Ponty ever abandoned the problematic of expression, but rather, it remains prominent in *The Visible and the Invisible* and

3

in his dialogue with Leibniz in that text and in the first of the lecture courses on nature that span the years from 1956 to 1960.[5] Robert Vallier comments that Merleau-Ponty's return to the texts of the late Husserl and to the Husserlian notions of institution (*Stiftung*) and reinstitution (*Nachstiftung*) in the course on "Institution in Public and Private Life" is unsurprising, given that his still horizonal problematic of nature concerns, in his own words, "the primordial . . . that which carries us,"[6] and which thus, in the manner characteristic of institution, issues into a plethora of ever new expressions. Instead of his thought having undergone some sort of *Kehre*, its itinerary shows rather that the problematic of expression became enriched and deepened by his studies on institution and passivity, as well as by his engagement with the biological sciences, and that ultimately, as Renaud Barbaras puts it succinctly, his late ontological "turn" really stems from the phenomenology of expression.[7]

In the French Merleau-Ponty scholarship, it is indeed Barbaras who, in his important book, *The Being of the Phenomenon,* in which he presents a critical, developmental or teleological reading of Merleau-Ponty's oeuvre, highlights the central importance of expression. He argues that, in *Phenomenology of Perception,* and specifically in the chapter on "The Body as Expression and Speech," expression is not as yet understood at a level that would allow it to overcome the dualisms that Merleau-Ponty problematizes, such as nature and culture, appearance and reality, subject and object, as well as intellectualism and empiricism. As Barbaras explains:

> He does not genuinely conceive this body *as* expression, which would suppose that one consider the body *starting from* the phenomenon of expression, that is . . . by grasping speech as an originary phenomenon; what he is doing here is apprehending expression starting from the body conceived as the subject of natural behaviors.[8]

However, Barbaras acknowledges that ultimately, due to Merleau-Ponty's reworking of its problems in his ontologically oriented late thought, "the phenomenology of perception fulfills itself as a philosophy of expression." Barbaras explains further:

> All the axes of Merleau-Ponty's ontology appear to be really the fulfillment of a consistent philosophy of expression . . . the description of the perceived is overcome by the philosophy of expression [which], grasped in all of its implications, is fulfilled in an ontological enterprise.[9]

In the English-language scholarship on Merleau-Ponty, expression has remained largely neglected, with the exception of Lawrence Hass's book *Merleau-Ponty's Philosophy*.[10] Hass not only draws much needed attention to the importance of expression for Merleau-Ponty, but he also offers lucid and inspiring accounts of its role in the philosophy of mathematics and of language.

This book owes its genesis to my intensive reading and rereading, over some thirty years, of the Merleau-Pontyan texts, a practice of reading that has been further inspired and enhanced by the relatively recent publication of previously unavailable sources, such as the résumés of, notes for, and auditors' transcripts of his lecture courses. There emerged a growing sense that expression was not only a theme that meaningfully interlinked such disparate facets of Merleau-Ponty's thought as aesthetics, the philosophy of biology (especially zoology), and ontology, but also that it constituted for him a central problematic in its own right. Nonetheless, just as Merleau-Ponty points out, in "Eye and Mind," that color, for all its visual significance, does not offer a master key to the visible,[11] expression likewise cannot be considered a master key to Merleau-Ponty's thought. There is indeed no place for a master key in a philosophy that emphasizes irreducible multiplicity, difference, and ineluctable divergence or nonclosure (*écart*).

Since I share Barbaras's developmental perspective on Merleau-Ponty, the focus of this book is trained (with the sole exception of the first chapter, devoted to the 1945 essay "Cézanne's Doubt")[12] on Merleau-Ponty's later and late thought. This means, of course, that the textual basis consists to a large extent of fragmentary texts, working notes, or lecture notes and transcripts (indeed, working on the late Merleau-Ponty can sometimes feel like working on the pre-Socratics, not least also because his style conjoins intellectual clarity and precision with elusiveness and a poetic sensibility). The book is, as the title indicates, a trace-work, not only because of the givens of textual basis and style, but also because Merleau-Ponty himself struggles with the question of expression, and it becomes entangled with other guiding ideas (such as institution or the elemental nature of flesh). Sometimes it also becomes submerged in the treatment of complex scientific issues but, far from being relinquished, it approaches what, in terms favored by Martin Heidegger, one could call the essential unthought of Merleau-Ponty's thought. The reader should therefore not find it surprising that, in the studies that make up this book, expression is not always at the forefront, or in explicit and constant view, but may at times be at best traced out, to borrow one of Merleau-Ponty's favored metaphors, in filigree. To constrain it to remain in full and constant view would be analogous to the medieval practice of interpretation that twisted "the nose of wax," though not here with a view to the unity of *sacra doctrina*, but of a unity simplistically superimposed on complex texts. It would also approach the sort of "positivity" that Merleau-Ponty everywhere criticizes.

It is time then to give the reader a sense of what she or he can expect to find in these studies, beginning with Part 1, "Expression in Merleau-Ponty's Aesthetics." In the "Prospectus," Merleau-Ponty points to his essays "Cézanne's Doubt" and "Metaphysics and the Novel"[13] as having already touched upon his guiding concerns with truth and human interrelation, but as still being in need of an adequately developed philosophical foundation. Chapter 1, "Primordial Perception and Artistic Expression: Merleau-Ponty and Cézanne," retains the pairing of these two essays, but with a focus on freedom which, quite apart from its importance in the context of Merleau-Ponty's engagement with Sartrean existentialism, also helps to clarify the abrupt shift, in "Cézanne's Doubt," from Paul Cézanne to Leonardo da Vinci, as well as the concluding meditation on psychoanalysis. Art, as "an operation of expression," seems to be emblematic of human freedom; yet this claim is precarious, given that an artist's heightened sensitivity exposes her or him to the debilitating force of the traumas of life and of psycho-history. Merleau-Ponty resolves the problem by exploring the reciprocities between expressive creation and facticity, and by developing (as he did in the final chapter of *Phenomenology of Perception*)[14] a conception of freedom that leaves intact its bonds with the world. Beyond this concern with freedom, however, the chapter goes on to call into question his understanding of Cézanne's painterly work as a proto-phenomenological investigation of perception itself as primordial expression, arguing that Cézanne sought rather to realize a project of painterly expression that, in its quest for a "realization parallel to nature," was fundamentally autonomous.

Chapter 2, "Expression, Institution, and the Field: A Searching Itinerary," is devoted to Merleau-Ponty's 1952 essay "Indirect Language and the Voices of Silence," which constitutes both a part and a distillation of his abandoned book project *The Prose of the World*. Although he argues here that painting, like literature, is a labor of thought and that every human use of the body is expressive, he castigates abstract painting and finds no legitimate role for it in the painterly tradition already inaugurated, in his view, in prehistoric times. The chapter problematizes not only this exclusion (which connotes also an exclusion of the vast scope and diversity of contemporary visual art), but also his advocacy of a cross-cultural and trans-historical unity of art, or of a unity of "human style" that derives from the body's expressivity. It further questions the instituting power of works of art that may be purposely ephemeral, and finally Merleau-Ponty's subordination of "the mute forms of expression" to verbal expression in the literary arts. In conclusion, the chapter examines the interrelation between the aesthetic themes developed in the essay and the author's lecture courses on institution and passivity of 1954–55, focusing on the themes of natality, the seriality of institution, and the notion of a "field."[15]

Completing the aesthetics section, chapter 3, "Painterly and Phenomenological Interrogation in 'Eye and Mind,'" notes that the painter's body functions, for the late Merleau-Ponty, not so much as a matrix of expression than as the agent of a trans-substantiation, and as caught up in a lateral proliferation of reciprocities and "equivalences" or exchanges. If expression is in abeyance here, the reason appears to be that, in the context of thinking the invisible of the visible and developing an ontology of flesh, it will need to be rethought in a manner adequate to these guiding insights, and specifically as springing, not from the natural body, let alone from its natural behaviors, but from the body as a non-positive expressive matrix. Returning to his long-standing meditation on spatial depth and perspective construction in the visual arts, particularly in painting, Merleau-Ponty finds that the depth that painting continues to seek is not a third dimension, but rather the reversibility of dimensions (or "branches of being"), which also grants autonomy to visual and painterly registers such as color and line. Although the chapter is critical of Merleau-Ponty's failure to recognize modalities of painting that are genuinely auto-figurative, as well as of what Michel Haar calls his "nostalgia for the originary,"[16] it recognizes his articulation of new insights that transcend some of the difficulties encountered in the 1952 essay, as well as the thought of a radically differential "deflagration" of being, and finally a rethinking of absence or lack in a context of natality and fecundity rather than finitude.

Part 2, "Expression in Animal Life," focuses on the second of Merleau-Ponty's lecture courses on nature and on the scientific literature with which he engaged. Chapter 4, "The Expressivity of Animal Behavior: Embryogenesis and Environing Worlds," points out his key problem of understanding an organismic totality that remains, in its formation as well as its maturity, irreducible to its constituent parts and not thinkable in terms of an essence or telos. The chapter suggests that the relation between organismic totality and behaviors that are at one with morphological development is fundamentally expressive. Drawing on Saussurean linguistics, and thus on the diacritical emergence of meaning from signs, Merleau-Ponty works toward a differential, non-positive understanding of organismic totality as a dimension (or, as he often says of the human body, a *mesurant*) in terms of which the animal's environment meaningfully configures a world.

Engaging here with Jakob von Uexküll's research on the multiplicity of animal worlds (*Umwelten*),[17] Merleau-Ponty stresses that even the simplest such worlds (Uexküll worked chiefly with lowly invertebrates), and certainly the "worlds of encounter" (*Gegenwelten*) characteristic of higher animals, enable a genuine openness and flexible behavioral response to the environment that is not mechanical, but fundamentally expressive. His understanding of animal worlds contrasts sharply with Heidegger's (in a 1929–30 lecture course not published during Merleau-Ponty's lifetime).[18] For all of his praise of Uexküll, Heidegger interprets the animal world (in contrast to the *Umwelt* of *Dasein*) as an incarcerating ring (*Umring*) penetrated only by the specific stimuli that mechanically "disinhibit" drives. Merleau-Ponty, taking up Uexküll's musical metaphors, compares the animal world to a melody singing itself. He thus stresses its nonsequential temporality, the noncausal relations among its parts, and its character of an oneiric theme indissociable from its expressive realizations.

Chapter 5, "The Expressivity of Animal Appearance and of Directive and Instinctual Activities," begins by exploring Merleau-Ponty's engagement with Edward S. Russell's notion of "directive" activities,[19] whose finality is "blind" but normally efficacious, and which lead him not only to assimilate physiological processes to behavior in an internal milieu, but also to interpret them as "seeking to express . . . a structure of the whole." Mimicry, in contrast, is a behavior "in external circuit" that, along with animal appearance in general, cannot be exhaustively explained by a principle of utility but is, once again, understood more adequately as expressive. The chapter reflects that, in contrast to the traditional philosophical quest for univocal truth, an exuberant play of expressive, and often deceptive, appearances pervades natural life. In dialogue with Adolf Portmann (whose revised and expanded 1960 edition of *Die Tiergestalt* [Animal Form] he was, however, unable to familiarize himself with), Merleau-Ponty meditates on the intrinsic value of visual appearance, together with the fact that its refinement in animal life may not have any survival value, but may even, as Portmann notes, increase the animal's vulnerability. Portmann's challenging claim is that not only the vital organs, but also an animal's visual appearance are intricately prepared for in early embryonic development, and that finally there are prominent "unaddressed appearances," whose expressivity is entirely nonpurposive, in animal morphology and display. Since he discusses these unaddressed appearances only in the 1960 edition, Merleau-Ponty does not acknowledge them; yet they may in the end converge in some respects with his own reflections, in *The Visible and the Invisible,* on the invisibility integral to the visible and on an absolute invisibility "without an ontic mask."[20]

In conclusion, Merleau-Ponty takes up the work of Konrad Lorenz on the dissociation of instinctual activity from determinate objects or goals, focusing on its expressive value and its functioning as a matrix of symbolism.[21] The sexual relation, in particular, is ritualized and may exhibit the value of sheer monstration. Not surprisingly, these reflections lead Merleau-Ponty (though mostly in the third lecture course) to a critical engagement with Darwinian and neo-Darwinian evolutionary theory, in a search for "lateral" interrelations within nature, and between humanity and animality, in place of a model of sheer descendence. Merleau-Ponty's intensive and insightful work on nature, and specifically on the expressivity of animal life, is indispensable to the development of his late, positive ontology.

Although Merleau-Ponty carries on a philosophical dialogue with a range of thinkers, both historical and contemporary, it is his sustained dialogue with the major rationalists that deserves special attention in connection with expression, since they—in particular Baruch Spinoza and Gottfried Wilhelm Leibniz—developed a sophisticated metaphysics of expression. Merleau-Ponty's most prominent rationalist interlocutor, however, is René Descartes, who institutes an understanding of nature (indissociable as such from an ontology) and of life that have been fateful not only for Western philosophy but also for the life sciences, and which Merleau-Ponty seeks to deconstruct. Lawrence Hass also calls attention to the problematic Cartesian legacy, in philosophy and cognitive science, of an understanding of perception as mental representation.[22] Descartes's metaphysics is creationist rather than expressive; and his delimitation of finite reason over against the infinite and incomprehensible divine creative intellect allows him to leave certain tensions between philosophy and actual experience unresolved. Merleau-Ponty tends, however, to view these delimitations (such as Descartes's acknowledged inability to give a rational account of human embodiment) in a positive light, as indicators of the readiness of "classical science" to leave intact a sense of ontological enigma.

Part 3 deals with "Expression in Merleau-Ponty's Ontology." The first chapter of that section, Chapter 6, "The Role of Expression in Merleau-Ponty's Dialogue with the Rationalists," calls into question his rather cursory critique of Spinoza as a thinker whose notion of infinity and whose ontology remain "positive." Although he is appreciative of Spinoza's thought of the infinite "unknown attributes" of God or Nature, he does not explore Spinoza's understanding of these attributes as expressive orders of manifestation that are also infinite in kind, and thus incapable of any totalizing or "positive" presentation. Furthermore, it is surprising that he neglects Spinoza's understanding of the human mind as the complex idea of the human body, together with its implications for rethinking human embodiment, and finally also Spinoza's recognition of universal sentience.

Although Merleau-Ponty dissociates his own thought of expression from the Leibnizian *géométral*, as a system that anchors monadic expression in divine creative transcendence and treats the monadic substances as "windowless" and thus incapable of genuine openness to the world, one must, as Barbaras states, "think about the world of Merleau-Ponty in the image of the Leibnizian universe."[23] Merleau-Ponty, Barbaras thinks, came to realize the closeness of his own ontology to Leibniz's late metaphysics of expression in the very process of developing it. Chapter 6 calls attention, however, to his surprising neglect of the difficult question of embodiment in Leibniz's late thought, together with the philosopher's rejection of the reality of both discarnate minds and nonsentient biological life. The importance, in the history of ideas, of these facets of Leibniz's thought for the "new biology" of the mid-twentieth century still remains to be explored.

The seventh and final chapter, "The Irreducibility of Expression: Merleau-Ponty's Ontology and Its Wider Implications," takes up his understanding of language and of perception as "a language before language."[24] Language carries forward the expressivity of perception and the symbolic articulation of the life world in the unbroken manner of a "surpassing in place," and as bringing about an intertwining or *Verflechtung* (a Husserlian term that Merleau-Ponty favors) of human being, world, and language itself. This intertwining is carried forward into further registers of expression, including the artistic and intellectual.

Philosophy for its part must engage in a vigilant and self-problematizing "hyper-reflection," so as to guard against obliterating the thread of "silence" that sustains its effort to bring "mute experience" to the expression of its own meaning. As a work of linguistic creation (Merleau-Ponty treats it as akin, in this respect, to literature), it must nonetheless realize that the expressive voice that realizes linguistic creation is not wholly one's own, but is also, and more fundamentally, "the voice of no-one, being the very voice of things, of the waves and the forests."[25] This thought leads on to Merleau-Ponty's late ontological notion of flesh as elemental, as an anonymity inherent within the self, and as shown forth in the multiple expressive styles of natural beings. The chapter suggests that these styles are fully and genuinely apprehensible only in the elusive manner of what Merleau-Ponty calls the carnal essences, idealities that remain indissociable from their sensuous presencing and thus bridge the divide between idea and flesh.

Flesh, however, also exhibits defining structural features, such as nondivision and reversibility, marked everywhere by an irreducible nonclosure or divergence (*écart*). Reversibility cannot therefore be interpreted as a symmetry that would exclude alterity. To the contrary, Merleau-Ponty shows himself to be a thinker of the key twentieth-century problematic of difference which is, for him, indissociable from expressivity. Within the ontology of flesh, relations have priority over their relata, rather than presupposing them as positive entities, and similarly visibility or tangibility do not ultimately derive from factual bodies or the factual world but are "more real" than these, thus undercutting binary metaphysical schemata. The Merleau-Pontyan chiasm is a figure of diacritical cohesion by divergence, emblematic of the originary expressivity of flesh. The expressive polymorphism of flesh leaves no metaphysical residue of positive identity. Divested of such residues, it gives rise to the pervasive intercrossings of nature, carnality, sensuousness, and ideality.

The path of this inquiry into Merleau-Ponty's thought of expression, moving from aesthetics to the philosophy of biology and on to ontology, thus describes a circle (which is not without its own moment of *écart*), in that being, to be experienced and apprehended in its expressive manifestations, requires to be creatively (and thus expressively) bodied forth. The multiple styles of natural being that come to presence in the manner of carnal essences must in their turn be figured forth by artistic, intellectual, or other expressive creations to be meaningfully apprehended, and for such apprehension to be communicated. Expression, nonetheless, is not introduced into nature by humans, nor even by animal life, but is primordial, having always already begun anonymously. If natural being is expressive through and through, there is, as Merleau-Ponty remarks in a late working note, "no absolutely pure philosophical word."[26] Philosophy, as an intellectual creation invested in language, is responsive to and expressive of "wild being" as well as of cultural life. It seeks to achieve a noncoincident adequation to the ontological irreducibility of expression which does not, however, leave it either a mere fabrication nor self-contained and without ethical relevance. The possible relevance of Merleau-Ponty's philosophy of expression in the context of environmental ethics and environmental aesthetics will be explored, if only in a preliminary manner that may point out some pathways for future work, in "Concluding Thoughts."

Part 1

Expression in Merleau-Ponty's Aesthetics

Primordial Perception and Artistic Expression: Merleau-Ponty and Cézanne

> Now, old as I am . . . the color sensations which create light in my paintings, create abstractions that keep me from covering my canvas or defining the edges of objects where they delicately touch other objects, with the result that my image or picture is incomplete.
>
> —Paul Cézanne to Émile Bernard, October 23, 1905 (Letter 8)

Although Merleau-Ponty's remarks on Cézanne's painting in the chapter "The Thing and the Natural World" in *Phenomenology of Perception* are of a piece with his discussion of the painter in the contemporaneous essay "Cézanne's Doubt,"[1] the first of his three essays on aesthetics, and particularly on painting, the context of his discussion of Cézanne in the *Phenomenology* is not primarily aesthetic. It is rather that of a reflection on the intersensory unity of the thing in its "absolute reality" which, Merleau-Ponty argues, is not the unity of an indefinite substrate of qualities (nor yet that of a system transparent to the intellect which he characterizes by the Spinozan notion of *facies totius universi*).[2] The unity is rather that of a "unique accent" or "manner of existing" (what he will later call a style), of which the thing's supposed qualities function as the "secondary expression."[3] Merleau-Ponty hears an echo of this insight in Cézanne's reported remarks that a painting of a landscape must contain in its visual configuration all of the landscape's sensory aspects, even its odor, or that any mark of color in a painting must contain the light, the air, and in short the entire, enveloping presence of what is offered to sense.[4] The thing, by virtue of its unity of style, realizes "in advance of the Other . . . this miracle of expression: an interior which reveals itself on the outside."[5] What enables it to do so is the body's "dialogue" or lived, interrogative engagement with it that makes possible the accomplishment of perception as primordial expression. Cézanne, Merleau-Ponty reflects, failed to recognize this in his youth, when he pursued dramatic expression first of all and as such, learning only gradually that "expression is the language of the thing itself,"[6] the language articulated by its sensory aspects which are ultimately indissociable, so that "the better the color harmonizes, the clearer the drawing becomes."[7]

In this achievement of clarity, the thing, however, does not relinquish its alterity or enigmatic self-containment; it remains "a resolutely silent Other," and is "for our existence less a pole of attraction than a pole of repulsion."[8] The painter's vision solicits and enters into this very alterity (whereas ordinary vision contents itself with recognition, or with an appreciation or aversion that conceals alterity). To accomplish perception as primordial expression requires that one "open oneself to an absolute Other that he prepares for from out of what is deepest within himself."[9] In "The Thing and the Natural World," Merleau-Ponty seeks the key to understanding this birth of expression from out of alterity in temporality, noting that thing and world are "lived" by the perceiver in an enchainment of perspectives but transcend all perspectives "because the enchainment is temporal and not achieved."[10]

This key, nonetheless, fails to grant access to the enigma of the expressive advent of sense since, as Renaud Barbaras observes, Merleau-Ponty, in the *Phenomenology,* remains focused on "the subject of the movement of transcendence" (thematized as "existence"), rather than addressing "the very advent of sense."[11] In this context, moreover, Cézanne is approached mostly through his reported sayings, rather than through his painterly work (which, surprisingly, Merleau-Ponty leaves out of account even in discussing illumination and the modulations of color). When he takes up, for instance, "the brilliant green of a vase by Cézanne," whose chromatic modulations fully present, and not merely evoke, the glazed ceramic, he draws from this observation no more than an affirmation of "the co-existence of profiles across space and time."[12] The phenomenological import of Cézanne's art will have to be explored more concretely and at a deeper level; and Merleau-Ponty turns to this task in "Cézanne's Doubt."

In "Cézanne's Doubt," however, Merleau-Ponty also addresses the further issue of the nature of freedom, to which the final chapter of *Phenomenology of Perception* is devoted.[13] It is this issue which explains the essay's otherwise puzzling transition from a reflection on Cézanne's painting and person to a discussion of Leonardo da Vinci which largely ignores that painter's art. In *Sense and Non-Sense,* Merleau-Ponty groups the essay with another contemporaneous essay, "Metaphysics and the Novel," which takes up the existentialist understanding of freedom through an appreciative discussion of Simone de Beauvoir's novel *L'invitée* (*She Came to Stay*).[14] The issue of freedom remains important as well in the immediately following essay, "A Scandalous Author," which dates from 1947 and addresses the critical reception of Sartre's literary work.[15]

In "Metaphysics and the Novel," Merleau-Ponty reflects that phenomenological and existentialist philosophy seeks to formulate "a contact with the world that precedes any thought about the world," and that, for this reason, philosophical and literary modes of writing can no longer be separated:

> When it is a matter of making the experience of the world speak philosophical expression takes on the same ambiguities as literary expression, if the world is made such that it could not be expressed otherwise than in "stories" and shown, as it were, by being pointed to.[16]

Beauvoir's character Françoise has largely succeeded in sublimating the experience of the Other's alterity and thus in refusing to recognize any limits to her own freedom as a pure consciousness or bestower of meaning, given that her relationship with Pierre has fostered the illusion of unreserved communication with no residue of opacity. When Xavière's entrance into the relationship destroys that illusion and traumatically shatters all of Françoise's existential assurances, she realizes that, since actions do not admit of any single motive or explanation but are (in Freud's term that Merleau-Ponty quotes) "overdetermined," the meaning that her own actions have in Xavière's eyes eludes her control and repudiates her denial.[17] The authentic realization of human freedom, Merleau-Ponty concludes, consists in "actively being what we are by chance, in establishing that communication with others and with ourselves for which our temporal structure offers us the opportunity and of which our freedom is merely the sketch."[18]

It seems, however, that this realization may become problematic in the case of the artist. Is his or her creative freedom not often curtailed by the vicissitudes of life, visited upon a heightened sensibility, even if the traumas and psycho-history lived through may partly inform and shape the work? If artistic expression cannot be regarded as emblematic of human freedom, does not freedom as such become questionable, which would mean that expression which, at every level, presupposes a certain freedom, cannot maintain its preeminence?

Merleau-Ponty addresses this issue by turning to Cézanne, notwithstanding the challenge posed by the fact that his painterly project still remains in some respects enigmatic, and that his personal reclusiveness had already rendered him an almost mythic figure in his own time. Merleau-Ponty's diagnosis of Cézanne's "schizothymia" (in respect to which he compares him to El Greco) is perhaps almost as questionable as the suggestion he puts forward that his devotion to painting from nature, together with "the inhuman character of his paintings," might be considered a pathological alienation of his humanity.[19] Merleau-Ponty is, to be sure, arguing dialogically here, as is his custom, and he goes on to acknowledge that Cézanne looked at nature "as only a human being can."[20] Two factors that nonetheless render his analysis questionable are, first, the fact that Cézanne's turn to the painstaking study of nature owed an incalculable debt (which he remained ready to acknowledge) to his close working association, in the 1870s and in 1881, with Camille Pissarro—an association that Merleau-Ponty, who mentions Pissarro only in passing,[21] fails to take into account. Second, he also neglects Cézanne's sustained and almost obsessive preoccupation with an image (explored in over two hundred paintings) that owed little to nature, and almost everything to imagination, namely that of nude bathers (sometimes male, more often female) in a landscape. Merleau-Ponty's failure to consider this central theme in Cézanne's painting is especially troubling in that his characterization of Leonardo da Vinci (which is based on Paul Valéry)[22] also deprives this artist of any haunting image, whereas a student of Leonardo's drawings can hardly fail to notice the prominence of images of the deluge or of tempests, ranging from the meteorological to the metaphorical, such as *The Deluge of Material Possessions*.

If Valéry characterized Leonardo as, in Merleau-Ponty's citation, "a monster of pure freedom,"[23] seemingly without strong passions, personal ties, or worldly attachments (so that with regard to this sovereign freedom his existential condition seems to contrast sharply with Cézanne's), Merleau-Ponty turns to Sigmund Freud's psychoanalytic interpretation, based on the configuration of the Virgin's cloak in Leonardo's *The Virgin and Child with Saint Anne,* and drawing on the artist's early childhood memory or fantasy of a "vulture" striking his mouth with its tail.[24] Although, as is now recognized, the bird was not a vulture, but rather a kite (*un nibbio*), so that the ancient Egyptian symbolism of the vulture becomes irrelevant, and although the painting is perhaps more compelling and enigmatic in its cadence of embraces (the Virgin, on Saint Anne's lap, pulls the child toward herself, while he similarly embraces the lamb), and in its setting of an almost primeval landscape, the childhood narrative remains significant. Jean-Claude Frère notes that Leonardo, as a man of his time, readily accepted omens (among which classical culture privileged those connected with the flight of birds) and considered the experience an intimation of his destiny.[25]

For Merleau-Ponty, the psychoanalytic interpretation provides hermeneutic entry into "a forest of symbols" and allows one to understand Leonardo's very stance of freedom (his analytical power and his cultivation of detachment and cognitive sovereignty) as his manner of taking upon himself and living out the formative circumstances of his birth and childhood.

Art, Merleau-Ponty stresses, is "an operation of expression."[26] He assimilates the exigency of expression to Cézanne's aim of "realization," although for the late Cézanne this notion seems to have carried the specific and literal sense of a "making real" in the modality proper to painting which, according to Lawrence Gowing, meant for him "the logic, the organization, and the calculation which the sense of color was subjected to."[27] Merleau-Ponty notes that artistic expression is not, as it were, the translation of a thought that is already formed or clarified into the medium of the chosen art. The meaning or sense of the work is not antecedent to its creation, and neither can it be understood on the basis either of an artist's life or of his or her place in the history of art.[28] This does not mean, however, that an artist's creative freedom or power of expression constitutes an absolute spontaneity; rather, what it gives "a figured sense" to is his or her ineluctable facticity. Cézanne's work, he remarks, "reveals the metaphysical meaning [*sens*]" of the illness that afflicted him, so that the latter ceases to be an absurd (senseless) fact and becomes "a general possibility of human existence," a possibility that the viewer can now connect with.[29] Genuine freedom "does not break its bonds with the world," for which reason "we never see either the idea or freedom face to face."[30] In Merleau-Ponty's provocative formulation, it is the work to be done which calls for the artist's life which, tortured as it may be, makes it possible,[31] even though the interconnection between life and work eludes any causal explanation.

A key theme of Merleau-Ponty's phenomenological interrogation of Cézanne's painting is the undercutting of conceptual dichotomies. Cézanne, he notes, repudiates such ready-made alternatives as sensation or thought (or even eye and mind),[32] nature and art, or chaos and order, in an effort to recapture "the spontaneous order of things perceived" that underlies "the human order of ideas and sciences."[33] In a recent article, Jack Flam speaks similarly of Cézanne's technique as one that, by its startling or incongruous combinations, yields "a picture space full of shifts and ellipses," creating tensions between the painted surface and the represented scene.[34] As Merleau-Ponty understands it, however, Cézanne's orientation is not toward a deconstruction of the unitary picture space, but toward an undivided "primordial world" and its visual exploration. His painting therefore suspends the reificatory and stimulus/response-governed habits of ordinary visual perception, so as to reveal "the ground of inhuman nature on which man establishes himself." According to Merleau-Ponty, this is the reason for the fundamental strangeness experienced by viewers of Cézanne's paintings who, in the museum, tend to pass on, with a certain sense of relief, to other works—such as those of Monet or Renoir—that are less refractory to customary ways of seeing the world.[35]

One must ask, however, whether Cézanne's work is properly understood as a proto-phenomenological investigation of what Merleau-Ponty will call "wild being," or of perception itself as primordial expression. What calls such an understanding into question is the fact that Cézanne regarded the proper achievement of painting as the achievement of "a harmony parallel to nature," a harmony that, particularly in his late paintings, was realized in terms of chromatic scales (the musical metaphor is pertinent) or sequences of unblended patches of color that do not record what the eye sees nor conform to the laws of aerial perspective but that rather constitute an *autonomous* "réalisation sur nature" (realization on the basis of nature).[36] Concerning these patches of color, Lawrence Gowing comments that "it is the relationships between them—relationships of affinity and contrast, the progressions from tone to tone in a color scale, and the modulations from scale to scale—that parallel the apprehension of the world."[37] To parallel is not to rejoin; or, as Yve-Alain Bois comments, these touches of color which make for "the touch of Cézanne, by which he transcribed . . . his 'coloring sensations' were . . . an abstraction," which nevertheless reconfigures nature.[38] This reconfiguration or parallel thus constitutes *a self-contained artistic order of expression,* rather than functioning as the painterly interrogation of vision's primordial and inherently expressive interrogation of "wild being," as which Merleau-Ponty understands it. Given that his focus is trained on "expressing what *exists,*"[39] his emphasis rests on the study of existence rather than on the autonomous character of artistic expression. Concerning the ontological bearing of Cézanne's art, Flam comments insightfully:

> If the solid forms in his paintings seem to be on the verge of dissolution and the empty spaces on the verge of becoming solidified, they reflect Cézanne's intuitive understanding of the interchangeability of matter and energy and his intense awareness of the metaphysical void that underlies what we can know of the natural world.[40]

This comment is more in tune with Merleau-Ponty's late understanding of the ontological basis of painterly expression than with the "phenomenology of pre-reflective being" he pursues in "Cézanne's Doubt."[41]

Merleau-Ponty finds evidence of Cézanne's effort to return to the "primordial world" or to "matter in the process of taking form, order coming to birth through spontaneous organization" (the metaphoric of natality is pervasive not only in this essay, but in Merleau-Ponty's work as a whole) partly in his use of color.[42] Cézanne, he argues, set himself apart from impressionism by the very composition of his palette which (according to Bernard) comprised eighteen pigments, including earth colors (yellow ocher, raw sienna, green earth, Indian red) and black.[43] Impressionism, Merleau-Ponty argues, limited itself to the pure seven colors of the spectrum (thus excluding browns, earth tones, and black), so as to be able to show things submerged in and bound together by light and air. The impressionists' use of optical mixture and of the juxtaposition of complementary colors to enhance luminosity further submerged the object, depriving it of "its proper weight." In contrast, Cézanne's use of warm colors and black shows, Merleau-Ponty argues, that he wanted "to represent the object, to find it again behind the atmosphere."[44] In this context, he interprets Cézanne's chromatic modulations in terms of a search for materiality and gravity:

> The object is no longer covered with reflections, lost in its relationships to the air and to other objects; it is, as it were, secretly illumined from within; light emanates from it, and from this results an impression of solidity and material substance.[45]

A concern for materiality can certainly be traced throughout Cézanne's work, beginning with the materiality of facture in his early paintings, which are often executed with broad, impastoed strokes of a painting knife (and which include, besides the scenes of violence mentioned by Merleau-Ponty, some powerful and austere still lifes and portraits). One can even wonder, with Bois (who is commenting on the late portraits of the gardener Vallier) whether perhaps the ultimate destiny of even those Cézannian works "of which we celebrate the airy respiration" was to end up "somber and saturated with matter, as were the canvases of his 'couillarde' period."[46]

Merleau-Ponty's analysis remains nonetheless open to questions. First, while it is not in fact the case that impressionist painting excluded browns, ochers, or blacks,[47] the composition of a given painter's palette cannot reliably inform one about his or her use of these colors, since they can readily be obtained by pigmentary mixture. Cézanne, however, eschewed pigmentary mixture in his pursuit of chromatic modulations, suggesting that his use of earth pigments and black reflects his "logic" of color modulations rather than attesting to his search for the object. Here Bernard's recollection of Cézanne's response to his own severely limited palette (consisting, at the time, of only four colors—essentially the primaries and lead white) is telling: Cézanne, he writes, told him that it was impossible to paint without a further array of pigments, of which he named about twenty. "I understood then," comments Bernard, that the master, "instead of mixing many colors, had a set array for his palette . . . and that he applied them directly."[48] It seems that Cézanne's aversion to mixing colors stemmed from his concern to avoid modeling or chiaroscuro in favor of the juxtaposition of patches of unblended color in chromatic sequences. As Gowing remarks, from about 1900 onward (and thus in the last six years of Cézanne's life), objects merge for him into a flux of color[49]—that is to say, into a painterly register that, once again, allows him to create an order parallel to nature, rather than seeking to recapture it as something pre-given.

Reflecting on Bernard's verdict that Cézanne aimed at reality while denying himself the means to attain it, Merleau-Ponty examines the spatial distortions often found in Cézanne's paintings. He singles out the portrait of Gustave Geffroy (1895–96, Musée d'Orsay) for its forward-tilted worktable, as well as a portrait of Mme. Cézanne (which he does not identify) for the discontinuity of the frieze bordering the wallpaper on both sides of the figure.[50] The painting may possibly be *Mme Cézanne in a Yellow Armchair*, of which there are two versions, one of 1888–90 (in the Fondation Beyeler), and one of 1893–95 (Metropolitan Museum of Art). Interestingly, Theodore Reff, in an article on Cézanne's relation to the painterly legacy of Jean-Baptiste-Siméon Chardin, observes that perspectival distortions (such as a flattening of circular shapes seen perspectively as ellipses) can also be found in Chardin's work where, however, they lack any "logical basis." He speculates that they may have a history in post-Renaissance art that remains yet to be explored[51] (and if so, this history may—in contrast to the "logic" governing Cézanne's distortions—be connected to a re-vindication of natural vision over perspectival construction).

Merleau-Ponty argues, however, that Cézanne was faithful to the "lived" perspective of natural perception, avoiding both perspectival construction and a photographic rendering. Photography, he notes, is unfaithful to perception in that the human eye compensates for the drastic disparity in size of near and distant objects, or for the change of circular shapes to ellipses (a point that artists today who work from "reference photos" would do well to pay heed to). He observes:

> It is the genius of Cézanne to bring it about that, through the arrangement of the painting as a whole . . . the perspectival deformations cease

to be visible as such . . . and contribute only, as in natural vision, to give the impression of an order coming to birth.[52]

One wonders, nonetheless, whether the complex spatial dynamics, with their distortions and ambiguities, of works such as the well-known *Still Life with Plaster Cupid* (c. 1895, Courtauld Institute), or *Still Life with Flowered Pitcher* (c. 1899, Hermitage Museum) are illuminatingly understood as explorations of "lived perspective," rather than of pictorial space and the relations among pictorial elements (which make for what Reff calls their "logic"). Merleau-Ponty's fundamental concern, moreover, is one to which natural vision or lived perspective is inessential: Cézanne, he finds, reveals "matter in the process of taking form," or "the object in the process of appearing," and this coming to presence involves an indivisible intersensory plenitude, rather than requiring a synthesis of discrete sensory givens. In primordial perception, he argues, there is no distinction between vision and touch; but rather the "lived thing" first offers itself as "the center from which [the sensory givens] radiate."[53] The world, he writes, is "a mass without gaps," an "organism of colors," so that, if a painter is truly to express it, his or her arrangement of colors must contain the indivisible whole of its sensory presencing. Otherwise the painter's work will be a mere "allusion to things," and will fail to show them in their "imperious unity."[54] In this way the painter will be able to bring the human orders of ideas and sciences back into contact with primordial nature, confronting it "with the sciences that, as [Cézanne] says, have issued from it."[55]

Is this primordial unity of vision and touch (or other sensory registers) quite so unproblematically espoused by Cézanne's painting? Bois offers a deeper insight concerning this question. He considers a well-known passage in Cézanne's first letter to Bernard, in which the painter explains that, while lines parallel to the horizon give breadth, those perpendicular to it give depth, and since "nature exists for us humans more in depth than on the surface," it is necessary to introduce into the vibrations of light represented by reds and yellows "sufficient bluenesses [*bleutés*] to make one feel the air."[56] In disagreement with the usual interpretations of these remarks as bearing on aerial perspective, Bois points out that the abundant milky blues in Cézanne's paintings do not in fact conform to the rules of aerial perspective (that is, distant objects are not consistently bluer in tone and more shrouded by atmosphere than near ones), and furthermore that aerial perspective presupposes homogeneous space, whereas Cézanne's space is traversed by ruptures (so that distant objects may be incongruously propelled forward by virtue of the spatial dynamics of color or of definition).[57] Bois's reconsideration of this passage in the light of Cézanne's painterly practice (he singles out in particular the 1896 painting *The Lac d'Annecy*, in the Courtauld Institute, which Merleau-Ponty also refers to for its strangely claustrophobic atmosphere)[58] sensitizes one to the late Cézanne's preoccupation with and "anxiety" of distance. This anxiety shows itself to be linked to the pathos of verticality characteristic of the human body, and to the human reliance on the distance sense of sight (in contrast to animals whose reliance on chemical or tactile perception tends to confine them to the immediate surface). Second and importantly, Bois (referring here to Rosalind Krauss's analysis of Pablo Picasso's work of 1909)[59] acknowledges Cézanne's recognition of a hiatus between the purely visual space of projection, articulated vertically, and the carnal and tactile space that unfolds depth horizontally "beneath our feet" (and that the human body rejoins in the passivity and proneness of sleep or death).[60] It is interesting to consider that this same tension is thematized in certain sculptures of Alberto Giacometti, notably in *Man Walking*, represented by two works in the Fondation Beyeler.[61] Bois reflects that the tension or disjunction between vision and touch in an artist's work results from "a crisis, from a putting into doubt of vision itself as to its capacity to give us access to depth."[62]

Reflecting on factors such as the organic and curvaceous volumes prominent in Cézanne's painting—his "principle of sphericity," and its contrast with both his practice of cruciform composition and his veiling patches of pure color, Bois suggests that Cézanne wanted to "tie the look to touch at the very moment when the two sensory registers were in the process of disjoining themselves: to invent, in some way, a tactile vision."[63] If so, he strove to close over the hiatus that had begun to open up in his painting between vision and touch. Such an effort can certainly not rely on the indivisible plenitude of sensory presencing that Merleau-Ponty considers to be granted to primordial perception. In fact, all assurances become elusive here; and one may suspect that Cézanne's doubt was less a matter of individual pathology than of facing the artistic challenges that he lucidly recognized and responded to.

Painting remains, of course, inherently a matter of touch, embedded in materiality. In Leonardo's sfumato technique, carried to perfection in the *Mona Lisa*, the actual touches of the brush are invisible to the naked eye; but Cézanne, particularly in his late period, painted in discrete touches that assert themselves as such and that constitute, as Bois puts it, "the bridge between his pigment and substances, [between] forms and the spatiality of the world," while being at the same time "almost a musical mode of notation," which enabled him, nonetheless, to evoke "worlds at the threshold, similar, for our perception, to nature itself."[64]

The consideration of the threatening disjunction, for the painter, of vision and touch has implicitly led back here to the "harmony parallel to nature" that was, for Cézanne, the distinctive achievement of painting, true to its proper mode of expression. Merleau-Ponty's analysis does not give adequate scope to the autonomy of painterly expression (or to what Cézanne called the "abstractions" that, in his attentiveness to "coloring sensations," came to prevent his completing a painting as a straightforward study of nature).[65] He tends instead to understand painterly expression as a proto-phenomenological "intuitive science" interrogating "the ground of primordial nature" that subtends human projects. If "expressing what *exists* is an endless task,"[66] however, the reason is not only the infinite intricacy of existence or of primordial nature, but also the limitless expressive autonomy that is proper to art or, in this instance, to painting, which is, although inspired by nature, never bound to it (whether or not nature provides the "motif"). Even if perception is primordially expressive, artistic creation is not essentially a retrieval of the expressivity of perception.

Cézanne may have first explored the spatial dynamics of juxtaposed discrete touches of color in his luminous watercolors; but he consummates this exploration in some of his late canvases, such as the extraordinary *Undergrowth (The Path of the Mas Jolie at the Château-Noir)* of 1900–1902 (Fondation Beyeler). In this painting, the sinuous shapes of a couple of trees together with some rectilinear architectural elements are barely sketched into the mostly diagonally applied patches of greens, yellow-greens, clear and somber blues, delicate greys, and striations of sienna and ocher, interspersed throughout by the white of bare canvas. As Bois puts it well, Cézanne's paintings (and particularly the late works) "are lungs": and the discrete touches of color facilitate their palpable respiration because they "presuppose the void" or emptiness.[67] Bois—mindful that Cézanne was an accomplished Latinist who loved classical literature and could recite much of it by heart—somewhat playfully links this void to the atomism of Lucretius; but the notion of an emptiness that appearances circumscribe in freely configuring themselves will also resonate, at a deeper level, with the ontology of the late Merleau-Ponty.

Given that artistic expression as such surpasses its sources of inspiration (and even "primordial nature") and that, in Cézanne's painting, it issues into a "harmony" that is autonomous and compelling, but whose subtle inner logic was evidently not understood by even the most sympathetic of his interlocutors (such as Bernard), it is hardly surprising that the painter should have been menaced by doubt. Indeed, the condition of perceiving oneself "nine days out of ten" surrounded only by the dregs of one's empirical life and by projects that remain still in question is one that is hardly foreign to artists and writers in general.[68] Nonetheless, Cézanne, throughout his personal travails, was convinced that, as he wrote to Bernard, "only in making paintings can you find refuge";[69] and he remained true not only to painting as his mandate and his very mode of being, but also to the inner logic and the exigencies of his work, which he lucidly discerned and strove to follow, so that his practice of painting, however searchingly pursued, was at its core affirmative, assured, and courageous rather than crippled by doubt.

Expression, Institution, and the Field: A Searching Itinerary

> One will thus understand by institution those occurrences of an experience that endow it with durable dimensions, with respect to which a whole other dimension of experience will have sense, will form a thinkable sequence or a history—or else the occurrences that deposit a sense within me, not in virtue of survival and residue, but as an appeal to a sequel, exigency of a future.
>   —Maurice Merleau-Ponty, *Institution and Passivity*, translated by Leonard Lawlor and Heath Massey (2010)

When Merleau-Ponty reworked "Indirect Language," the third chapter of his never-completed book, *The Prose of the World*, in 1951 and 1952, to become "Indirect Language and the Voices of Silence," and eventually the lead article in the collection of essays titled *Signs*,[1] he found himself engaged in working out what Galen Johnson calls "a general theory of expression."[2] Indeed, two further chapters of *The Prose of the World* are explicitly devoted to the question of expression, namely "Science and the Experience of Expression" (chapter 2), and "Expression and the Child's Drawing" (chapter 6). In the text known as "A Prospectus of His Work" that Merleau-Ponty submitted to Martial Gueroult on the occasion of his candidacy for a chair at the Collège de France in 1952–53, he characterized his research in progress as focused on "studies on expression and truth" which offer an epistemological approach to "the general problem of human interrelations," together with institutions and values. He notes that the phenomenon of expression presents a spontaneity "that gathers together the plurality of monads, the past and the present, nature and culture into a single whole."[3]

Apart from these acknowledged concerns, Merleau-Ponty's focus on working out a philosophy of expression reveals also his awareness that structuralist analysis (in particular Saussurean linguistics, to which the opening pages of "Indirect Language and the Voices of Silence" are devoted), as well as André Malraux's theories on aesthetics and the history of art, and less directly Jean-Paul Sartre, to whom the essay is dedicated and whose views on the relationship between the verbal and silent arts, and of art to action, posed significant challenges to Merleau-Ponty's phenomenology that he needed to address.[4] Some of these challenges were also mutually challenging, in that, for instance, whereas structuralism effaces the place of the subject as the originator of signification, Malraux charged post-classical painting with sheer subjectivism, or in that this supposed subjectivism comes up against the evidence of hidden affinities or historical continuities which can, contrary to Malraux, not be ascribed to the agency of a quasi-Hegelian spirit.[5] Given the need to respond to these complex claims, it is perhaps not surprising that Merleau-Ponty's essay is less than unified but involves some startling shifts in intellectual perspective.

In the reflection on Saussurean linguistics prefaced to the final version of "Indirect Language and the Voices of Silence," Merleau-Ponty judges that language in its entirety is fundamentally "a style of expression."[6] The child becomes proficient in his or her natal language, not by putting together meaningful linguistic elements as in a jigsaw puzzle, but rather by learning and exploring the language "from within," moving always already within it as an integral whole. In both language and culture, Merleau-Ponty reflects, there is an immanence of the whole to its parts (a thought that he will take up again in his later reflections on embryology), for which reason language, far from being a transparent conveyor of meaning, retains an intrinsic opacity.[7] It does not admit of a complete expression that would enable it to coincide with things themselves but remains interwoven with "threads of silence," so that the writer cannot look to an ideal of perfect literary expression, any more than the painter could meaningfully envisage an ideal and ultimate painting.[8]

Merleau-Ponty concludes that there is no choice to be made between "absolute painting" and an art that remains related to the world (which is not only the perceptual world but also the life world and the domain of action); and he denies that there could be any culturally or historically invariant sense data (as he will elaborate in his reflection on a patch of red in *The Visible and the Invisible*).[9] Even classical (Albertian) perspective (which will be taken up again in part 4 of "Eye and Mind")[10] does not qualify as absolutely true to the visual spectacle; it not only does not replicate natural vision but is also a culturally specific expressive register, whereas the visual perception or experience of depth "is not of the order of laws."[11] The perceived world exceeds every expressive configuration which works itself out, in the history of art, as a recognizable style. Taking issue with Malraux's understanding of a painter's style as an invention issuing from sheer subjectivity, Merleau-Ponty stresses that there is no style that does not constitute a modality of contact with the world. Furthermore, an artist's style does not remain limited to his or her work but has, if its modality of expression proves "successful," a power of "institution," which Merleau-Ponty understands in the Husserlian sense of *Stiftung* or inauguration, and which ultimately attests to carnal inter-corporeity.[12] The style becomes, for the artist, an "inner schema"[13] that imposes itself on her or him, while at the same time it begins to function as a generally recognized modality of expression.

If painting is, for these reasons, comparable, as Merleau-Ponty suggests, to "a labor of thought,"[14] his ensuing condemnation of abstract painting is all the more astonishing; and it marks one of the essay's intellectual shifts. Although he has just criticized Malraux for defining modern painting as a glorification of subjectivity "outside the world," and has noted that perception is already expressive and "stylizes," and that all style, furthermore, is "a shaping of the elements of the world," he charges abstract art as such with "a negation or refusal of the world."[15] A refusal remains, of course, still a modality of relation; but if abstract painting is understood, in keeping with Merleau-Ponty's characterization, as an obsession with either pure geometrical forms or (in its biomorphic aspect) with "infusoria and microbes," retaining a mere "odor" of a "shameful and despairing life,"[16] it becomes impossible to understand how it can still engage meaningfully with the elements of the world in either their material or their pure primordial aspects.[17] Merleau-Ponty is certainly open to Cézanne's or Paul Klee's "tolerance for the incomplete," or to the way the arabesque functions, for Henri Matisse, as "the lightning sign" of the world's self-revelation, but he fails to do justice to pure abstraction. In 1952, abstract art commanded attention in Paris with the exhibition "Un art autre" ("A Different Art"), featuring forty European and American abstract artists. It was followed during the same year by an exhibition devoted to Jackson Pollock, and the following year by a show of American abstract painting at the Musée d'Art Moderne. Although Merleau-Ponty points out that modern painting, and modern thought generally, bring one up against "a truth that does not resemble things," since it is without any external model, he does not take the measure of the ways in which purely abstract painting (or sculpture) can accomplish this, or of how, in this very accomplishment, it still remains inextricably engaged with the world of visual and life experience.

Arguing against the "historicity of death" instituted by the museum (which, he claims, makes painters as mysterious "as octopuses and lobsters"),[18] as well as against a quasi-Hegelian spirit operating "behind the painter's back," Merleau-Ponty seeks to explain the supposed unity of painting throughout its complex (if, as he understands it, exclusively Western) history by "the single task that all painters are faced with."[19] This task derives, he argues, from the primordial expressivity of perception itself and of the lived body. As he writes, "All perception, all action which presupposes it, and in short every human use of the body is already *primordial expression*."[20]

It is, he finds, the expressivity or the expressive gesture of the body, "begun by the least perception, that develops into painting and art." Prehistoric cave painting thus inaugurated a tradition only because it had already primordially "received one, that of perception."[21] Inauguration, he stresses, constitutes an *advent* that cannot be derived from the mere accumulation of events, and which renders the instituted tradition self-sustaining. The tradition is, he notes, borne "by the caryatid of our efforts which converge by the sole fact that they are efforts to express."[22]

Merleau-Ponty does not question this unity of art that he understands as a plurivocal convergence marked by certain resemblances (so that the works produced by one culture remain aesthetically meaningful for another across space and time)—a unity that is, however, quite different from the univocity of universal reason. He conceives it as "a unity of human style" which brings "the gestures of all painters together in one sole expressive effort—a single art."[23] One may, nonetheless, question such a cross-cultural unity of art on the basis that the very concept of art is proper to the Western intellectual and cultural tradition (as is also the privileged position accorded to painting). Thus the formal inventiveness of African sculpture that partly inspired Picasso's creation, in 1907, of *Les demoiselles d'Avignon* did not, for its creators, constitute a venture of art-making destined for aesthetic contemplation, but functioned rather within a context of ritual, religion, power, and magic—a context within which the question of art's (one cannot now avoid the term) relevance to action could never even be posed. The idea of a cross-cultural and trans-historical unity of art risks insensitivity to the vital functioning of artifacts that are retrospectively gathered together as art objects available for aesthetic contemplation (and, of course, as commodities on the art market) within the cultures and historical periods of their origin.[24] This danger bespeaks itself in Merleau-Ponty's remark that the artists of other cultures, who may have consciously thought themselves to be continuing "primitive terrors," or even, as he adds sweepingly, those of "Asia and Egypt" on the whole, unknowingly inaugurated "another history, which is still ours."[25] In a similar vein, he notes that it is by virtue of this cross-cultural unity that "we take the trouble to transform fetishes into art."[26] It seems that the idea of a unity of art as a plurivocal and differential convergence has here become the idea of a univocity that silences or is dismissive of genuine otherness.

It is also, to say the least, questionable whether the human body in its sentience, motility, and expressive gestures is really so unitary as to give rise to a single art and a universal symbolic or pictorial "syntax." Merleau-Ponty does not address art's thematization of the differential character of embodiment which is explored, for instance (if beyond the time of his writing), by the work of the Cuban-American artist Ana Mendieta. Her art (which consists mostly of performance and earth works) often involves or is enacted upon her own gendered body in its exposure to criminal, sexual, or sacrificial violation, its exilic displacement, its kinship to the animal body, its mortality, and its obliteration or reabsorption by the elemental forces of nature. Although she worked intensively with the elements of earth and water, it was fire that, beginning with the photographic documentation of her *Silueta de Cenizas* (*Silhouette of Ashes*) in 1965, became a key focus of her work, uniting the powers of destruction and regeneration as they impinge upon the body.[27]

As concerns art's thematization of the differential character of embodiment, one can also fruitfully turn to the work of the Thai artist Montien Boonma, insofar as his installations and sculptures often explore the body's devastation by illness and the iconography of the spiritual aspects of the quest for healing, as well as the kinship of the human body in its vulnerability to the violated and endangered body of the planet.[28]

The very notion of expression seems to bring with it a differential scope and thus a disunity that Merleau-Ponty does not want to recognize. He passes too easily from a primordial expressivity of perception and gesture to an expressivity that transfigures the facticity and the traumas of the artist's individual life (among which figure, in his rather stereotypical listing, mistresses, creditors, the police, and revolutions, but not illness, aging, exile, or brutalization), rendering them "transparent and luminous."[29] Even if such a transfiguration of individual experience, in all its variability, renders it communicable and generally meaningful, this does not support his claim that "the historicity of life reconciles paintings by virtue of the fact that each one expresses the whole of existence."[30] Art's register of expression remains a register of singularities rather than of a comprehensive or essential unity.

Finally, Merleau-Ponty's reflections on the instituting power of works seem to presuppose that works are created with an intention of (relative) permanence, rather than of ephemerality or of their swift undoing. Such is not necessarily the case even for works that function within a cultural or religious tradition (such as the Tibetan sand mandala that, for all its exquisite detail of imagery, is ritually destroyed soon after its creation); and it certainly is not true of twentieth-century and contemporary art, even if (leaving out of consideration performance art, installations, conceptual art, earth art, or works such as Andy Goldsworthy's ephemeral "leaf throws" and "rainbow splashes") one restricts oneself to the relative solidity of sculpture. Eva Hesse, for instance, created sculpture out of materials that she knew would disintegrate, such as latex; and, as Briony Fer comments, her works are also prone to decay through the agency of light—the very light that is essential to their "shadow life." They thus show "solid form in the process of collapse, sculptural form laid waste."[31] Somewhat similarly, the Hawaiian artist Karen Kosasa found it necessary to withdraw her sculptures, made of wood, from a group show at the Honolulu Academy of Art, since she could not accede to the museum's demand for fumigation. Indispensable as fumigation was for the museum, given the need to protect its holdings, it would have counteracted the biological disintegration of her work from within that Kosasa had envisaged in creating it (and it would also have constituted a violation of various forms of life in the name of the self-assertion of art).[32] The power of institution exercised by a work that is purposively ephemeral may perhaps rely upon the photographic trace, but even then, the work must still somehow remain efficacious as such, even in its absence or undoing. In "Indirect Language and the Voices of Silence," Merleau-Ponty does not enter upon the efficacy of absence or of the trace—concerns that will gain prominence in his later exploration of the invisibilities that are indissociable from the visible.

Merleau-Ponty moves from the consideration that Malraux's aesthetic analyses can only be rectified by bringing together perception, history, and expression to an implicit dialogue with Sartre and Marxism concerning the bearing of his own philosophy of expression on a philosophical analysis of history and action.[33] He reflects that the realization that the continuum of endeavors to express founds "one single history," much as the body's hold on every possible object founds a single space,[34] enables one to reject the idolization of history as an autonomous power, and to conceive it instead on the basis of *actions* which are analogous to *works:*

> The action remains as an exemplary type and will survive in other situations in another form. It opens up a field. Sometimes it even institutes a world . . . it outlines a future. History, according to [G. W. F.] Hegel, is this maturation of a future in the present, not the sacrifice of the present to an unknown future.[35]

Hegel, Merleau-Ponty reflects, rejects judging action by its results alone as well as by its sheer intentions, evaluating it instead as one would a work: by its success "in making values become facts." Hegelian dialectic, he suggests, "is what we call by another name the phenomenon of expression" which integrates the singular with the universal.[36] On this basis, Merleau-Ponty not only, quite surprisingly, assimilates the politician to the painter (they both, he argues, move others—namely the public that their oeuvre addresses—toward values that they will only later recognize as their own);[37] but he also affirms the legitimacy of treating painting as a language. As such, it is capable of recapitulating and presenting in its perceptual meaning an entire process of expression.[38]

Even the literary arts, Merleau-Ponty reflects, cultivate a certain tacit rather than fully articulate expression, vesting signification in elisions, lacunae, or peremptory traces, and thus in the unspoken rather than in what is explicitly said. The means of expression remain, he notes, enveloped by "a halo of signification"; and truth becomes manifest, not by a sharpening of focus, but rather by a movement "which throws our image of the world out of focus."[39] Expression, thus understood, constitutes the mind's very "existence in act"; and language, together with the literary arts, can claim only a relative privilege over the visual arts in their expressive silence, or over praxis.[40]

In what must count as the essay's most startling shift in perspective, however, Merleau-Ponty goes right on to subordinate "the mute forms of expression" to language (at the same time, moreover, as he expressly denies any relationship of superiority or subordination between language and meaning).[41] The arts of language, he now claims, "go much further toward true creation" than is possible for painting (and by implication, other visual arts), whose works supposedly contest one another in an unstilled rivalry, so that each new creation strives to supersede those of the past.[42] He argues that literature, in contrast, preserves its past in critical transformation, accomplishing what one is tempted to call a certain *Aufhebung*. It does so, moreover, in self-transparency for, he maintains, "one does not paint painting, but [one] speaks about speech."[43]

It may quite likely be true that, as art critic Holland Cotter has claimed, "the impulse to destroy is what made early Modern art the guerrilla movement it was,"[44] but this particular historical moment of European and American twentieth-century art neither defines painting or visual art as such nor sets it apart from the arts of language (to say nothing about music, theater, or dance, the last of which Merleau-Ponty neglects entirely). His characterization of the history of painting as rivalrous, in fact, indicates obliquely that painters have always "painted [about] painting"; for one does not rebel against or rival what one is not deeply engaged with. Painters, moreover, have in their work quite explicitly and consistently addressed the history or contemporary context of painting, whether straightforwardly (as Vincent van Gogh re-created Jean-François Millet and the Northern masters, or as Édouard Manet's *Olympia* and *Déjeuner sur l'herbe* have given rise, like a musical theme, to a panorama of variations) or else obliquely (as Cy Twombly, who worked abstractly and emphasized the graphic trace, could nonetheless acknowledge the influence of Nicolas Poussin). If one moves outside the Western tradition (to which Merleau-Ponty confines himself), one comes up, in particular, against the intricate historical self-referentiality of classical Chinese painting and calligraphy (which is here the master art), so that, for instance, Wang Hui (1632–1717) innovated, not by displacing, but by boldly reconfiguring and reinventing the classical masters, while the twentieth-century painter Zhang Daqian (1899–1983) was not only an innovator conversant with Western art, but also a master of the styles of his illustrious predecessors Shitao and Bada Shanren. To complicate matters still further, the contemporary American abstract painter Brice Marden takes much of his inspiration from the classical tradition of Chinese art, particularly calligraphy.[45]

Merleau-Ponty concludes his essay by accusing painting of taking up its abode in "a dreaming eternity," negating time and history and offering instead the questionable pleasure of an anachronism.[46] His elaboration makes clear that the sort of painting he is thinking of has a narrative or quasi-literary focus, which literature itself, of course, can easily render more vivid and precise. Despite his earlier engagement with Cézanne who certainly kept his distance from quasi-literary painting, Merleau-Ponty seems, at this point, unable to dissociate painting from literary or historical reference. Thus he concludes that "language speaks, and the voices of painting are the voices of silence."[47]

Nonetheless, he reiterates that language, in all its modalities, cannot pretend to reach "the thing itself" (in the sense of the phenomenologically proverbial *Sachen selbst,* which really are not things [*Dinge*] so much as matters at issue). Even though language does not, in its act of expression, dissipate its revelatory power in a Saussurean network of lateral references but surpasses itself toward what it signifies, its temporal and situated character debars it from any possible coincidence with the very issues in their truth. This holds true even for the philosophical use of language, so that, as Merleau-Ponty writes, "The meaning of philosophy is the meaning of a genesis. Consequently it could not possibly be summed up outside of time, and it is still expression."[48]

One is left wondering about what may have impelled Merleau-Ponty to introduce a Sartrean hierarchization into his comprehensive philosophy of expression, privileging what he calls "language and the system of truth," and subordinating the silent arts. Is the phenomenon of expression by its very nature too multifarious to support his project (as outlined in the "Prospectus") of developing a theory of truth, or does Claude Lefort touch upon the nerve of the issue by his claim that Merleau-Ponty came to recognize—at least by the time he offered his lecture courses on institution and passivity in 1954–55—that "the attempt to carry forward the phenomenology of perception by a theory of expression . . . still left him dependent upon a philosophy of consciousness"?[49] Merleau-Ponty does acknowledge, in a working note to *The Visible and the Invisible,* that the problems he addressed in *Phenomenology of Perception* remain insoluble within that work, "since I set out from the distinction 'consciousness—object.' "[50] Renaud Barbaras comments that the radical change of perspective in *The Visible and the Invisible* stems from Merleau-Ponty's realization that "the impossibility of rejoining the world's being, which until now was ascribed to reflexive or thetic consciousness, is now judged *inherent to the philosophy of consciousness as such.*"[51] This change is perhaps horizonal in "Indirect Language and the Voices of Silence," so that its effort to surmount a perceived limitation of the "silent arts" appears to be connected with a questioning of a philosophy of consciousness.

The quest to gain deeper insight into these issues would require a study of the lecture courses on institution and passivity of 1954–55, which will, however, be considered here only with respect to their bearing on aesthetics and the instituting power of works.

As Lefort notes, in the lecture courses the idea of institution, inspired by the Husserlian notion of *Stiftung* (instauration or inauguration), disengages itself from the context of the philosophy of expression and the understanding of history in which it first took form.[52] Time, Merleau-Ponty points out, is the very model of institution, which interlinks activity and passivity, so that the instituting and instituted subjectivity are indissociable and are radically different from the subject as constituting consciousness.[53] "To constitute," Merleau-Ponty writes, "is almost the contrary of instituting: the instituted is meaningful without me, the constituted is meaningful only for me and for the me of that moment."[54] The key notion is no longer that of the subject (not even of the body-subject) but that of the "field" (*champ*), which is trans-subjective and structured by the import of symbolic forms. Not only painting, or planimetric perspective as a historical form of the organization of space, but philosophical analysis itself constitute symbolic forms. However, if, as Merleau-Ponty writes, "perspective has the same function as critical philosophy: link of subjectivity and objectivity, of viewpoint and reality,"[55] it is also true that the intentionality of painting is not pure ideality but a concrete and materially based praxis whose guiding logic "is blind, a logic that creates itself in making its way [*en cheminant*]."[56] Institution interlinks concrete singularity with universality, offering, in Lefort's phrase, "a knowledge of the particularities that unite" within the scope of history.[57]

The problem of passivity arises with respect to phenomena that cannot be conformed to the model of institution—there is, after all, no institution of the oneiric, or of a delirium. Yet passivity is not the exception or a privation or special case, since there is ultimately no sharp dividing line between the supposedly real and the oneiric or imaginary, so that, to cite Lefort once more, "one must recognize an oneiric consciousness of wakefulness."[58] It was Freud's important contribution to recognize a structure proper to oneiric thought; and for Merleau-Ponty, this insight serves in the end to integrate oneiric thought and imagination with his analysis of institution, in a manner that is of far-reaching importance for his philosophy of art.

In his lecture course on institution, Merleau-Ponty situates the analysis of the institution of a work in between his analyses of the institution of a feeling (of love, as explored by Marcel Proust, or as a "phantasmagoria of the Other")[59] and the institution of a form of knowledge. This schema will allow him decisively to repudiate the privileging of discursivity or pure logos that remained problematic in "Indirect Language and the Voices of Silence." Thus, in the "Third Sketch" of his third lecture course on "The Concept of Nature," devoted to "Nature and Logos: The Human Body," he notes that "there is a logos of the sensible world and a savage mind that animates language . . . communication in the invisible continues what is instituted by communication in the visible."[60] On this understanding of language and institution, it is no longer possible to privilege the arts of language over the silent arts or, indeed, to support any hierarchical ordering of the arts.

Taking up again the thematic of natality that was prominent in his reflections on artistic creation in "Cézanne's Doubt," Merleau-Ponty emphatically rejects construing birth (which is, after all, like death, from which it is indissociable, a passion in the double sense of a passivity and a suffering) as an act of the subject's initial self-assertion, or as the sheer upsurge ex nihilo of consciousness understood as the Sartrean for-itself. Rather than being the initiatory act of bestowing meaning (*Sinngebung*), birth—and perhaps already conception—initiates

> the opening of a field . . . there is a leap toward a future that comes about by itself . . . Birth is . . . the institution of a future. Reciprocally, institution abides in the same mode of being as birth and is not an act any more than it. Later on, there will be decisive institution or contracts; but they must be understood from the vantage point of birth, and not vice versa.[61]

What then are the implications of this modeling of institution on natality for understanding the institution of a work, together with artistic creation and the historicity of art? Every work derives from and draws on precedents from which it can, nonetheless, not be causally deduced (any more than, as Merleau-Ponty argued in "Cézanne's Doubt," it can be deduced from or explained by the facticity of the artist's life). In discussing "the institution of a feeling," he notes similarly that any attempt to account for Proust's rich explorations of the complexities of love by reference to his homosexuality or psycho-history will show only that these personal contingencies opened up for him a unique manner of access to contingencies that are universally recognized.[62] The artist's facticity thus sustains the "metaphysical" significance of his or her work, rather than being either its causal condition or being antithetical to it. The nexus that interlinks the two is now, for Merleau-Ponty, the temporalizing character of institution, so that

> here as well the contingencies are re-centered by it [the work] and end up receiving a sense that surpasses them so thoroughly that one no longer knows where the work had its beginnings in the vital and artistic past of the artist, or even in the tradition that inspires it.[63]

The writer and the visual artist (and probably the practitioner of any art) do not start out from fully formed and available significations (nor generally from the "inspiration" of popular parlance), but rather from a certain lack, need, or void. It is only by the sustained labor of writing or of painting that one can hope to find one's voice or vision. The project of artistic creation thus comes to understand itself largely through partial realizations, with the work in progress forming a series of institutions and revealing that institution tends as such toward seriality.[64] Although seriality—as the work's historical fecundity—requires that it be encountered again and again by others, it issues from an intrinsic matrix of sense that is neither positive nor delimited, but open: "[the "internal" sense] is divergence [*écart*] with respect to a norm of sense, *différence*. It is this sense by divergence, deformation, that is proper to institution."[65]

The move from expression (in the rather undefined sense that this notion has so far carried for Merleau-Ponty) to institution (which, he notes, has so far lacked any name or identity in theories of consciousness)[66] allows him to distance sense or meaning more decisively from positivity. This dissociation offers a further reason why the eloquent arts can no longer be privileged over the silent arts. If meaning is differential at its core, speech cannot realize it more perfectly than painting or sculpture, nor does it have any advantage as regards the transformative appropriation of its own past.

Furthermore, since Merleau-Ponty situates the institution of works (which forms part of "personal" or intersubjective" rather than "universal" history)[67] in between, and in unbroken continuity with, the institution, respectively, of a feeling and of a form of knowledge, there can also be no sharp dividing line between institution in the purely personal domain and in the domain of general validity.[68] Notwithstanding its overwhelming power, a passion such as love is nothing positive; it constitutes rather an erosion of the self by the alterity of the beloved, who is, Merleau-Ponty writes, "within me under the forms of suffering or privation . . . by means of lack," and who, to begin with, also lacks a positive essence.[69] The passion, moreover, institutes itself across concatenations of contingencies, so that, if there ever was any original bestowal of meaning, it can be rejoined only in deviation or difference—as is the case with the contingencies of facticity and heritage taken up and transcended by the work of art.

If the work itself (whose insertion into the public domain still remains, for Merleau-Ponty, "the most personal of vows")[70] does not simply outstrip contingency, neither is it outstripped (by virtue of its retaining a tie to contingencies) by the essential truths or pure ideas that knowledge grants access to. To draw such a quasi-Platonic dividing line is, Merleau-Ponty asserts, untenable, for "the true, the essence, would amount to nothing without what leads up to it. There is sublimation, not outstripping toward another order."[71]

He acknowledges that, in arguing that the formulation of scientific ideas, no less than the creation of works of art, opens up a field and inaugurates an "infinite task," rather than attaining pure, atemporal self-evidence, he has assimilated the history of knowledge to the history of painting.[72] Only at this point does he reconsider the notion that the integration of the past into the opening up of a future might be accomplished more perfectly by institution that is a work of language, rather than by painterly institution. He allows for this residual difference and reflects that it allows, in the intellectual disciplines, for the impression of "the conquest of a free signification . . . before which language effaces itself;" but he concludes that nonetheless such a conquest derives from institution, so that one must "go back to institution to deepen the proper sense [le propre] of knowledge."[73]

In his concrete discussion of the institution of a work, Merleau-Ponty explores the transition from the pictorial (or sculptural) expression of space in antiquity (which implied that space was conceived as nonsubstantial), via its assimilation to sheer luminosity by Christian Neoplatonism, to the systematic construction of space by Renaissance perspective. This discussion, which engages closely with Erwin Panofsky's art-historical analyses,[74] functions as an example of how, once a field has been laid open, it allows for systematic endeavors and for a "teleology of the whole" without prescribing any ultimate telos or inviting totalization.

He also returns, if only briefly and elliptically, to Cézanne through a meditation on Liliane Guerry's study of Cézanne's pictorial space.[75] The editors of Merleau-Ponty's *L'institution dans l'histoire personnelle et publique* "Institution in Personal and Public History"—Dominique Darmaillacq, Claude Lefort, and Stéphanie Ménasé—provide excerpts of Guerry's text in their "Bibliographical References." Guerry lucidly recognized the challenge that Cézanne's notion of a "harmony parallel to nature" posed for his expression of space:

> It was no longer just a question of reproducing a fugitive luminous ac-
> cord, but of expressing at the heart of an abstract space a synthesis of
> all possible harmonies. So as not to be fragmented in the infinity of the
> accord of colors, the masses must then affirm themselves with stability,
> since they alone are borrowed from reality, while the luminous combina-
> tions, like the space . . . are the fruit of an intellectual reconstruction.[76]

These comments shed a different light on what Merleau-Ponty, in "Cézanne's Doubt," spoke of as the artist's supposed desire to find and again represent the object, which impressionism had dissolved into a play of light.[77] As concerns the discussion of Renaissance perspective in the context of the pictorial expression of space or depth, it will be best to integrate the brief and sketchy comments offered in the institution lectures with Merleau-Ponty's fuller reflections on these topics in "Eye and Mind."

In turning to "Eye and Mind" (and subsequently to Merleau-Ponty's philosophy of nature and to his late ontology), the question of the relation between expression and institution will continue to pose itself. Although, in the lecture courses of 1954–55, the thematic of institution does seem to have superseded that of expression, one cannot assume that this displacement will prove to be definitive. It may rather be the case that Merleau-Ponty's engagement with the question of institution had a transitional role, in that it facilitated or even mandated a deepening and clarification of his late understanding of expression.

3

Painterly and Phenomenological Interrogation in "Eye and Mind"

> Small wonder that a Merleau-Ponty . . . decided to investigate the phenomena of perception and of artistic creation with a view to the experience of Cézanne. He spent a summer upon the traces of the painter at the foot of Mt. Sainte-Victoire, and he found that the acts of perceiving and of artistic creation spring from the *chiasm* . . . which consists of the encounter of gazes, which brings in its train the encounter of bodies and spirit. In this play of perfected encounter, the subject who looks is also being looked at, for the world that is envisaged shows itself to be also one that "envisages." Truly creative perception comes to pass through a From-body-to-body and a From-spirit-to-spirit.
>
> —François Cheng, *Fünf Meditationen über die Schönheit* (2008)

Neither expression nor institution are foregrounded in "Eye and Mind," written in the summer of 1960 at Le Tholonet (close to Cézanne's natal city of Aix-en-Provence). Since this essay or short monograph concerned with painting is the last work Merleau-Ponty published,[1] it is indispensable for a study of the phenomenological ontology that he sought to develop in *The Visible and the Invisible*, left a fragment at his death. Furthermore, as Galen Johnson points out, the writing of "Eye and Mind" is interlinked with the writing of the introduction to *Signs*, which Merleau-Ponty had essentially concluded in early 1960, but to which he added a final section immediately after completing "Eye and Mind."[2] Both of these texts contemporaneous with the essay take up the theme of expression which therefore, as well as for intrinsic reasons, remains at the horizon of Merleau-Ponty's philosophical exploration of painting. Of the essay's five parts, each addresses a distinctive set of issues, and so this study will follow the fivefold structure of the analysis.

Technicity, Totalization, and the Guidance of Art

The opening section of "Eye and Mind" echoes Heidegger's reflection, in his 1954 essay "Die Frage nach der Technik" ("The Question Concerning Technology"), that technicity in its contemporary maximization is "the set-up that provokes" (*das herausfordernde Ge-stell*) and that it "conceals unconcealing as such, and together with it that wherein unconcealment, that is truth, comes into its own [*sich ereignet*]."[3] Merleau-Ponty's focus, however, is trained more on the method and discourse of the sciences than on technology as such, which is one reason why his text here is replete with implicit references and allusions to Descartes, the inaugural philosopher-scientist. The implicit references can be found in the contrast Merleau-Ponty draws between contemporary techno-science and "classical science," to the effect that, whereas the former (in keeping with Heidegger's diagnosis of its reduction of even the mere object to *Bestand,* or to posit and resource at one's disposal) touches only distantly upon the world of actual experience and absolutizes its own constructs, the latter, though boldly constructivist, still safeguarded "a sense of the world's opacity."[4] For Descartes this meant acknowledging that the divine infinity, as the transcendent foundation of truth, repudiates comprehension, and that embodiment, or the "substantial union" of body and soul, is likewise incomprehensible to the pure intellect, and even the intellect aided by imagination.[5] "Classical science" thus remained aware of its limitations, whereas the techno-science that Merleau-Ponty criticizes tends toward totalization by reducing the world to the mere "object X of our operations."[6] Just as Heidegger reflects that the reduction of nature to disposable energy reserves reduces human beings as well, and "in an even more original manner than nature,"[7] to the same status, Merleau-Ponty warns that humans are on the threshold of actually becoming the *manipulanda* as which they have cast themselves, and of entering upon a cultural regime "where there is no longer anything either true or false concerning man or history."[8] If so, he remarks with an allusion to Descartes's intricate rhetoric of sleep, dream, and deception in "Meditation One," they will fall into a sleep or a nightmare from which there is no longer any possible awakening.

Opacity is akin to silence, as well as to concealment. For Heidegger, human beings enter upon their essential dignity, which consists "in safeguarding unconcealment, and together with it always in advance the concealment of all beings [*Wesen*] on this earth," insofar as they let themselves belong and respond to "the destinal sending of unconcealment."[9] This involves their coming to understand technicity itself as a (deeply ambiguous) modality of the granting of unconcealment; and what can open the path to such understanding is a further modality of unconcealment that belongs to the configuration of *technē* yet is other than technology, namely artistic *poiēsis* as "the bringing forth of the true into the beautiful."[10] Heidegger tends to privilege, not the silent arts, but the *poiēsis* of the poet. However, he also points out, in the cited essay, that "the poetical [*das Dichterische*] essentially pervades [*durchwest*] every art." It is that which brings the true "into the pure radiance . . . of its shining forth."[11]

Merleau-Ponty, by contrast, now privileges the silent art of painting as the modality of artistic interrogation most capable of revealing "the fabric of raw being of which activism doesn't want to know anything."[12] Painting can rejoin things in their silence and bring this silence, or the opacity of the world, to expression (the term, however, is not used here) because it is not called upon to offer any interpretation or take a stand as to issues, but is free to abide in its pure visual contemplation. One might reflect that such detachment from knowledge and action (which is of course challenged today by some forms of visual art and has rarely, if ever, been really pure) is equally characteristic of music; but Merleau-Ponty finds the detachment of music "from the world and from what can be designated" to be too extreme, thus rendering music self-contained rather than allowing it to function as a modality of proto-phenomenological interrogation.[13] These questionable comments on music may well also illuminate his general disregard for sheer painterly abstraction, which is more akin to music than exploratory of the perceived world or even the psyche.[14]

Merleau-Ponty's revocation of the privilege he had earlier accorded to speech and its arts in favor of the phenomenological guidance offered by painting may, however, need to be qualified, given the fact that—as attested by Edouard Pontremoli—he entered, in late 1960, into correspondence with the novelist Claude Simon, expressing profound admiration for the latter's work (particularly for *La route des Flandres* [The Flanders Road], his seventh novel), together with the wish to address it in a lecture course. "Five Notes on Claude Simon," part of Merleau-Ponty's notes to himself in preparation for his lectures, are extant.[15] As Pontremoli notes, Merleau-Ponty believed, at this time, that he could recognize "in this singular novel, and also in various statements by the author, a research and preoccupation closely similar to his own."[16] Pontremoli describes Simon as a writer who "toils, adjusts, mends, is intent upon making silent experience speak," and whose art is caught in the tension between artistic refinement and the innocence of one who sees. It is certainly significant that Simon claimed that the book to be written (the seventh novel, as a "fragmentary writing of the disaster") appeared to him all at once, like a vision or like a landscape, but in bodily contact with the actual (and now pacific rather than devastated) landscape of Normandy. Thus Merleau-Ponty, in his first note, cites Simon's testimony, given in an interview, that he still sees before him "the moving countryside" (seen from a vehicle) where, "in a fraction of a second, I envisaged *La Route des Flandres*. Not the idea of the book, but the book as a whole."[17] Simon also claimed, however, that "in order to see, to imagine the material of the novel, one must write, or that lived and deeply felt experience, even if verbalized, is not enough to make one a writer; one must work to make "what is felt actually speak."[18] One gleans from Merleau-Ponty's fascination with Claude Simon's writing that, had he lived and been able to offer the planned lectures, he might have rethought once again the relation between the arts of language and "the voices of silence" that are those of the visual arts.

What Merleau-Ponty seeks the painter's guidance for is to enable scientifically informed thought to find its way back to the originary and unmotivated upsurge of the world, its sensory and sense-fraught presencing for embodied human beings. Once thought awakens to the phenomenal reality of one's body, "there [also] awaken the associated bodies," who "haunt me and together with whom I haunt a sole actual and present being," in stark contrast to "that possible body as to which one is free to maintain that it is an information system.[19] This possible body has its ancestry in the Cartesian conception of natural science as being essentially hypothetical (a conception that underlies his mechanistic physiology), rather than being concerned to or capable of doing justice to nature in its actuality. Only by engaging with experience in its actuality, and by vigilant self-questioning, can scientific thought once "again become philosophy,"[20] as it was in the epoch of "classical science"; but now (given the challenges posed by quantum theory to the conception of objects or states in classical physics) the philosophical modality of interrogation can no longer conform to any classical model but requires perhaps a rethinking and further development of the phenomenological approach.

Indivision, Reversibility, and Carnal Essences

The painter's body in its operative actuality is now, for Merleau-Ponty, not so much the agent of expression as of a transubstantiation that takes place between itself, the world, and the painterly work. He or she is at pains to avoid the Cartesian understanding of vision as essentially a form of thought dependent upon bodily indices, together with the Sartrean division between consciousness, as the pure for-itself without any pre-given identity, and the world as the in-itself that lacks self-awareness and self-determination. Instead of these dualisms, Merleau-Ponty affirms "in-division" (that is, nondivision) and a pervasive complication and contamination that give rise to paradoxes, reversals, antinomies, and together with them, to the problems addressed by painting which in their turn "illustrate the enigma of the body."[21]

In exploring the intricate interrelations between vision and motility, Merleau-Ponty avails himself of the Leibnizian terminology of "total parts": vision and motility yield, as it were, two maps that are co-extensive and adequate to perceptible reality as a whole and are, in this sense, "total," yet are not superposable and remain, in this further sense, partial.[22]

In Leibniz's metaphysics of expression (elaborated as early as 1676 but refined thereafter), the individual monadic substances express God and the universe as a whole but nonetheless do so only partially, in keeping with their different monadic perspectives and degrees of lucidity.[23] Unlike Leibniz, however, Merleau-Ponty can acknowledge no absolute original that could be perspectivally expressed. The only systemacity he is prepared to admit is that of a "system of exchanges" that operates, not hierarchically, but laterally as an intercrossing "between seer and seen, between touching and the touched, between one eye and the other, between hand and hand."[24] In this laterality of exchanges without a sharp division between sensible phenomena and the sentient body, vision cannot open upon things from a detached vantage point but must already be prefigured in them, just as the sentient body of her who sees is from the outset offered to vision.

Hence the registers of visual presencing, such as color, form, or light which, Merleau-Ponty notes, the painter's gaze interrogates as to the purely visual means by which the visual scene configures itself—and thus as to their powers of visual constitution—evoke an echo in the painter's body (given that her vision is highly sensitized), while simultaneously her look appears to her to be reciprocated by theirs. This echo or "internal equivalent," which Merleau-Ponty thematizes as a "carnal essence,"[25] motivates in its turn the creation of a new entity, the painterly or graphic "icon" that seeks to body it forth. A carnal essence is not fixed in invariant self-identity but is open to alteration (so that, for instance, Van Gogh's powerful paintings of sunflowers do not fixate the essence of the flower's sensuous presencing, which is, for instance, bodied forth anew and differently in the abstract *Sunflowers* canvases painted by Joan Mitchell). Furthermore, the carnal essence is not contemplated in a dis-

passionate *Wesensschau* or pure intellectual intuition; but rather its aesthetic apprehension engages (true to the double sense of *aisthēsis* as both
sensory apprehension and feeling) the painter's and the viewer's sensory,
imaginative, oneiric, and emotive life. The painting, in Merleau-Ponty's
words, offers to the gaze (and not to the mind) "the traces of vision from
the inside, so that it may espouse them, [and] to vision its interior linings,
the imaginary texture of the real."[26]

As a traditional icon may allow for the presencing of sacred reality
rather than being simply a self-contained image, the painterly "icon," as
Merleau-Ponty understands it, is not a thing to be contemplated purely
for its aesthetic (let alone decorative) value. One does not so much see
it as "see along with it," or under its guidance; and it opens, not unto
transcendent reality, but unto the "wild being" that underlies cultural
and intellectual constructs. The aspect of sacrality is not, however, necessarily excluded here: Merleau-Ponty himself evokes it not only by his terminology of the "icon," but also by repeatedly contrasting the painter's
vision with "profane" vision. With regard to twentieth-century painting,
one need only consider Mark Rothko's intense concern for the contem-
plative attitude and environment conducive to viewing his work (the environment was ideally realized by the Menil Chapel in Houston) to gain
a sense of the continued importance of sacrality, quite apart from any
religious imagery or symbolism, in certain facets of twentieth-century
art. This sense of sacrality is perhaps an intensification of the painter's
awareness of being, as it were, looked at—and thus solicited by and responsive as well as responsible to—not only the mountains or the sea in
the ever-changing light, but the sheer presencing of the world, so that
her or his vision becomes, in this laterality of exchanges, "a mirror or
concentration of the universe."[27]

Merleau-Ponty concludes the second part of "Eye and Mind" with
a reflection on mirrors as being not only (when shown in paintings) a
self-inscription of the painter's vision and of "the travail of vision" as such
by analogy, but also a figuration and amplification of "the metaphysical
structure of our flesh," in that they both attest to and, by means of their
artifice, explore and enrich the carnal or sensory origins of reflection.[28]
In drawing the seer's flesh outside the body proper (so that one may
virtually sense certain stimuli in one's reflected body, as well as actually
sensing them), the mirror also prefigures intercorporeity: "man is a mirror for man."[29] The mythic infatuation of Narcissus with his aqueous reflection is then perhaps not self-absorption, but rather a fascination with
vision as the "universal magic" that interchanges things with spectacles,
and self with others, and thus, paradoxically, a fascination with alterity.

Echoing his observation, in "Cézanne's Doubt," that the painter

does not find himself obliged to choose between such canonical oppo-
sites as sensation and thought, or reality and appearance,[30] Merleau-Ponty
now concludes his reflections on painting and mirrors with the statement: "Essence and existence, imaginary or real, visible or invisible,
painting blurs all our categories in deploying its oneiric universe of carnal essences, efficacious resemblances, and mute significations."[31]

It is clear, however, that what preoccupies him now is the inter-
involvement of vision, the visible, and its painterly interrogation with
invisibilities. The latter comprise, on perhaps the simplest level, what
"profane vision" passes over in an oblivion of its own "premises" or means
of self-constitution, namely the whole "texture of being of which the discrete sensory messages are only the punctuations or the *caesurae*."[32] With
respect to Rembrandt's *Night Watch,* for instance, Merleau-Ponty points
out that the spatial reality of the captain's hand is conveyed by "the intercrossing of two incompossible views" since, whereas the hand points
toward the viewer, its shadow shows it simultaneously in profile.[33]

The invisible of the visible also comprises the latter's imaginary,
oneiric, and emotive resonances; but beyond these relatively straightforward senses of the invisibilities involved in visibility, Merleau-Ponty
appears to be searching for a more hidden sense that has ontological
import but whose articulation seems as yet partially to elude him. He
observes, for instance, that artistic inspiration should be understood literally as "inspiration and expiration of being, respiration within being,"
so that it is vitally interconnected with being and that action and passion
(much like visibility and invisibility) become indiscernible.[34]

His search for this more radical sense of invisibility may be one
reason why, despite the echoes of "Cézanne's Doubt" (among them the
statement that "the painter's vision is a continual birth"),[35] the thematic
of expression that is central to the earlier essay is now in abeyance. Rather
than being superseded, however, expression (as well as institution, which
is also not explicitly thematized) will have to be rethought or developed
in a manner adequate to the full recognition of the invisible of the visible
which, in the context of the ontology of flesh, will dissociate it decisively
from subjectivity.

Descartes's Optics and the Painterly
Interrogation of Vision

If painting is attuned to the transubstantiations and metamorphoses that
characterize vision, Descartes's conceptual and mechanistic reconstruc-

tion of vision in his *Optics,* which Merleau-Ponty addresses in part 3 of
"Eye and Mind," is the locus classicus of the effort to exorcise these "spec-
tres."[36] Although Descartes, in his usual scientific manner, presents his re-
construction of vision as a *modus concipiendi* that, while clear and distinct
as well as technologically fruitful, makes no claim to do justice to nature
in its actuality, it has metaphysical import. For Merleau-Ponty, its import
is that of "an absolute positivity of being," effacing any latencies, together
with the inter-involvement of seer and seen.[37] Vision is cast as essentially
a mental operation that deciphers bodily indices (such as the brain
traces that result from the physiological mechanisms involved). For Descartes, imaginative envisagement, far from penetrating "toward the heart
of being," as Merleau-Ponty would like to understand it, merely makes
these indices say more than they warrant.[38] It goes without saying that
painting, in consequence, in no way defines one's access to being; what
efficacy it may possess (the subjunctive is called for since in fact Descartes
discusses only copperplate engravings) is that of drawing understood as
an art of perspectival projection. This projective schema presupposes a
space that is pure extension, "the in-itself *par excellence,*" independent
of any situated viewpoint and refractory to phenomena such as orientation, envelopment, or inter-encroachment.[39] Perhaps, Merleau-Ponty
speculates, Descartes might have discovered in vision a richer modality
of access to being had he explored such "secondary qualities" as color
(which he does in fact give some attention to in the context of discussing
aerial perspective and afterimages); but the very fact that they exhibit no
regular mathematical correlation to extension leads him to dismiss them
as "secondary."[40]

The point of these analyses is not, of course, to castigate the Cartesian construction of vision, which is integral to the rise of the mathematical sciences of nature and constitutes, in its mathematization of
space, a bold and significant venture of thought. The point is rather,
first of all, to call attention to the temptation inherent in this venture to
reify and absolutize its own constructs, so as "to set up as structures of
being certain properties of beings."[41] Second and importantly, Descartes
himself did not succumb to this temptation and did not simplistically
seek to eliminate the enigma of vision. Rather, and in keeping with his
usual readiness to accept restriction of scope as the price of certainty, he
is ready to concede that vision, in its dependence on bodily indices, is a
mode of thought that "functions according to a program and a law that
it has not given to itself." There remains, at its heart, "a mystery of passivity." In particular, the sentient body, "according to which" one must think
in exercising vision, is not an indifferent part of extension exchangeable
with any other, but is a primary and irrecusable "here."[42] The fact that the

mechanics of light (the refraction and reflection of light rays) and the physiological mechanism involved in vision, as Descartes understands it, yield qualitative perception and meaning can ultimately be ascribed only to "the institution of nature" or to the mystery of embodiment that issues from the divine infinite and creative intellect. As Merleau-Ponty remarks:

> On all these topics, we are disqualified by position. Such is the secret of the Cartesian equilibrium: a metaphysics that gives us decisive reasons to stop doing metaphysics, [that] validates our evidences by limiting them [and] opens up our thought without tearing it to pieces.[43]

Descartes's strategy for guarding his constructivist science against self-absolutization and for safeguarding "the obscurity of the 'there is'" is one that is no longer available to the contemporary "'technicized' thought" that Merleau-Ponty problematized in the opening pages of "Eye and Mind." What is needed instead is a phenomenological "prospecting of the actual world," as seen and as lived "from within," in its layered and intercalated complexity.[44] This is the quest that motivates Merleau-Ponty to turn for guidance to the painter's nonverbal interrogation of visuality.

What an interrogation of painterly interrogation may reveal is what Jacques Garelli calls "a visibility that pronounces itself within the flesh of the world, in its processes of differentiation," and in the context of which the registers of visibility (such as color or form), and visible givens themselves, have a differential value.[45] As Merleau-Ponty remarks in a working note to *The Visible and the Invisible*, dated November 1959, a certain color gives itself as both "a certain being and a *dimension*, the expression *of every possible being*, functioning, in these dual aspects, as "a total part":

> It is thus that the sensible initiates me to the world, as language [does] to the other: by encroachment, *Überschreiten*. Perception is not, in the first instance, perception of *things*, but perception of *elements* (water, air . . .), of things that are *dimensions*, that are worlds. I glide unto these elements, and here I am within the *world;* I glide from the "subjective" to being.[46]

The trajectory of the interrogation orients itself toward a revisioning of ontology that, as Garelli puts it, will ultimately leave "no locality assignable to the thing or to man, unless by reduction."[47] Has Merleau-Ponty's own thought, in its turn to painting as a nondiscursive modality of thought that investigates "the fabric of raw meaning" in its self-configuration, entirely detached itself from any kinship with reduction—a reduction that now bears, to be sure, not on ontology, but on the understanding of painting itself? As Michel Haar argues, Merleau-Ponty considers painting to be in unbroken continuity with perception, so that it reinscribes the spontaneity of the primary perceptual expression:

> The paradoxical, disorienting project of Merleau-Ponty is to relativize the history of painting by leading it back to its cradle, to the gestures of the body immersed in a trans-historical living and quasi-eternal present.[48]

The unbroken unity of painting that Merleau-Ponty recognizes "since Lascaux" and that, for him, spans epochs and cultures contrasts strangely with the fluidity he accords it in that it interrogates phenomena in the very process of taking form. Haar speculates that what may have led him to the questionable recognition of an originary "virginity without reference" may have been his postulation of a fundamental difference between the visual (and perhaps also musical) arts and the arts of language, such that "whereas the former 'take up the task again at the outset,' the latter inscribe themselves in a tradition that they perpetuate."[49] Such was, of course, the reason for the privilege accorded to the arts of language in "Indirect Language and the Voices of Silence."

No reductive unification of painting, or of any visual art, can hope to stand up against an attentive exploration of these arts' historical, cultural, and contemporary diversity—an exploration that a phenomenological engagement with them cannot dispense with. In "Eye and Mind," however, Merleau-Ponty, aware no doubt of this challenge, tends to engage more closely and consistently with the writings and reported sayings of painters than with their actual works (notwithstanding his thoughtful selection of reproductions of works by Giacometti, de Staël, Cézanne, Matisse, Klee, and Rodin and Richier that grace the essay, but that he does not, for the most part, directly comment on). Thus, for instance, Max Ernst and Henri Michaux are quoted; but a consideration of surrealist *painterly practice* (which Merleau-Ponty avoids) would challenge his construal of painting by showing only a tenuous and questionable continuity with perception. Since it is part 4 of "Eye and Mind" that most searchingly addresses both painterly practice and the reflections of painters on their art, and since it also forms the heart of the essay, the issues touched upon will have to be examined more fully in its context.

Fields and Dimensions of Visual Presencing

Echoing Heidegger's point in "The Origin of the Work of Art," that the world proper to the work of art is not the original and irretrievable one of its creation, but rather the one that it now opens up and grants access to,[50] Merleau-Ponty reflects that the work "opens up a field" in which it inscribes its own metamorphoses.[51] This reflection not only supersedes his negative comments on the museum's "historicity of death" in "Indirect Language and the Voices of Silence,"[52] but it also consummates his argument, dating back to "Cézanne's Doubt," that artworks are neither causally explicable nor situated in a history of straightforward filiation. The artwork, he now considers, is possessed of an active and self-renewing identity, and thus exhibits a continued differential fecundity. In particular, this "structure of the event" within contingency now inspires him to explore the ontological implications of confronting "classical thought" (which embraces both the philosophical tradition and what he has called "classical science") with "the researches of modern painting." Part 4 of "Eye and Mind" is devoted to this exploration.

If the painter is still in quest of depth (*la profondeur*), what he or she seeks cannot be either prosaic three-dimensional extension or perspectival construction (as concerns both of these, the enigma is their bond which allows perspectival distortions and the eclipsing of things from view to reveal their spatial deployment). The depth that the painter seeks is not a dimension, but rather "the reversibility of dimensions," a "global locality" or voluminosity that allows for the presencing of things and that involves all the registers of visibility, such as color, the "latent line," or void no less than form.[53]

One difficulty with Merleau-Ponty's analysis is that he does not distinguish between the spatiality of the scene that a painting may give expression to and pictorial space as such, resulting from the visual interaction of colors, forms, internal edges, and other aspects of painterly facture. As perhaps a limit case, even a monochrome painting (such as, for instance, Brice Marden's early monochromes) exhibits pictorial spatiality, due to aspects of its facture such as the relationship between color and format, the spatial dynamics of color itself, the facture of the surface and hence the way it absorbs or reflects light, and the treatment of edges. The elements that make for a painting's pictorial space may, to be sure, also express the spatiality of nature (thus Merleau-Ponty refers obliquely to the painterly tradition of color-space, which can be traced back to Titian and forward to Cézanne); but pictorial space need have no reference beyond itself. Merleau-Ponty remains rather hesitant to dissociate pictorial space—or any aspect of the visual work—from a reference to the perceived world (and thus from the primacy of perceptual expression). Even when he reflects that the painter does not representationally confront the world but rather "comes to birth" within it (the metaphors of natality remain prominent), as though by a concentration and "coming into its own" of the visible, and that painting tends ultimately toward autofiguration, he seems to take away with one hand what he has just granted with the other: "[The painting] is a spectacle of something only in being the spectacle of nothing . . . so as to show how things make themselves things, and the world [makes itself] world."[54]

As truly autofigurative, or as the "spectacle of nothing" beyond itself, the painting would not be charged with revealing the visual constitution of things, or of the world. Nevertheless, Merleau-Ponty does acknowledge that the effort of modern painting has not been a matter of choosing "between the figuration of things and the creation of signs, but of multiplying the systems of equivalences [between the registers of visibility and of painterly facture] of breaking their adherence to the envelope of things."[55] Not that nonfigurative painting is necessarily, or even usually, a creation of signs, but this characterization is indeed pertinent to the art of Paul Klee's, whose painterly thought now fascinates Merleau-Ponty.

Merleau-Ponty's return to the perceived world and to the expressivity of perception nonetheless also takes him beyond it. Reflecting on the way one sees, on a languid summer's day, the water in a swimming pool, he notes that one cannot definitively localize its shimmering substance or "aqueous power," so that it is not contained by the pool in which it "materializes itself" but also dances, in a play of wavelike patterns or arabesques of light, across the screen of cypresses, expressing its elemental character in the luminosity and dynamism of the entire scene.[56] What the painter seeks under the name of depth—and also of space or color—is "this internal animation, this radiance of the visible," which Merleau-Ponty undertakes to explore in its various registers and finally as "a system of equivalences."[57] Modern painting and sculpture have, he notes, multiplied this system, further elaborating what he calls "a logos of lights, of reliefs, of colors, of masses, a presentation without concept of universal being."[58] In doing so, an artist may use novel materials or invent entirely "new means of expression"; but she may also reinvest those long recognized as integral to her art. Among these, Merleau-Ponty here considers the most basic: color, line, and the presentation of motion in media that are intrinsically static.

In discussing "the dimension of color," or the power of color to create form and space, to unite depth with surface and, in short, to enable visual presencing in its complexity, he turns his attention back to Cézanne. Surprisingly, however, he makes no effort to explore the artist's "harmonies parallel to nature," his processions of patches of subtle and luminous color, the role of color in his creative process, or even his rich reflections or remarks on color. He focuses instead on the whites (or the areas of blank gessoed canvas) interspersed in the *Portrait of Vallier*.[59]

Cézanne, in fact, painted five portraits in oil, and three in watercolor, of the gardener Vallier during the last two years of his life (one of the oils—it is unclear which—is considered to be the last painting he worked on before his death).[60] Unfortunately Merleau-Ponty does not specify which of the oil portraits he has in mind (the inclusion of areas of white paper in a watercolor would not call for special comment). Quite apart from the consideration that, in these late oil paintings, Cézanne's handling of paint is thicker and crustier (and thus less revealing of the blank canvas) than in earlier works, and that he had already begun to intersperse blanks in his paintings much earlier (compare, for instance, the 1896 portrait of Joachim Gasquet), Michel Haar's criticism is apt: if indeed, as Merleau-Ponty has it, the function of these whites were to reveal "a more general being of color" or of color-space than is revealed by chromas, why would Cézanne have reserved them for only a few of his paintings?[61] Furthermore, Haar remarks, "One can question oneself about the nostalgia for the originary that leads Merleau-Ponty to privilege whiteness, the absence of color, in relation to colors . . .Whiteness would not appear if it were not surrounded by colors."[62]

To these points one might add the consideration that, although white light comprises within itself all the hues of the spectrum, this is far from being true of pigmentary whites, which are dense and opaque and lack the originary character, with respect to chromas, that Merleau-Ponty ascribes to white. The "dimension of color" calls for a more nuanced exploration of color than Merleau-Ponty offers here.

Merleau-Ponty does, however, devote more sustained attention to line, pointing out that (as, he admits, painters need not be told) contour lines are an artifice; there are no outlines in nature. Such lines may be indicated, or even "imperiously demanded" by things without, however, being entities in their own right. The challenge faced by the artist is therefore to liberate line from the prosaic and mendacious task of demarcating things, and of restoring to it its autonomous power to "render visible."[63]

Is it true, however, that, as Merleau-Ponty claims, no one before Klee has allowed a line to muse, to undulate, or to "go line" (*aller ligne*)?[64] Line has been fundamental to classical Chinese painting and calligraphy since its remote inception, having there what has been called a "presentational" rather than a mimetic function.[65] In his *Recorded Sayings,* the early Qing dynasty individualist painter Shitao (or Zhu Ruoji, 1642–1707) speaks of a primordial line (*yihua,* literally "one-stroke painting") which "encompasses nature's infinity."[66] Even in Western art, moreover, one can trace what Merleau-Ponty calls the "latent line" perhaps back to "Lascaux," but certainly to classical Greek relief sculpture and painting, in which the play and expressivity of line are highlighted. A fine example—though only one among many—are the white ground terracotta "bobbin" paintings attributed to the "Penthesilea Painter," two of which (showing a youth in the company of Nike, and of Eros) can be seen in New York City's Metropolitan Museum of Art.[67]

The fact that line here describes figures, or perhaps a fillet and a lyre, does not prevent it from "musing," or from autonomously deploying itself, effracting and activating space, any more than the graphic line of Picasso or of Matisse (two outstanding visual poets of line) needs to detach itself from descriptive reference or renounce the inspiration of natural forms to do so. Merleau-Ponty recognizes that line is essentially "a certain effraction practiced within the in-itself . . . [a] restriction, segregation, modulation of a primary spatiality."[68]

Finally, as to the virtual presentation of motion, Merleau-Ponty points out that a cinematic "still" showing a body in motion belies motion's temporal dynamics by arresting time, while cubist analyses of motion, or Marcel Duchamp's *Nude Descending a Staircase*, are "Zenonian reveries on motion" that do not allow one to experience its actuality.[69] What allows for "the surging forth of transition and duration" is, as Auguste Rodin recognized, a spatial-temporal incompatibility among the respective positions of the limbs or trunk of a moving body, an "internal discordance" that, in violating canonical logic by conjoining incompossibles, is nonetheless true to "the logic of the body" in motion.[70] Rather than clinging to the external features of motion, art seeks "its secret ciphers" and, in so doing, attests once again that "all flesh, and even that of the world, radiates beyond itself."[71]

With respect to the sculptural presentation of motion, one may consider, by way of an example, a Han dynasty bronze of a "heavenly" or "dragon" horse, dating to the second century C.E.[72] Since this mythical horse "flies" (without wings), it is shown with three of its hooves in the air, and one resting lightly on the back of a flying swallow. The sculpture conveys a powerful sense of equine energy and motion, even though the position of the horse's limbs is manifestly unnatural; no real horse would ever gallop in this way. The example serves to suggest that a convincing presentation of movement may be accomplished, not only by the conjunction of temporal incompossibles, but also by an utter discordance with reality, or even in independence of any representation (as in abstract painting or sculpture). Merleau-Ponty's tendency to privilege art's interrogation of phenomenal reality leads him to focus on its mimetic power, rather than to consider that motion, or dynamic energy, need not be mimetically presented to be conveyed by a work of art. Chinese and Japanese brush calligraphy are abstract arts of motion in space, transmitting dynamic energy; and such energy is also intensely conveyed at times in different ways, by some twentieth-century abstract painting, such as the works of Franz Kline, Joan Mitchell, or Willem de Kooning.

What Merleau-Ponty's analyses of painting and sculpture converge on is an erosion of customary ontic assurances. In this sense, he concludes part 4 with the epitaph, taken from Klee's *Diaries,* that is inscribed on his tomb, translating the German "Diesseitig bin ich gar nicht fassbar" as "Je suis insaissisable dans l'immanence" ("I cannot be grasped in immanence"). The translation is idiosyncratic, since the German terms "diesseitig" and "jenseitig" ordinarily refer to what lies "on this side" or "that side" of the dividing line marked by death. An examination of Klee's *Diaries* reveals that he used the terms in their customary sense; and the larger context of the epitaph concerns the closeness of his artistic persona to "the dead and unborn."[73] Furthermore, one of Klee's paintings, dating from 1940 (the year of his death) and now in the Fondation Beyeler, is titled *Gefangen: Diesseits/Jenseits Figur* (*Imprisoned: Figure of This-Side/ Beyond*). The schematically rendered figure in this painting has one eye turned downward and the other, without pupil and thus unseeing, turned heavenward.

Galen Johnson also points out the idiosyncrasy of Merleau-Ponty's translation, noting that it is not that of Pierre Klossowski's French translation of the *Diaries,* which renders *diesseits* correctly as *ici-bas.*[74] Johnson offers a perceptive discussion on two senses that "transcendence," in its opposition to "immanence," carries for Merleau-Ponty: besides the "horizontal" outreach toward others and toward the world, there is also, for him, a "transdescendence" that probes the depths.[75] One might, perhaps, go further and reflect that, if indeed painting, for Merleau-Ponty, undercuts traditional dichotomies, it will also undercut that of immanence and transcendence, allowing one to glimpse the emptiness at the heart of presencing. Although he notes that an artist must acknowledge that spirit, being intrinsically without place, must nevertheless remain bound to a body to be initiated to others and to nature, visual presencing springs for him ultimately from the sheer "dehiscence of being."[76] Dehiscence— a botanical metaphor—induces dissemination, a differential proliferation and outreach into the unknown, which inscribes itself in the "invisible reverse" of visuality, or perhaps even in a radical invisibility "without an ontic mask."[77] Art can allow invisibilities to reveal themselves as such, that is to say, in the modality of "a certain absence." Absence cannot function as a positive nucleus of expression in the traditional sense. This confirms that the notion of expression must await a critical rethinking that will decisively dissociate it from positivity and render it adequate to an ontology of the "dehiscence" or "deflagration" of being.

The Historicity of Artistic Creation

In the short fifth part of "Eye and Mind," Merleau-Ponty returns to the issues of the historicity of art and of the relation between artistic or intellectual creation involving language, and creation in the silence of visuality. His discussion incorporates the insights he first articulated in his 1954–55 lecture courses on institution and passivity, together with the critical revisions of certain of his positions in "Indirect Language and the Voices of Silence" that they imply.

The "convergences" or stylistic affinities between artworks belonging to different epochs or cultures that had puzzled Malraux now no longer call, in Merleau-Ponty's view, for the postulation of a trans-historical and trans-cultural unity of art that would explain them. If "the first of paintings went to the farthest reach of the future,"[78] it did not do so by an essential circumscription of the art, but by opening up a differential field within which every creation solicits others or, as Merleau-Ponty puts it, "confirms, exalts, recreates, or creates in advance all the others."[79] If certain of Rodin's sculptural fragments converge surprisingly with works by Germaine Richier, one need not look for an explanation beyond the fact that, as *sculptors,* both artists are interlinked by the same "network of being."[80] Every register of visuality, such as form, color, mass, line, or tonality (technically called "value") is, Merleau-Ponty now affirms, one of "the branches of being"; and as such—that is to say, as what he also calls a "dimension"—it involves all the others. No genuine artistic quest can be merely partial but rather has a bearing on the art as a whole; and since every creation reconfigures the entire field, there are also no definitive innovations or advances: "At the moment when he [the artist] has just acquired a certain expertise, he notices that he has opened up another field where everything that he was previously able to express has to be resaid differently."[81]

These considerations counteract the privilege that Merleau-Ponty had earlier (in "Indirect Language and the Voices of Silence") accorded to the arts of language over the silent arts as being more capable of accomplished and historically significant creation. Furthermore, if every creation inscribes itself in a trans-subjective, differential field, it will not be able to set itself up as a self-contained and definitive achievement. Merleau-Ponty reflects that anything that has been discovered or established, whether in the arts, in philosophy, or even in the sciences, still remains in some respects elusive and horizontal. Thus the sciences also find themselves constrained to recognize "a zone of the 'fundamental,' populated by dense, open, torn beings" which the theory in question cannot exhaustively encompass.[82] While this thought is only indicated rather than significantly developed here, Merleau-Ponty's engagement with the biological sciences in the lecture courses on nature will allow for a fuller exploration.[83]

In the context of the philosophy of art, two key points are that no human creative endeavor can attain the lucid self-transparency with which, in "Indirect Language and the Voices of Silence," Merleau-Ponty had credited the arts of language, and that, if meaning is differential at its source and its core, these arts also lack any privilege as to the appropriation of their own past, so that dispropriation prevails.

Finally, if there are, by virtue of the dimensional and field structures elaborated, "no [artistic] pathways that are truly opposed," and if the history of the visual arts advances by labyrinthine detours, encroachments, or sudden transformations rather than by definitive and one-directional progress,[84] these arts can also no longer be criticized for their supposed spirit of rivalry that would frustrate meaningful historical integration.

Do these insights amount, in the end, to a resigned parody of Heracliteanism, so that "everything flows"; and the soil beneath one's steps is shifting quicksand? Such a despairing relativism springs, in Merleau-Ponty's judgment, from a deluded attachment to the fantasy of some ultimate positivity that would surmount the lack, void, or emptiness within historicity and at the origin of artistic creation.[85]

In one of the paeans to natality that seemed to flow from his pen as readily and memorably as meditations on mortality flowed from those of Heidegger and Derrida, Merleau-Ponty (whose very image of the "branches of being" suggests a tree of life) concludes his last essay with the reflection that the lack inherent in all artistic and intellectual creations is not simply a matter of their finitude and fragility, or of the creators' mortal condition, but indicates rather that they still "have almost their entire life before them." It remains now to consider—in the contexts of Merleau-Ponty's philosophy of nature and ontology—how these insights, indebted to his engagement with institution and passivity and developed in the context of his meditations on art, will also inform and transform his understanding of the nature and scope of expression.

Part 2

Expression in Animal Life

4

The Expressivity of Animal Behavior: Embryogenesis and Environing Worlds

We are surrounded by innumerable realities which exceed our ability to intuit them [*unser Anschauungsvermögen*]; they remain "non-intuitable" [*un-anschaulich*] because they are "super-intuitable" [*überanschaulich*]. All living beings, plants and animals, belong here; we possess of them only the image of their momentary appearance; as to their mode of being [*Dasein*], which reaches in a closed manner from the germ to the adult, and of which we know that it shelters a unitary lawfulness, we can form no image. All the kinds of animals and of plants, with which we operate as though with known magnitudes, are super-intuitable realities.

—Jakob von Uexküll, *Umwelt und Innenwelt der Tiere* (1909)

Of the three consecutive lecture courses on nature that Merleau-Ponty offered at the Collège de France between 1956 and 1960,[1] it is the second course, titled "The Concept of Nature: Animality, the Human Body, and the Passage to Culture" that offers a rich source for studying the thematic of expression, since it not only deals with sentient life but also focuses predominantly on behavior. Although Merleau-Ponty singles out both the notions of behavior and of information and communication—notions that in "the mutation of biological concepts" have come to displace the antithesis of mechanism and vitalism—as topics to be examined, his chief focus is trained on behavior, a thematic that he had, of course, already taken up in his first book, *The Structure of Behavior* of 1942.[2] Notwithstanding the course title, the human body is not thematized; and even in the third course, titled "The Concept of Nature: Nature and Logos; The Human Body," it is discussed only (with a particular focus on libido, and thus with a slant toward psychoanalysis) in the margins of explorations of the animal body and, in particular, of Darwinian and neo-Darwinian evolutionary theory.[3] Nevertheless, human embodiment is already an important concern at the outset of the first and longest course, devoted to "The Concept of Nature," where Merleau-Ponty problematizes the conceptual rupture between Descartes's understanding of nature as "the *auto-functioning* of the laws, which derives from the idea of the infinite," and his account of what he terms the "substantial union" of body and soul, which is opaque to the intellect yet vividly attested to by experience or feeling.[4] The concern with human embodiment remains horizonal throughout the nature courses.

In entering upon a reading of these lecture courses, one needs to bear in mind that, in the first two courses, one is not reading Merleau-Ponty's actual words, but rather the notes diligently (but, it seems, not without certain lapses) taken by an anonymous auditor, whereas the third course (for which no student notes were available) consists of the editors' compilation of Merleau-Ponty's characteristically sparse, sketchy, and "sometimes illegible" lecture notes.[5] Despite these textual limitations, the courses on nature are crucially important, not only due to their penetrating analyses of the history of philosophical and scientific conceptions of nature and of the then current debates in the biological sciences, but because, as Merleau-Ponty states, "the concept of Nature is always the expression of an ontology—and its privileged expression."[6] The nature lectures are therefore integral to and indispensable for the passage to ontology that characterizes Merleau-Ponty's late thought in *The Visible and the Invisible,* left a fragment at his death.

Embryology and Behavior

In 1929, George E. Coghill published his pathbreaking study of the embryology and the physiological and behavioral development of the axolotl lizard (*Amblystoma tigrinum*), a Mexican species, and of the closely related species *Amblystoma punctatum,* in which, however, the essential behaviors of swimming (the animal spends the early part of its life in water), predation, and walking develop at different relative rates.[7] Coghill's choice of this vertebrate for his analyses reflects the fact that it is quite "typical" rather than being highly specialized, and that it is also "rather primitive."[8] Merleau-Ponty initiates his discussion of animality by a reflection on Coghill's work which, according to the lecture notes, "still has not been exceeded, [although] we haven't yet measured all its weight."[9] One of Coghill's key insights concerns the close congruence between physiological maturation and the emergence of behavior, so that "the form of the behavior pattern in *Amblystoma* develops step by step according to the order of growth in particular parts of the nervous mechanism."[10] Merleau-Ponty (according to the lecture notes) puts it somewhat more forcefully: "the maturation of the organism and the emergence of behavior are one and the same thing."[11] No less importantly, Coghill shows that, in its development from egg to maturity, the animal is not assembled piecemeal but constitutes from the outset an integral whole, so that there is a predominance of the organic totality over the parts. This means, according to him, that there are two processes operating simultaneously in the development of behavior, one being the expansion of the total pattern in its unity, and the other "the individuation of partial systems which eventually acquire more or less discreteness."[12] In their emergence, these partial systems, such as the motility of the forelimbs (which develop first) are initially under the dominance of trunk movement and only gradually acquire their relative autonomy. It is, Coghill writes, as though the central government were to establish "its sovereignty over the rising community before that community had acquired a central organization of its own." The simile is closely echoed in the lecture notes (which perhaps lends credence to the anonymous auditor).[13] Furthermore, Coghill points out, the individuation of a particular local pattern within the total pattern of the developing organism appears to be anticipated by the growth of nervous organization "with specific reference to that partial pattern long before the latter makes its appearance in behavior."[14] This implies that the organism is not an entity closed in upon itself but must be understood in terms of a reference or openness to the future. Moreover, it draws on behavioral accomplishments already realized, such as swimming, to accomplish new tasks essential to its survival, such as terrestrial locomotion.

This process of development is regulated by the growth and differentiation of the nervous system. The nerve cells cannot, Coghill emphasizes, be regarded as a mere conducting mechanism but constitute from the outset "a dynamic system reacting to its surroundings in the manner of the living organism."[15] The system is not only dynamic (Coghill rejects a static anatomy) but also flexible, in that the different specialized functions of the nerve cells are not inherent to them but result from their placement in the context of the polarities and gradients that Coghill traces in organismic development.

In the lecture notes, Merleau-Ponty emphasizes this point: "At the origin, the nervous cells are of the same kind, and what distinguishes them is the direction of conduction toward the head or toward the tail, following which they are motor or sensory."[16] The neural system thus emerges from a pre-neural dynamic; and this dynamic does not cease to operate at any point in the maturation of the organism. Rather, according to Coghill's insight that Merleau-Ponty affirms, the greater capacity for learning that distinguishes higher animals from, say, insects is due to the matrix of pre-neural tissue within which the functional nervous system is embedded, so that, to echo some of the previous discussion, "the conception that a neuron grows during a so-called embryonic period . . . and then ceases to grow and becomes simply a conductor . . . is erroneous and wholly inadequate" to account for the role of the nervous system in learning.[17] According to the lecture notes, one must thus regard the function of conduction as a mere consequence rather than as the governing principle of nervous organization.[18]

Merleau-Ponty points out that, in the dynamic system that is the developing organism, a characteristic total pattern spreads throughout the whole of it at the same time that its parts "acquire an existence proper to them and [do so] in the very order in which they are invaded by the total pattern." This, he notes, presents the philosophical problem of how to understand an operative totality that is irreducible to its parts. The question of what status one must accord to such a totality is, in his view, not only "at the center of this course on the idea of nature . . . [but also of] the whole of philosophy."[19]

The reader may perhaps wonder what this question, and indeed Merleau-Ponty's close engagement with a behaviorally focused embryology, may have to do with the problematic of expression. One can, at this juncture, offer only a hint: the relation between the totality and the emergent behaviors is an expressive (and not a mechanical) relation. Merleau-Ponty does not address this issue here but rather asks his auditors to conjoin the researches of Coghill with those of Arnold Gesell and Catherine S. Amatruda, originally published in 1945.[20] Despite their acknowledged indebtedness to Coghill, the latter researches are focused, not on a humble lizard (even though the authors include two of Coghill's images of *Amblystoma*), but on the prenatal and circumnatal development of the human being. This focus is indeed already prefigured by Coghill, who claims that in man as well there is a "forward reference" in physiological and neurological development, so that the human organism is one that, within certain parameters, is self-creating and operative in and of itself.[21]

Given Gesell and Amatruda's dominant focus on form in a biological context, it may be best to begin by enumerating their seven principles of a dynamic morphology—principles that are echoed closely in the lecture course.[22] These principles, which Gesell and Amatruda acknowledge to be closely interrelated, but which nonetheless vary greatly in their actual and individual expression, are the following:

The first principle is that of "individuating fore-reference" or of the anticipatory and provisional realization of competences and adjustments that are neither brought about by environmental factors nor are due to experience but are, rather, endogenous. The second principle is that of the directionality of development (e.g., its cephalo-caudal or proximal-distal sequencing), while the third principle is that of "spiral reincorporation," which is to say, of the spiral pattern of incorporating lower-level organization or achievements into the higher, thereby transforming rather than simply superseding the former. This is, of course, the structure of Merleau-Ponty's "dépassement [ascension, surpassment] sur place" or "surpassing in place" which will be articulated in *The Visible and the Invisible*.[23] In the lecture course, the second and third principles are conflated. The fourth principle is that of the "reciprocal interweaving" of underlying structures; and Merleau-Ponty (who shares the authors' fondness for textile metaphors) elaborates this: the design must appear "with a certain surprise" out of threads that seem uncoordinated; for "life does not present a united front."[24] The fifth principle is that of functional asymmetry: notwithstanding the bilateral symmetry of the human body schema, man confronts the world obliquely and takes initiative from a decentered position (symmetry is, after all, the figure of stability). The sixth principle, that of "self-regulatory fluctuation," is closely connected with this, in that it indicates that the achievement of balance and progress always involves instability and disequilibrium. Finally, the seventh principle, that of "optimal tendency," specifies that life tends toward maximal realization or, according to the lecture notes, toward "a certain optimum."

Gesell and Amatruda offer a richly detailed account of embryonic, fetal, and circumnatal human development, showing that morphogenesis is at one with the emergence of behavior. Although species-specific, and thus inherent and fixed in its sequence, it is in each case realized in an individual manner by the observed "fetal-infants" (premature infants who are developmentally still in a fetal stage), and by neonates. Echoing Coghill, Gesell and Amatruda note that the embryo already "is perfectly integrated even before it has a nervous system," and that many of the human being's twelve billion or more neurons (which have already come into existence by the mid-fetal period) "continue to grow in an embryonic manner" from then on into adulthood, forming the basis for the possibility of creative accomplishments or "genius."[25]

Although Gesell and Amatruda's *The Embryology of Behavior* shows some philosophical ambition, its philosophical sophistication does not equal its scientific (or human) interest; and Merleau-Ponty thus treats it more as a basis for developing certain insights or questions than as a partner in dialogue. Taking up the insight that the animal body must be defined dynamically and can be understood as a modality of the circumscription of space, he elaborates it by likening this circumscription (which echoes the demarcation of a "field") to the ritual gestures of the Roman augur tracing out "a holy and meaningful contour." Similarly, the developing organism defines a *templum* within which gestures and other elements of behavior will have a meaning.[26]

Prominent among these elements is the asymmetry of behavior (see the fifth principle of dynamic morphology). Merleau-Ponty remarks critically that Gesell fails to ask just why such asymmetry is typical of the human being, and that he treats it implicitly as a mere contingent phenomenon, rather than calling attention to its essential connection with action. In comparing the asymmetry of behavior to the Saussurean understanding of language as based on the diacritical, and thus differential, relationships among signs, Merleau-Ponty begins to highlight the central role of sheer difference in the organization of behavior, and to work toward a non-positive understanding of totality.[27]

As Gesell and Amatruda make clear, there is no real difference between bodily organization and the organization of behavior (Merleau-Ponty cites here the infant's gradual development of clearly defined periods of sleeping and waking, as discussed in *The Embryology of Behavior*).[28] The developing body is a sketch or anticipation of behavior; and reciprocally behavior can be considered as "a second body" elaborated by the intercrossings of motor powers, the whole forming "an organic body of behavior moving toward the heights in a spiral cycle."[29]

Merleau-Ponty takes from his reading of Gesell and Amatruda the notion of a field (which was already prominent in the lecture course on institution of 1954–55).[30] In outlining why, for Gesell and Amatruda, the animal cannot be considered a mechanism, the lecture notes comment:

> The animal must be considered as a field, that is, it is both a physical being and a meaning. It is a true electrical field. Only a field has properties such that it is always distinguished from things *partes extra partes*, because it always includes a relation between parts and the whole.[31]

It may be the case that, in contemporary physics, field theory must be considered "a vestige of state logic," even though, as the physicist David Finkelstein comments, it had until now been "the only way to combine the principles of locality and relativity." Among the reasons why it cannot be ultimate are, according to Finkelstein, the marks of its "degeneracy" which indicate that it is a projection of a deeper theory—a theory that, in Finkelstein's view, will reject a continuum of space-time in favor of a discrete theory "in which the discreteness is so fine that we have to approximate it by a continuum."[32] Had Merleau-Ponty been able to follow these contemporary discussions, he might have found that the notion of a field, based, as it is, on that of a continuum, may not be radical enough to function as the figure of a purely differential organization. He requires such a figure because he equates the notion of form—which, he notes, Gesell considers to be "the fundamental mystery of science"—with that of totality; and he considers totality to be in no way positive, but to be rather "a principle that is either *negative* or based on *absence*."[33]

Merleau-Ponty does caution that, with respect to the "new biology," notions such as those of gradients and field function as the index of a problem rather than as solutions. The problem remains that of the status of a totality that is neither merely supervenient upon the assembly of parts nor is a positive and antecedently directive principle. In search of models for such a totality he turns, first, to cognitive psychology, then to "the becoming of a painting," and finally to an example of animation, given that, in the purely perceptual domain, "nothing impedes the whole from being other than the sum of its parts without being, for all that, a transcendent entity."[34] Among these models, those of the perception of movement and of painterly creation are of special interest, since they allow one to link the scientifically informed discussion of behavior back to Merleau-Ponty's aesthetic thought, and in particular to "Eye and Mind" (with its reflections on the painterly and sculptural expression of motion). Thus they facilitate the discernment of yet another whole that is neither antecedent nor supervenient to its articulation: that of the compass of the philosopher's own thought.

Movement, according to the lecture notes, is not perceived as merely sequential, but rather as an oriented whole; and the filmed documentation of the working processes of Matisse and Picasso shows the almost miraculous emergence of a compelling work from seemingly random and erratic painterly gestures. Working processes differ, of course; but Merleau-Ponty could just as well have taken his model from certain classical painters (based on the more laborious study of underpaintings and preparatory work). Thus, for instance, Tintoretto's consummately articulated figures tend to emerge from improbable skeins and tangles of lines. Referring to the model of painterly creation, Merleau-Ponty comments in the lecture notes:

> It is the same for the body of behavior in Gesell. Threads are tied up, which come from everywhere, and which constitute independent forms

> . . . at the same time [as] . . . a unity. With the first sign, a halo of the possible appears, which was not contained in the first sign, and which was unforeseeable from it.[35]

As to the status of this totality, he acknowledges that, at this point, he can only offer "some cues." If the present contains the future in latency, this is due, he suggests, not to positive factors, but rather to a disequilibrium—one, moreover, that does not allow for the "lazy solution" of returning to a prior state of balance (thus the adolescent facing puberty cannot return to and ensconce herself in the relative quiescence of childhood). "It is not a positive being but an interrogative being that defines life," Merleau-Ponty suggests; and the totality that may surge forth from multiplicity is "the establishment of a certain dimension" in terms of which the organism's surroundings will acquire meaning or, one might say, configure a world.[36] Negation, he now reflects, need not be synonymous with irreality but may be understood as divergence; and life, perhaps, "is only a fold, the reality of a process . . . unobservable up close."[37]

It has been a rather tortuous itinerary that has led to Merleau-Ponty's repeated, and repeatedly qualified, formulations of the non-positive or non-entitative status of totality in the context of organismic maturation and behavior; but it is this non-positivity of the governing principle that will radicalize his late understanding of expression. Expression now can clearly not function as the realization or concretion of anything pre-given but will have to be thought in terms of sheer divergence, difference, or perhaps natality.

Environing Worlds: Jakob von Uexküll

The great German zoologist Jakob von Uexküll's (1864–1944) fundamental theory that each species of animal forms and lives within its own environing world or *Umwelt,* together with his detailed studies of animal *Umwelten,* has engaged philosophers including Heidegger, Merleau-Ponty, and Deleuze and has been formative for the fields of ethology and biosemiotics.[38] In 1926 Uexküll, who had been working at the Zoological Center in Naples but had been forced by the wartime loss of his family fortune to take up a position at the University of Hamburg, founded there the influential Institute for *Umwelt* Research. Concerning Uexküll's thought and philosophical import, Giorgio Agamben comments:

> Uexküll's investigations into the animal environments are contemporary with both quantum physics and the artistic avant-gardes. And like

them, they express the unreserved abandonment of every anthropo-
centric perspective in the life sciences and the radical schematization
of nature . . . Where classical science saw a single world that comprised
within it all living species hierarchically ordered, Uexküll instead sup-
poses an infinite variety of perceptual worlds . . . linked together as
though in a gigantic musical score.[39]

Merleau-Ponty explores Uexküll's notion of *Umwelt* and its implications
chiefly on the basis of two books from the range of Uexküll's writings:
his early work, *Environing Worlds and Inner Worlds of Animals* (*Umwelt und
Innenwelt der Tiere*), which appeared in 1909, and the late *Strolls Through
the Environing Worlds of Animals and Humans* (*Streifzüge durch die Umwelten
von Tieren und Menschen*) of 1934.[40] Given that almost a quarter-century
separates these two works, their understanding of the *Umwelt* is not iden-
tical; and it is therefore appropriate here to outline their different perspectives.

Having discussed, in *Environing Worlds and Inner World of Animals*,
the environing worlds of mostly primitive invertebrates, including the
amoeba (*Amoeba terricula*), which is little more than a clump of protoplasm, as well as *Paramecium,* sea anemones, medusas, sea urchins, star-
fish, mollusks, crustaceans, crabs, and leeches, and finally cephalopods,
earthworms, and dragonflies—life forms among which Uexküll acknowledges being "at home"[41]—he considers that it is the human observer's
own milieu or environment (*Umgebung*) that has furnished the basis for
these analyses.[42] He states explicitly that it is "our own *Umwelt* which simultaneously constitutes the milieu [*Umgebung*] for all animals," and that
therefore the *Umgebung* represents the *Umwelt* of the observer, not of the
animal observed.[43] Furthermore, he maintains that "the world that sur-
rounds us [thus our *Umgebung*] is the objective reality" that is the sole
concern of the scientific investigator.[44] If indeed every species of animal
has its own *Umwelt*, the latter represents that part of the general *Umgebung* "which affects the sensitive [*reizbare*] substance of the animal body,"
and its character and complexity are determined entirely by the organism's "plan of construction" (*Bauplan*).[45] Not only the environing world,
but also the "inner world" (*Innenwelt*) of animals results from the interrelations between the *Bauplan* and external factors. Specifically, the inner world reflects the way in which these interrelations are responded to
by the animal's nervous system (where a nervous system is present). The
inner world of animals can therefore be studied on the basis of their behavior; and Uexküll resolutely rejects all psychological speculation as to
animal experience.[46] In the Husserlian terms that Merleau-Ponty is fond
of, these experiences remain for the observer *nichturpräsentierbar* (incapable of originary presentation).

Even *Amoeba terricula,* which lacks a nervous system (it consists of ec-
toplasm and endoplasm), does not lack responsiveness to certain stimuli:
it avoids light; it becomes "a dangerous robber" for prey such as infusoria
by making itself sticky; and it does not amalgamate its own protoplasm
with that of other members of its species. Summing up the discussion of
its *Umwelt,* Uexküll comments:

> Thus the amoeba hangs within its *Umwelt* as though on three kinds of
> elastic threads which hold it round about and which guide and deter-
> mine all its movements. This little excerpt of the world [presumably of
> the *Umgebung*] is a world that is intrinsically coherent, simpler and less
> contradictory than our own, but just as well planned, just as artful.[47]

In more advanced animals, however, the *Umwelt* is complemented by a *Gegenwelt* or world of encounter. Lest the reader expect here to leave behind
invertebrates and move on perhaps to canines, elephants, or primates,
Uexküll names as the point of departure for his study of *Gegenwelt* the
humble earthworm (*Lumbricus terrestris*), whose nervous organization involves two different but collaborating centers that jointly form a schema.[48]
It is, according to Uexküll, characteristic of the *Gegenwelt* to represent the
givens of the *Umwelt* by means of schemata that derive from the animal's
needs and thus reflect its governing principle or *Bauplan.*[49] Among the
types of *Gegenwelten* and their bases, Uexküll discusses, in ascending order
of complexity, those governed by motor or chromatic sensibility, or by
iconic representation, as well as the role of statoliths.[50] This leads him to
raise and discuss the question that he terms "the most difficult point of
the entire problem" and one that certainly resonates with the wider scope
of Merleau-Ponty's own researches: "What is the influence of [the organism's] own movements on the world of encounter?" His discussion (which
is too technical to be followed out here) focuses on the role of an ana-
tomical structure found only in vertebrates: the labyrinth of the inner ear.[51]

Uexküll has a tendency to complement scientific exactitude with
philosophical speculation; and he concludes his book with the speculation that, since higher or more complex *Umwelten,* in his view, comprise
lower ones within themselves, even ordinary human *Umwelten* are likely
to be comprised within higher ones—not, to be sure, those of super-
natural beings, but rather of more realized humans. Interestingly, his
example is that of an artist, Hans Holbein [the Younger?]; and his comments are worth quoting:

> One only needs to look at the paintings of a Holbein to convince one-
> self that the world in which he lived was one of far greater richness than

our own. When he paints the simplest objects, they possess such an in-
comprehensibly high reality that the objects [*Gegenstände*] surrounding
us pale in comparison. If Holbein now wanted to examine the relation
between our *Umwelt* and *Innenwelt*, . . . he would find in the *Gegenwelt* of
our brain schemata to which the objects of our *Umwelt* correspond . . .
The gaps of our *Gegenwelt* would not, however, remain concealed from
him; and he would say: "For these higher realities the object [*das Objekt*,
or the object of research, man] is not suited."[52]

Once again, as for Merleau-Ponty, scientific investigation has linked up
with the figure of the painter.˙

There is at least one sentence in *Strolls Through the Environing Worlds
of Animals and Humans* that could fit readily into the earlier book; it reads:
"The environing world of the animal . . . is only an excerpt of the milieu
[*Umgebung*] that we see spread out around the animal—and this milieu
is nothing else than our own human environing world."[53] Nonetheless,
in *Strolls* the human being is no longer unconditionally the measure, nor
does Uexküll recognize a unitary human *Umwelt*. Even if one were to re-
strict one's observation of humans to researchers in the natural sciences,
he reflects, one would find that the role that nature plays for them is "extremely contradictory"; and he concludes on a Kantian note that "behind
all its worlds, engendered by it, conceals itself, eternally unknowable, the
subject—nature."[54]

His discussion of the environing worlds of natural scientists is pre-
ceded by the analogue of the oak tree that is variously experienced by
animals—the fox or owl that may shelter in it, the squirrels, birds, and
insects that, in different ways, relate their lives to it—and by people such
as the forester or the child frightened by a bark formation, without ever
being seen in and for itself.[55] As Rudolf Langthaler remarks, "with [the]
attestation of an infinite number of *Umwelten*, every contestation as to a
'more objective *Umwelt*' or as to 'the higher degree of reality' of these
Umwelten will become pointless."[56] It is no longer clear that Hans Holbein
could pass judgment.

Uexküll, concerned to discredit a reductive understanding of animals as physical entities governed by physicochemical processes, delin-
eates the "circle of function" (*Funktionskreis*) that interlinks an animal's
"world of receptivity" (*Merkwelt*) with its "world of efficacity" (*Wirkwelt*),
via factors such as the receptive or effective organ (*Merkorgan, Wirkorgan*),
or the marks that stimulate or signal effectiveness, and their carriers. Together, these are constitutive of the animal's *Umwelt*.[57] Every living "subject," he comments, "spins its relations like the thread of a spider into
determinate properties of things and interweaves them into a firm net

that carries its *Dasein*."[58] It is a mistake, Uexküll argues, to suppose that the relations of an animal to its environment are articulated within the familiar spatial-temporal framework of human life. He credits Karl Ernst von Baer (1792–1876) with having made subjectively engendered temporality readily intuitable.[59] In this context, he points out that, whereas humans cannot distinguish more than eighteen vibrations per second, the "fighting fish" encounters this limit at thirty or more, and the snail (identified only as "vineyard snail") at just four. Thus the fighting fish perceives its environment (in particular its fast-moving prey) as though in a slow-motion film, while the snail perceives ponderous movements (including its own) in an accelerated manner. For these and other reasons Uexküll, who compares the environing world of animals graphically to soap bubbles surrounding them, states that "he who denies the existence of subjective realities has not recognized the foundations of his own *Umwelt*."[60]

Strolls begins with an account of the life cycle of a European species of tick (*Ixodes rhitinis*), whose greatly enlarged image appears on the opening page. For Uexküll, the tick does not merely furnish an example of a starkly simple animal *Umwelt*, but it also serves as a test case (*Prüfstein*) for his rejection of mechanism. For these reasons, discussions of its life processes are subtly interwoven throughout much of the book; and this humble animal can serve to render Uexküll's perspective clearer and more vivid. Although its life cycle has become philosophically somewhat familiar due to both Merleau-Ponty and Agamben,[61] it will be briefly recounted here.

The animal emerges from its egg in an incomplete state, lacking one of its four pairs of legs as well as its sexual organs. It is, however, capable of preying on ectothermic animals such as lizards; and when, after repeatedly shedding its skin, it reaches maturity, it is capable of feeding on endotherms. After mating, the female's body stores the sperm; and the animal climbs to the tip of a protruding branch on a shrub, guided by the general light sensitivity of its skin (it has no eyes). There it remains, insensitive to its surroundings except for one stimulus: the scent of butyric acid given off by the skin of a passing mammal. Naturally, it is a rare event that a mammal should pass underneath the branch or brush against it; and the tick is equipped to "wait"; under laboratory conditions, ticks have done so, without nourishment, for as long as eighteen years. The chemical signal or *Merkmal* of butyric acid provokes a behavioral response: the tick lets itself drop; and if its sense of temperature registers warmth (the mark of a mammalian body), it will move about until it finds a relatively hairless spot. There it will burrow into the skin and consume a substantial meal of blood (but in the laboratory other liquids at the right temperature are equally accepted). With this blood meal, the tick's stored sperm is released, its eggs are fertilized, and it now drops to the ground, lays its eggs, and dies.

Uexküll points out that the stark impoverishment of the tick's *Umwelt* is also the condition for the assurance guiding its behavior; "and security is more important than riches."[62] From all the manifold ways in which a mammalian body may manifest its presence, the tick singles out just three that will sequentially guide its life processes. Uexküll notes that, for all the simplicity of its *Umwelt*, the tick represents "a higher type" than the sea urchin, which is not a unified animal but rather a "reflex republic." The tick has the possibility of experiencing the mammalian body, of which it sequentially receives chemical, thermal, and tactile stimuli, as a unity.[63] The very paucity of the tick's environing world can thus serve to bring into focus the animal's power of responsiveness (for an object such as a stone, Uexküll notes, there are no stimuli); and with organisms such as the hermit crab, response (here to the presence of a sea anemone) becomes highly flexible.[64] Thus Uexküll emphasizes that the simple animal is not only securely cradled within its world (even though this world may, of course, contain mortal dangers), but that simple animal worlds are also finely articulated and, in their coherent variety, consummately beautiful.

Excursus: Heidegger and Uexküll

Almost thirty years before Merleau-Ponty, Martin Heidegger engaged searchingly with the "new biology" in his 1929–30 lecture course on *The Fundamental Concepts of Metaphysics: World, Finitude, Solitude*.[65] There is no evidence that Merleau-Ponty had any acquaintance with this lecture course, nor indeed that he could have known it, given that it was not published during his lifetime. Even though no dialogue thus takes place between Merleau-Ponty and Heidegger concerning animality, a reading of Heidegger in this context is illuminating and indispensable.[66]

Heidegger calls attention to two "decisive steps" taken by biology in "the two generations" preceding his lecture course. The first step is that of Hans Driesch (1867–1941), whose embryological research on sea urchins revealed the enigmatic dominance of the whole to be realized over the parts that Merleau-Ponty recognizes as posing a persistent problem for interpretation. Heidegger notes that Driesch's work unfortunately opened the door to neovitalism, and also that he did not, in seeking to grasp the organism as an integral whole, include in that wholeness its interrelation with the environment.[67] It is of course Uexküll (whom Heidegger refers to as one of the most clear-eyed contemporary biologists whose observations are marked by "an astonishing assurance and plenitude")[68] who took this second decisive step, a step toward ecology. Heidegger contrasts Uexküll's approach with a straightforwardly Darwinian interpretation of evolution, according to which the animal simply is present or given (*vorhanden*) in an equally pre-given environment to which it must optimally adjust itself. Such an interpretation offers, he finds, no insight into the complex referential interrelations *Beziehungszusammenhänge*) in keeping with which, to speak with Uexküll, the animal defines its world.[69]

It would, Heidegger notes, be just silly to charge Uexküll with this or that philosophical shortcoming, instead of realizing that "an engagement with his researches belongs among what is most fruitful for the relation of philosophy to contemporary biology."[70] This deep appreciation notwithstanding, Heidegger is nonetheless troubled by the theory that animals no less than humans live within a genuine environing world. It is not clear what influence Uexküll's researches may have exerted on Heidegger's analysis of the *Umwelt* of *Dasein* in *Being and Time*.[71] Theodore Kisiel, in his magisterial work *The Genesis of Heidegger's Being and Time*, mentions only that "the young Heidegger was clearly aware of Uexküll's then popular notion of *Umwelt*."[72]

In *Die Grundbegriffe der Metaphysik* (The Fundamental Concepts of Metaphysics), Heidegger is now concerned to argue that, whereas man is a builder of world (*weltbildend*), and whereas nonliving entities such as a stone are worldless (*weltlos;* Heidegger recognizes nonetheless that stones or rocks may be understood differently in certain "mythic" or religious, cultural, and aesthetic contexts), the animal is "poor in world" (*weltarm*), in the sense of lacking (*entbehren*) world, a lacking of which a worldless entity would be entirely incapable.

Heidegger acknowledges the strange logic of a having that is also a lack, or, one might say, of an access to unconcealment that is also a deprivation:

> Thus in the animal there shows itself a *having of world* and *at the same time* a *not-having of world*. This is contradictory and therefore logically impossible. But metaphysics and what is of the essence [*das Wesenhafte*] have another logic than sound common sense.[73]

Heidegger stresses that he is not making a judgment as to relative perfection nor setting up any hierarchies among animals or between animals and man. Echoing Uexküll, he states that it is "a fundamental error" to suppose that amoebas and infusoria are less perfect than elephants or apes and that, to the contrary, every animal or sort of animal is equally perfect.[74] Jacques Derrida comments insightfully on this claim, noting that the very terms of poverty and deprivation "imply, whether one wants to avoid it or not, hierarchization and evaluation." This "humanist teleology" is, however, the price to be paid in "an ethico-political denunciation of biologism, of racism, of naturalism, and so on." In analyzing this logic, his own concern is "to exhibit, then formalize, the terrifying mechanisms of this program," which bespeaks itself equally in "Heideggerian" and "anti-Heideggerian" discourses, and even in their most subtle strategies and ruses.[75]

To return to Heidegger, his claim as to the perfection of unicellular life forms also allows him specifically to turn to the example of *Paramecium* (as discussed by Uexküll) in support of his thesis that the organism does not possess certain capacities by virtue of having organs (which would then resemble utensils or *Zeug*), but rather that the capacities (*Fähigkeiten*) themselves underlie the genesis of organs. *Paramecium,* being a "changing animal" (*Wechseltier*), forms and again dissolves structures and organs needed for its life processes (thus, for instance, it forms and dissolves mouth, stomach, intestine, and anus in the sequence needed for taking nourishment). Even in animals in which organs endure for life, they show, Heidegger claims, a "character of being that is fundamentally different from the being-ready-to-hand and the lying about of a utensil."[76]

It pertains, in Heidegger's view, to the fundamental character of a capacity to be proper or peculiar to the living being that exhibits it; and he calls this characteristic its *Eigen-tümlichkeit.* The organism is characterized by its "capacitated, organ-creating, peculiarity/ownness" (*befähigte, organschaffende Eigen-tümlichkeit*).[77] What it is thus enabled for are not mere sequences of processes, but rather genuine behavior, which Heidegger here terms *Sichbenehmen* and which he distinguishes from human agency or comportment (*Handeln, Sichverhalten*). The terminological distinction will be important in the sequel in that the mode of being of animals will be characterized by verbs and verbal nouns derived, like *Benehmen,* from *nehmen* ("to take"). Animals would not be "poor in world" if something were not "taken" from them.

Heidegger characterizes animal behavior as a "carrying-on" (*Treiben*) that stems from the animal's drivenness (*Getriebenheit*).[78] In their behavior (*Benehmen*), animals are "taken," enthralled, or enraptured (*benommen*) by phenomenal configurations pre-delineated by their drives, rather than being freely open to what may come to presence, not to speak of being open to beings as such. It is not possible here to follow out the remarkable concreteness and detail of Heidegger's argumentation (even if it involves reference to a horrifying example of vivisection performed on a honeybee, which contrasts strangely with the rather lyrical tone of his description of the worker bee as "flower-constant," visiting, for instance, only clover blossoms or meadow sage during a given outing). Similarly, it is not possible to take up the question of a genuine disclosure of space in the spatial orientation of bees (to say nothing of migratory birds).[79] What is important is that animal behavior, in its enraptured character or *Benommenheit,* involves "an essential deprivation [*Genommenheit*] of any apprehension of something *as* something."[80] For this reason, animals, though capable of relationships among themselves or to things (as, in Heidegger's earlier example, the lizard has a relationship to a warm stone which is not, of course, reciprocated), cannot form a relation to something other *as* other but are simply "taken" or "carried away" (*hinge-nommen*) by it; and their behavior or *Benehmen* therefore does not involve any lucid apprehension (*Vernehmen*).[81]

Animals are not, however, constantly buffeted about by their drives; but rather, these drives need first to be "disinhibited" (*enthemmt*) to become active; and they are disinhibited by the sort of stimulus that Uexküll termed a significant mark (*Merkmal*). Thus, to recall the tick (which Heidegger does not mention), the behaviors that consummate its life cycle (and that Heidegger would trace to its drives) would be disinhibited by certain chemical, thermal, and tactile sensations.

Being enraptured (*Benommenheit*), Heidegger suggests, "makes possible and pre-delineates its own domain [*Spielraum*] of behavior," such that the animal is surrounded by a ring (*Umring*) which is a ring of being driven-to that can be disinhibited.[82] Nothing that does not disinhibit has the capacity of penetrating this ring, for which the animal in question struggles (*ringt*) throughout its life in the modalities of preserving itself and its kind.

In essence, Heidegger has transformed Uexküll's environing world into an environing ring (*Umring*) that constrains and confines the animal and debars it from the sort of openness that would allow for a genuine world. Even the receptivity to stimuli (*Reizbarkeit*) that, in Uexküll's view, sets the organism apart from inanimate matter is, for Heidegger, conditional on "disinhibitedness and being ringed-in," and not vice versa.[83] He concludes that "the *organisation of the organism* does not consist in its morphological, physiological formation . . . but first of all precisely in *the fundamental capacitation of ringing-itself-around* [*Sichumringens*] and, together with that, of a precisely determined being open for a surrounding circle of disinhibition.[84] The logic of a simultaneous having and not having of something like a world has thus been spelled out: the animal, unlike the stone, is open and related to its surroundings; but these surroundings are, so to speak, its prison rather than its world. Since Heidegger, unlike Uexküll, who generalizes from observation, seeks throughout this discussion to grasp the essential being (*Wesen*) or animality (*Tierheit*) of "the" animal, whether the amoeba or the whale, he cannot avoid essentializing animals; and Derrida rightly criticizes him for presupposing the existence of "a domain, a type of being, that one calls animality *in general,* as to which it doesn't matter what is the example at issue."[85] Correlatively to this criticism, one can well ask whether, if animal life in its vastness is indeed held inexorably in thrall by rapture or *Benommenheit* and by drives and their possible disinhibition, these same assiduous jailers could really become utterly powerless once the human being makes its appearance. If this view seems unacceptable, so is the essentialization of animality.

Environing Worlds: Merleau-Ponty and Uexküll

Whereas for Heidegger the animal is literally "incarcerated" (*eingesperrt*) in its *Umwelt,* that is transformed into a surrounding ring impenetrable to anything but disinhibiting stimuli (note the contrast between this ring and the fragility of Uexküll's simile of the soap bubble),[86] Merleau-Ponty stresses that, with the appearance of the world of encounter (*Gegenwelt*) in higher animals, "the Umwelt is no longer a closing off, but rather an opening," such that "the world is possessed by the animal."[87]

Merleau-Ponty considers the environing world to be the world of behavior, which can be read across the bodies of animals, without the need for quasi-psychological speculation as to what may or may not be disclosed to them in some modality of consciousness. Consciousness, according to the lecture notes, can be regarded as a form of behavior; and behavior also comprises embryological and physiological organization. Indeed, Merleau-Ponty recognizes the need to allow for an *Umwelt* "at the level of the organ, at the level of the embryo"—levels at which one cannot speak of the unleashing of drives.[88]

Even primitive animals, such as *Paramecium,* which are held so tightly within their environing world as to constitute "a closed unity" with it, exhibit the plasticity characteristic of protoplasm (in contrast to machines). Merleau-Ponty takes up here the example of the amoeba which is made up of "flowing protoplasm," so that its plan of construction (Uexküll's *Bauplan*) is not fixed but is endlessly being re-created. Strikingly, Merleau-Ponty characterizes it as "a continual birth," using the phrase he also uses to describe the painter's vision in "Eye and Mind."[89] Once again, moreover, he emphasizes the nascence of *natura,* whereas Heidegger concludes his discussion of animality by denying to the animal the capacity genuinely to die, or to suffer the pathos of mortality.[90]

Merleau-Ponty notes that the nervous system does not account for the unity of the organism, and that protoplasm itself also exerts a regulative function. Thus the sea anemone (species unspecified) has three neural networks but only a single behavior; and its movements, even in an aquarium, follow the rhythm of the tides.[91] In more complex animals, however, the development of the nervous and sensory systems allows for fine discrimination and flexibility of response (there is no flexibility in Heidegger's *Umring*).

With the formation of a *Gegenwelt,* which Merleau-Ponty describes as "a mirror of the world" (one should recall here the discussion of the mirror that concludes the first section of "Eye and Mind") and as introducing "absolute novelty," stimuli no longer function as causal factors but have the value of *signs.*[92]

The conditions of possibility of the elaboration of a world of encounter are, according to Merleau-Ponty, to be sought in sensory-motor organization, as well as in the abilities to regulate physiological position and to achieve proprioception.[93] Whereas Heidegger implicitly reduced the *Wirkwelt* (world of efficacy) aspect of Uexküll's *Umwelt* to the unleashing of drives, Merleau-Ponty considers that "the *Wirkwelt* displaces the *Merkwelt,*" since animal behaviors "deposit a surplus of signification on the surface of objects." With animal *Umwelten,* and indeed with "life," there opens up a "field of action" with its specific temporality and spatiality, and with leeway for a diversity of relationships that Merleau-Ponty comprises under the term "inter-animality."[94]

One would expect plants to be mentioned under the rubric of "life" (and Heidegger indeed mentions but does not discuss them); but about plants Merleau-Ponty does not breathe a word. This is a serious omission, not only because animal life would generally be impossible in the absence of plant life, but also because plants, not unlike animals, selectively respond to stimuli and are not incapable of efficacy (which tends to take chemical form). There exists, moreover, the possibility of mutually responsive interrelations between plants and animals. For instance, certain passionflowers (*Passiflora* species), which serve as food plants for the caterpillars of butterflies of the genus *Heliconius,* have been observed to respond to larval feeding by developing a spotted foliar pattern resembling butterfly eggs which then leads female butterflies to seek out other, still pristine plants on which to lay their eggs. Perhaps inter-animality (which underlies "inter-corporeity" for Merleau-Ponty) will have to be replaced by a more inclusive, if still nameless, form of vital interrelatedness.

Merleau-Ponty goes on to delve into the philosophical implications of the notion of *Umwelt,* noting that it joins together embryogenesis and active behavior, as well as lowly and more differentiated forms of animal life. He takes up Uexküll's musical metaphor of the unfurling of an animal *Umwelt* as a melody singing itself.[95] What interests him about this comparison is not only the autonomous energy of the melody that "finds in [the singer's] body a type of servant,"[96] but also its nonsequential temporality. With the opening notes of a melody, the final notes are already called for; and reciprocally the opening is possible only by virtue of the ending. The genesis of a living being, Merleau-Ponty reflects, is similarly not intelligible in terms of a straightforward causal sequence.[97] One touches here again upon the problem of the relation of a totality to its constituent parts; but it is also important to Merleau-Ponty that the animal melody cannot be thought of as an essence outside of its particular expressive realizations, nor yet as a guiding telos, but is rather a quasi-oneiric pole, or a theme that haunts the animal's entire being without ever being confronted as such.[98]

An animal does not simply receive or register impinging stimulations, but rather "each action of the milieu is conditioned by [or responsive to] an action of the animal," so that, once again, a sequential causal mechanism proves to be an inadequate model. If one takes into account exclusively the causal or sufficient conditions that do, to be sure, obtain at any given moment, one loses "the relation of meaning" that interlinks the situation and the activity of the animal and that is precisely what is captured by the notion of *Umwelt.*[99]

The notion of *Umwelt* must, according to Merleau-Ponty, be dissociated not only from essence or telos, but also from "the idea of a substance or force." In this sense, "the unfurling of the animal is like a pure wake related to no boat."[100] Thus, Merleau-Ponty reflects, the notion of *Umwelt* has the potential (not realized by Uexküll) to move the understanding of life beyond "the old dilemma" of a Kantian principle that is not knowable in itself and a Schellingian *Subjektnatur,* to the recognition of "a milieu of events, which opens on a spatial and a temporal field."[101] He stresses that this opening up of a privileged milieu is not due to the agency of some new force or principle. If the animal is spoken of nonetheless as "a quiet force," its quietude is precisely its lack—and the lack on the part of its *Umwelt*—of any positive, determinate momentum and core, that is to say, to its sheer expressivity. In animals that form a *Gegenwelt* or world of encounter, this expressivity can take on the concrete form of an architectonic of symbols, such that the *Umwelt* becomes oriented toward their interpretation; "and there is thus within Nature a species of preculture."[102] Hierarchization, however, has to be avoided here no less than positivities such as essence; for ultimately it becomes difficult to draw a clear dividing line between behaviors that would be exclusive to "lower" or "higher" levels of organization, and indeed between behavior and mind.[103]

Reconsidering Expression

The organism's expressivity is, on Merleau-Ponty's analysis, vested in the creation of significance or meaning. The animal, he has argued, "is both a physical being and a meaning,"[104] and its form or totality constitutes a dimension of significance in terms of which it configures an environing world. Unlike Uexküll, however, Merleau-Ponty does not understand this formation of a context of meaning as a quasi-monadic perspective on a reality that would exist in and of itself (or perhaps as a facet of the human *Umwelt*), nor yet as a "symphony" that would grandly unite the animal melodies. Rather, the totality for him remains strictly non-positive; and he understands expression fundamentally as differential articulation. Its differential character makes for its plasticity, its openness to the future, and its creativity which links it in some ways to artistic creation (and which contrasts starkly with Heidegger's incarcerating ring).

It is this openness and expressivity that Merleau-Ponty has pursued in his searching engagements with embryology and *Umwelt* theory, and which he will go on to pursue more explicitly in the further contexts of the directiveness of animal activities, of morphology, and of the instinctual basis of behavior.

Rather than construing environmental stimuli as causes or as disinhibiting triggers, Merleau-Ponty accords them—at least in animals capable of forming a world of encounter—the potential value of signs or symbols which prepare the ground for the beginnings of culture. He has also allowed for animal behavior to invest objects with significance, rather than treating it as being merely responsive to what is pre-given. By virtue of its inherent expressivity, animal behavior can, for him, genuinely inscribe itself within a field of action (thus engaging in the *handeln* that Heidegger reserved for *Dasein*) and be situated in the continuity of sentient life, which already places it—contra Heidegger—in a continuum with human existence. Finally, it is this pervasive expressivity without any positive core that allows for genuine interaction among animals, or for an inter-animality that is capable of introducing genuine novelty. Although Merleau-Ponty does not explicitly address the issues of biologism and racism that Derrida brings to the fore, his engagement with the "new biology" and with animal life in its inherent expressivity may offer resources for taking a stand against the entrenched menace of these ideologies that can bypass the "humanist teleology" that Derrida problematizes.

5

The Expressivity of Animal Appearance and of Directive and Instinctual Activities

When we try to survey the multiplicity of animal forms, every precipitate attempt at explanation is silenced by this profusion. In this diversity there are indeed the cases just mentioned—there is protective coloration, there is also warning coloration, and there is, to be sure, deceptive similarity; but they are all reduced to single cases in which we find a utilitarian sense of the coloration or form of the animal body to be particularly striking. But what does this one-sidedly selected cabinet of curiosities amount to in the face of the wild, exuberant profusion of form-production in the garden of creatures!
—Adolf Portmann, *Die Tiergestalt* (1960)

From the embryology of behavior and of animals' environing worlds, as considered so far, Merleau-Ponty turns to animal activities in their mature specificity and with a view to their oriented or quasi-teleological character, as well as to mimicry, animal appearance, and the nature of instinct. His initial partner in dialogue is Edward S. Russell, whose *The Directiveness of Organic Activities* appeared in 1946.[1] Russell holds that biological processes are irreducible to processes of a simpler order, such as physico-chemical ones, and that the living organism must be understood as a dynamic system (he refers here to Coghill) oriented toward self-development, self-maintenance, reproduction, and finally senescence, within the compass of its life cycle. Unlike inorganic systems, which tend toward equilibrium and stability, the organism tends toward a mature end state that is "a highly complex and unstable organization, which can be maintained in being only by constant activity of an elaborate and coordinated kind."[2] One hears here the echo of Gesell and Amatruda's principles of self-regulatory fluctuation and of optimal tendency, as well as, more remotely, of Spinoza's notion of *conatus,* which Russell indeed explicitly acknowledges in his concluding chapter on "The Concept of the Organism," quoting (without giving the reference) from Proposition 7 of Part 3 of Spinoza's *Ethics:* "The striving by which each thing strives to persevere in its being is the actual essence of the thing."[3]

Russell rejects teleology or vitalism no less than mechanism or materialism, advocating instead a "free biology" that will not shy away from recognizing that "directiveness and creativity are fundamental characteristics of life."[4] Directiveness may express itself in the three registers of behavior, physiology, and morphoplastics (as an example of the latter, Russell points to the development of an uncharacteristic thick coat by giraffes wintering largely in the open at the Hamburg zoo). He explores directiveness or orientation with regard to the complexities of wound healing, structural repairs (such as those of variously damaged larval casings), the satisfaction of metabolic needs under unfavorable conditions, and reproduction. One of his most striking examples of directive behavior and physiology, and one that is taken up by Merleau-Ponty, is that of *Microstoma,* a marine fish.[5]

As Merleau-Ponty, following Russell, elaborates, *Microstoma* relies for self-defense on an array of stinging nematocysts deployed in a regular pattern over its entire body surface. It does not, however, produce these weapons but must take them from the hydra, which is dangerous to it, and which it will not generally prey on. If it is lacking in nematocysts, however, it will attack the hydra, seeking to paralyze it partially by its oral secretions, and, if successful, eating its flesh. The nematocysts of the hydra are not digested but are transported to *Microstoma*'s mesoderm, each by an endodermal cell, and eventually to the ectoderm, where they are properly spaced and oriented. Starving exemplars of *Microstoma* that have their normal complement of nematocysts still remain reluctant to prey on hydra; and when they at last do so, they eat its flesh but reject the nematocysts. If well fed but lacking their weapons, in contrast, *Microstoma* will reject the hydra's flesh but ingest the nematocysts. Finally, if a laboratory strain of *Microstoma* that have had no contact with hydra for forty-nine generations are presented with the green hydra (*Chlorohydra viridissima*), which has four different kinds of nematocysts, they will in due course ingest these; but only the two types of nematocysts that are suitable for *Microstoma*'s own defense needs will be transported to the body surface.

It would certainly be counterintuitive not to discern a directiveness in such complex and flexible behavior. What particularly interests Merleau-Ponty is, to begin with, Russell's assimilation of the relations among the cells of a given tissue or organ to behavioral relationships—an assimilation clearly supported by the evidence concerning *Microstoma*. Behavior can thus be considered "a physiological activity in external circuit," while conversely physiological activities are behaviors facing an internal milieu.[6] However, the processes involved (e.g., in wound healing) do not exhibit a decisive finality (thus healing may be arrested if the wound is covered with cellophane). Behavioral response is flexible; but it is also typically elicited by precise conditions and may therefore, under abnormal conditions, become counterproductive. Merleau-Ponty comments, according to the lecture notes, that "the finality of the animal is blind, not regulated by a plan of the whole," and that this "demi-blindness" is the price of its great efficiency.[7] This finality which may be alternatively (or conjointly) realized by behavioral, physiological, and morphoplastic means may thus constitute, with respect to the alternatives of mechanism or vitalism, "a vital activity of a third order."[8] Its blindness is perhaps the mark of its being bound to the animal's environing world which, Merleau-Ponty notes, "is not presented in front of the animal like a goal," but resembles rather a theme that haunts it.[9] These considerations explicitly evoke, for Merleau-Ponty, the thematic of expression:

> The organism is not defined by its punctual existence; what exists beyond is a theme, a style, all these expressions seeking to express, not a participation in a transcendental existence, but a structure of the whole . . .The reality of the organism supposes a non-Parmenidean being, a form that escapes from the dilemma of being and non-being.[10]

Merleau-Ponty's engagement with Russell's explorations of directiveness thus allows him to articulate consummately the thought of a directive totality that is non-positive and whose realizations are irreducibly both carnal and expressive.

Disappearing in the Sargasso Sea, and Other Mimetic Magic

With his meditation on mimicry as "behavior in an external circuit," Merleau-Ponty introduces a new aspect of the expressivity of animal life, an aspect that will preoccupy him for the remainder of the course. This aspect is the sheer exuberance of animal forms and behavior that cannot be submitted to a governing principle of utility but constitutes an excess over any restricted economy. Adaptation, to quote the lecture notes, "is not the canon of life, but only a particular realization in the tide of natural production."[11]

Although Merleau-Ponty refers to Pierre Hardouin's[12] work on mimicry, he does not engage closely and dialogically with this author but rather reflects on the phenomena of mimicry as such. Once again, however, he takes no note of the fact that mimicry is not restricted to animal life but is also practiced extensively by plants. For instance, one notable form of botanical mimicry is pseudocopulation, which is found among orchids of several genera and species, including *Cryptostylis* species, *Trichocerus parviflorus,* and *Oncidium benekenii.* The inflorescences of these orchids lure specific insect pollinators by emitting a scent that mimics the female's pheromone and, in some cases, by also presenting a likeness of its appearance, so that males pollinate the flowers in their frustrated attempts at copulation. Orchids of the genus *Bulbophyllum,* as well as the inflorescences of some stapelias and members of the arum family resort to another pollination "stratagem": their flowers attract flies as pollinators by presenting the appearance, and emitting the stench, of carrion. Incidentally, these examples also show that mimicry is not restricted to the visual dimension.

The zoologist Adolf Portmann, whose work Merleau-Ponty will shortly engage with, does give plant life its due and cautions, here also, against a totalizing submission to utility:

> One does well, to be sure, to pay attention to all the peculiarities that serve the pollination of a flower and that attest to so singular a relationship between plant and animal . . . It is not, however, a disregard of this important relationship that here especially we focus [on the fact] that the forms of an iris flower or a sunflower are indeed preserved, or perhaps even enhanced, by selection on the part of insects, but could not have been *created* by such selection . . . the coming to be of such beautiful forms is still as enigmatic to us as is that of animal forms.[13]

This caution, of course, does not discredit the reality and efficacy of mimicry which, in specific cases, has held its own against critical scientific challenges. Thus herpetologist Harry W. Greene examines the challenges to the occurrence and importance of both the Batesian and Mullerian forms of mimicry in the vexillary coloration of coral snakes and their imitators (in the first of these forms, harmless species imitate the warning coloration of a dangerous or inedible one, whereas in the second, two dangerous species "collaborate" as lookalikes). He concludes that not only are both occurrence and efficacy of these forms of coral snake mimicry strongly supported by the evidence, but also that venoms (the danger in question here) have played an important role in the evolution of snakes and of animals coexisting with them.[14] To get a sense of the extensiveness of this influence, one can consider the seemingly unlikely case of the caterpillars of sphingid moths which have developed the ability to mimic the appearance of a snake's head when threatened—a phenomenon that was already observed (although not correctly interpreted) by the artist and naturalist Maria Sibylla Merian (1647–1717).[15]

Merleau-Ponty cautions also against making efficacy the criterion for the reality of mimicry;[16] and the fundamental point is that—in marked contrast to the long-standing philosophical idealization of univocal truth—a multivalent, creative, and often deceptive play of appearances prevails throughout nature, repudiating any attempt to impose a single governing principle, such as utility or survival.

While Merleau-Ponty, unlike Portmann, does not make a basic distinction between cryptic and "semantic" (signifying) mimicry, his key example of cryptic mimicry, found among the fauna of the Sargasso Sea, converges with Portmann's description of the Sargasso fish (*Pterophryne* species), whose form is optically so utterly dissolved in its natural environment that, unlike caterpillars that resemble branchlets, or butterflies that mimic leaves, it has no need to adopt a suitable posture. To achieve the magic of invisibility, it need not, so to speak, even turn the ring of the shepherd of Gyges.[17] However, optical mimicry is not, Merleau-Ponty notes, necessarily achieved by actual (let alone conscious) imitation of visual form, as evidenced by the fact that some mimics have poor visual discrimination or are even blind. Portmann points out that, throughout the large domain of invertebrates, a dividing line separates those animals that can see one another from those that cannot, and that it constitutes a division between two levels of the intensity of life.[18] This line, however, does not demarcate the possibility of optical mimicry. Merleau-Ponty speaks rather of an "indivision" (that is, nondivision) between an animal and its surroundings and notes once again that the same indivision also underlies the formation of a sense organ which is no less "miraculous" than mimicry.[19] Indivision pertains, of course, to the ontological structure of flesh that he elaborates in *The Visible and the Invisible;* and his reflections on animal form and mimicry serve to concretize it. Here he notes that they serve both "to take away the dubious character of mimicry and to make what seems to go without saying appear as miraculous, to make the ordinary and the extraordinary communicate."[20] A defining feature of this indivision is expressiveness.

Life as "a Power to Invent the Visible":
Merleau-Ponty and Portmann

Although there are, as Jacques de Witte has shown, certain misconstruals
in the reading of Portmann that the lecture notes present[21]—misconstruals that may well originate with the anonymous note taker—the line of
Merleau-Ponty's thought is clear: he takes up the ideas that "we must
seek to grasp the mystery of life in the way animals show themselves to
each other," that animal form has an expressive and existential value of
manifestation (Portmann's *Formwert*), and that it attests to "a power to
invent the visible" (*d'inventer du visible*) that is fundamental to life.[22]

So as to understand the inspiration of Portmann's work for Merleau-
Ponty, it is necessary to follow out, in a rather unhurried manner, Portmann's reflections, researches, and arguments in *Die Tiergestalt* (Animal
Form).[23] He is critical throughout of the tendency of biological research
to privilege the inner and thus hidden processes of the organism and
to dismiss outer appearance as an epiphenomenon devoid of scientific
interest. He notes also that laboratory research has concentrated on a
narrow selection of animals (such as fruit flies, mice, or rats) that have
become "the pets of science," neglecting "the innumerable different
forms of life . . . that constitute one of the riches of the earth."[24] The
limitations of this approach already begin to reveal themselves—in the
absence of any complicated apparatus. Thus Portmann points out that
the iridescent black of a raven's plumage is built up entirely from the visible tips of feathers whose hidden parts are an inconspicuous grey; and
similarly the brilliant iridescence of the plumage of hummingbirds (the
colors of which are due to optical interference effects rather than to pigments) is limited to the visible surface. Complex patternings that appear
as a total effect are prepared for by each separate component feather
long before maturity and are thus realized by a convergence. Furthermore, the bilateral symmetry characteristic of more highly organized animals is also to a large extent geared to appearance, for the inner organs
tend to be asymmetrically formed and arranged; and furthermore, they
are closely similar in related species whose outward form differs mark-
edly, such as lion and tiger.[25] Thus, Portmann reflects, the segregation of
the organism's inner formation from its visible form constitutes "a first
major step toward recognizing the intrinsic value of the visible"; and it
also gives the lie to the slogan, long prominent in the history of design,
that form follows function.[26] Drawing on this discussion, Merleau-Ponty
notes that, just as the lungs are formed long before the embryo or fetus
has oxygen to breathe, the ensemble of markings that will form the pattern of a bird's plumage involves "a reference to a possible eye," and that

the coming to be of animal form is not reducible to the intra-organic processes involved.[27]

Merleau-Ponty does not comment on Portmann's rather technical chapter on "The Brain as a Measure of Differentiation" (chap. 3), with its comparative tables of the relative weight of the cerebral cortex in various groups of animals; but the chapter ends on an important observation: given that animals with highly differentiated organization also have high metabolic rates, they quickly face the danger of starvation (by way of contrast, recall the tick!) and are therefore also among the most endangered.[28] Furthermore, Portmann points out, the slender limbs of animals such as gazelles or antelopes have developed not merely in the service of faster running but are also part and parcel of a higher state of differentiation which may not prove to be more functional but may even endanger species survival.[29] Thus the expressive capacity of higher animals in whom, as Merleau-Ponty notes, "the body is entirely a means of expression,"[30] brings with it exposure and vulnerability. One may recall here Spinoza's important observation that "in proportion as a body is more apt than other bodies to act or be acted on simultaneously in many ways, so the mind is more apt . . . to perceive many things simultaneously."[31] Highly differentiated organization thus involves both a capacity for complex agency (including expression) and for being acted upon or affected in complex ways, and hence to suffer.[32]

In quest of the correlation between differential organization and the visual appearance of animals, Portmann devotes a chapter to mollusks and their shells (chap. 5). Merleau-Ponty, however, gives short shrift to mollusks—from the chambered nautilus to the thousands of species that originate shells of astonishing intricacy of form and resplendent iridescence and coloring—claiming that, since shells are brought about by "a local process," the animal "is not expressed in them."[33] Portmann points out that the greatest diversity of shell forms is found among the most primitive types of mollusks, whereas among highly developed types (such as cephalopods and nudibranchs) shells tend to become interiorized or to disappear altogether (although there are some exceptions).[34] Furthermore, bilateral symmetry (in contrast to spiral formation) is, according to Portmann, found only in mollusks with a highly centralized nervous system.[35] He comments that not only are the complexities of appearance "by no means lesser or simpler in low-ranking animals within a group than in the highly differentiated,"[36] but that among the former as well processes of formation are operative that far exceed the necessities of life. If one follows Merleau-Ponty in treating animal appearance as a language,[37] one will have to acknowledge that this expressive language is also competently "spoken" by relatively undifferentiated or archaic animals whose external skeleton (the shell) is developed and enlarged by rhythmic incrementation along defined growth zones, and furthermore that humans are far from understanding the visual "language" of the ocean depths (which gives prominence to bioluminescence).[38]

Merleau-Ponty contrasts the zebra (the different species and strains of which Portmann discusses with a view to their patterning) with mollusks as an animal whose form supposedly carries genuine significance and expressive value;[39] but Portmann's conclusion is more subtle. One must, he says, recognize that not only the eye, the heart, or the brain are formed by complex and, as Russell would say, directively oriented processes, but that such is also true of the animal's visual form, including patterning and coloration.[40] Optical appearance is thus not a byproduct but is intrinsic and essential to the animal's very being.

Merleau-Ponty converges perhaps most closely with Portmann on the issue of sexual dimorphism and sexual display and ritualization, although he limits himself to pointing out that, throughout the animal kingdom, sexuality is not a mere utilitarian function, and that "in higher order animals, the sexual relation . . . takes on an expressive value, a value of form."[41] Concrete examples would not, however, remain confined to the vague category of "higher" animals. Thus one might just as well point to the marvelous night-long courtship dance of the sea dragon (*Phyllopterix* species, a fish closely related to the sea horse), or even the light signals of fireflies which vary from species to species, as to the courtship dances of cranes, the bravura courtship flights of male hummingbirds, or the artistic ventures of male bower birds.[42] On the other end of the spectrum, however, one might also consider that the diminutive males of the various species of anglerfish (such as *Melanocetus johnsonii*) parasitically attach themselves to the much larger female and end up merging their tissues entirely with hers, or that (as Heidegger notes with evident horror),[43] among certain arachnids or insects (notably the praying mantis) the male is devoured after coitus. In the crucial context of sexuality, expressive ritualization and utility stand perhaps in more multivalent relationships than that of straightforward dominance or subordination.

Merleau-Ponty, however, concludes that both mimicry and Portmann's researches show that animal behavior exceeds utility and that finally "being cannot be defined outside of perceived being." To quote the lecture notes:

> There are as many relations among animals of each species as there are
> internal relations among every part of the body of each animal. The fact
> that there is a relation between the exterior aspect of the animal and

its capacity for vision seems to prove it: the animal sees according to whether it is visible.[44]

These remarks closely echo Merleau-Ponty's stress on the integration of the seer within the visible in "Eye and Mind." In the context of the discussion of animal life, however, this participation, which is also what de Witte calls "intervisibility," is constitutive of "inter-animality" which becomes the basis of the "inter-corporeity" that Merleau-Ponty will explore in *The Visible and the Invisible*.

Portmann's stress (in the second edition of *Die Tiergestalt*) is placed more radically on the autonomous importance of sheer visual appearance, even in the absence of any possibility of reciprocity or of a functional relationship. Thus he remarks, close to the conclusion of his book:

> We have arrived at marked formations whose concrete form plays no role in any of the accomplishments familiar to us within the play of life, because they pertain to beings who do not see one another with eyes, but who also do not scare away an enemy or conceal themselves from him by their colors and forms. This is the world of "non-addressed appearances"—and he who apprehends the life forms all about him with open eyes will find more and more such unaddressed creations of form.[45]

Thus Merleau-Ponty's concern for a pervasive inter-animality and for the "indivision" between an animal and its milieu, such that "the identity of the one that sees and of that which it sees appears to be an ingredient of animality,"[46] converges, in the end, only with what de Witte identifies as "the first stage "of Portmann's thought, which considers animal appearance as "an organ for being seen" (*Organ zum Anschauen*).[47] The "unaddressed appearances" that begin to preoccupy Portmann in the 1950s and that are thematized in the second edition of *Die Tiergestalt*,[48] however, display their optical inventiveness where there may be no eye to see them (one can think, for instance, of the wealth of appearance among unicellular organisms such as diatoms; and Portmann himself ventures in this context into a discussion of fungi).[49] It is here a question, as de Witte reflects, of an intrinsic visibility which no longer inscribes itself within an encompassing intervisibility.[50] Nonetheless, even though Merleau-Ponty stresses intervisibility, he himself, as de Witte recognizes, was engaged upon a *Denkweg* (to use the Heideggerian term) that, in the end, closely approaches that of Portmann and that leads him, particularly in *The Visible and the Invisible*, to the thought of a primary visibility dissociated from the polarity of seer and seen and interlaced throughout with an equally primary invisibility that is not ontic in nature. In answer to the question posed by Ted Toadvine whether phenomenology can twist free of what he calls "the anthropological machine," it may not simply be (as he sees it) the Merleau-Pontyan intertwining or *Ineinander* of animality and humanity that holds the promise of such a breaking free, but also, beyond it, the thought of an intrinsic in/visibility that Merleau-Ponty thematizes in *The Visible and the Invisible* as crossing out determinations such as subject and object, or the Sartrean for-itself versus the in-itself.[51] Thus he speaks, in a working note of January 1960, of an invisible that "is here without being object, which is pure transcendence, without an ontic mask. And the 'visibles,' in the last analysis, are themselves also centered only on a core of absence."[52] It is this thought that bespeaks itself at the horizon of Merleau-Ponty's engagement with Portmann.

The Expressiveness of Instinctual Life: Merleau-Ponty and Lorenz

Merleau-Ponty's last scientific partner in dialogue is the Austrian zoologist and psychologist Konrad Lorenz, who is considered a founder of ethology and who, in 1973, shared a Nobel Prize with his friend and collaborator Nikolaas Tinbergen, and with Karl von Frisch. Merleau-Ponty finds Tinbergen's approach uncongenial and so concentrates largely on the work of Lorenz (although, as de Witte shows, his reading of Tinbergen has also left its traces).[53] He makes no mention of the more problematic aspects of Lorenz's intellectual career, namely his membership in the Nazi Party (he joined in 1938) and support, at the time, of the party's biologist orientation. A number of Lorenz's well-known works are popularizations; and Merleau-Ponty worked with one of these, *Les animaux, les inconnus* (Animals, the Unknown), as well as with a study of "the companion" (*der Kumpan*) focused on a jackdaw (Lorenz worked predominantly with birds), which is now included in *Studies on Animal and Human Behavior*.[54] One of Lorenz's early texts devoted entirely to instinct, "Comparative Behavior Research," is included in a volume showcasing the work of his former student, the zoologist and psychologist Paul Leyhausen, who devoted much of his research to the predatory and social behavior of smaller wild cats and domestic cats.[55]

In this text, Lorenz distinguishes sharply between instinct, reflex, and a mere taxis which is an oriented activity directed toward placing the animal in a position and situation of optimal responsiveness to the factors that trigger an instinctual behavior; and these distinctions are echoed in Merleau-Ponty's reflections. Reflex behavior, Lorenz notes, tends to continue for as long as the stimulus is present, so that a researcher who, for instance, keeps turning a beetle on its back is likely to exhaust himself without the beetle's lessening its efforts to right itself. In contrast, instinctual behavior quickly exhausts the available energy, so that, in Lorenz's example, a ground-nesting bird that distracts a predator by "feigning" lameness (another instance of mimicry) will tire of doing so after only three or four consecutive provocations. On the other hand, instinct (unlike reflex) seeks by its own momentum to discharge itself, so that, in the absence of provocation, the threshold of stimulation is lowered; and the behavior may even play itself out *in vacuo*. Here Lorenz brings up the case (cited by Merleau-Ponty) of a jackdaw raised in captivity who had never encountered a flying insect, but who suddenly performs the instinctive behavior of capturing, killing, and consuming its nonexistent prey.[56] Lorenz points out that the stimuli that trigger instinctive behavior constitute schemata, rather than being finely discriminated. Thus, in another well-known example, a jackdaw that was able individually to identify, by minute visual differences, some twenty members of its flock with whom it had close social ties, nonetheless rushed not only to the defense of any one of these, but equally to that of a pair of black swimming trunks that the researcher made a show of carrying off.[57]

Lorenz argues against the view that instinct is the ontogenetic and phylogenetic precursor of variable and goal-directed behavior which involves "higher psychic accomplishment." He attributes such behavior to entirely different wellsprings.[58] In this respect, Merleau-Ponty seems hesitant to follow him. He stresses the dissociation of instinctive activity from any determinate object and sees in this dissociation the matrix of a variability of response as "a reference to the non-actual."[59] Drawing on Uexküll's metaphorics, he characterizes the object's significance as "a fragment of a melody that the animal carries within itself," and thus noncausally, as evoking "an oneiric *a priori*."[60]

As an endogenous activity, instinct constitutes, for Merleau-Ponty, a "style" that meets up with what evokes it in the animal's milieu and that is therefore not only "sacred and absolute" but is (in contrast to being goal-directed) "an activity for pleasure."[61] This characterization is somewhat questionable, given that instinctive behavior may expose an animal to pain, injury, or even death, as may happen in the defense of its young, or in the ritual "initiation" fights (researched by Leyhausen) that enable a young tomcat to claim a place among its peers. Perhaps play would qualify as an instinctual activity for pleasure; but surprisingly, Merleau-Ponty does not mention it.

His interest in instinct as an activity dissociated from a determinate object derives from its functioning as the matrix of symbolism. In empty activity, he notes, "the outlined act easily becomes signification," so that there is "a very narrow relation between instinct and symbolism."[62] He takes up again and elaborates here the ritualization of the sexual relation among animals that he touched upon in his engagement with Portmann. Thus he criticizes Tinbergen's efforts to explain the mating dance of the stickleback as a combination of the basic instinctual drives of fleeing, aggression, and sexual reconciliation and proposes an alternative: "Could we understand that sexual behavior contains several aspects, that it is entirely different from simple copulation, but [is] a monstration, a ceremony in which the animals show themselves to each other?"[63]

The behaviors of display and ritualization acquire a value of social evocation and are indispensable for copulation to take place. They are, however, not merely a preliminary preparation for copulation but rather are "copulation itself" as "an establishment of an action of presence."[64]

Merleau-Ponty concludes that the phenomenon of ritualization is fundamentally one of "reciprocal expression," and that it is legitimate to speak of "an animal culture." The existence of culture does, of course, presuppose some degree and forms of consciousness; and Merleau-Ponty acknowledges his dissatisfaction with the ethologists' evasion of the question of animal consciousness.[65]

A Note on Interpreting Evolutionary Theory

As the reader will have noticed, a strain of anti-Darwinist animadversions runs through much of the zoological theories and philosophical interpretations discussed. These animadversions in no way question the factual reality of evolution or the supporting evidence but concern rather the interpretation of evolutionary theory; and they hearken back, to a large extent, to Karl Ernst von Baer (an approximate contemporary of Darwin and a formative influence on Uexküll's education), who objected to the randomness and quasi-mechanical character of natural selection.[66]

Merleau-Ponty's occasional remarks on evolutionary theory in the second nature course point in the same direction by challenging the explanatory adequacy of natural selection. Thus his last such remark, in the context of instinct, is that instinctual behavior cannot be understood as adaptation, which presupposes the conformity of the organism to its actual milieu, given that the behavior may in fact anticipate future, and thus possible but as yet non-actual situations.[67]

In the third course on nature, however, Merleau-Ponty devotes considerable time to a critical and searching discussion of Darwinian and neo-Darwinian evolutionary theory. Out of the eight "Sketches" that make up the course for posterity, the "Fourth" through the "Seventh Sketch" are trained on this focus; and the thinkers and theories discussed range all the way from Hans Driesch and Teilhard de Chardin through the statistical Darwinism of G. G. Simpson.[68] It will not be possible here to follow out the complex and tangled lines of this discussion in the fragmentary text of the "Sketches," but some key thoughts can be singled out. Merleau-Ponty rejects the hierarchical model of descendence in favor of laterality and of a complex (nonlinear) proliferation, and he calls attention to the multiple and changing factors at work in evolution and to the plural strata of evolution itself, by virtue of which, he finds, "the causal explanation by [natural] selection disappears."[69]

Most importantly, perhaps, he explains at the conclusion of the "Seventh Sketch" that animality and human existence are given together within the entire fabric of being, and that it will therefore be necessary to seek to understand "the lateral union of animality and humanity," or the human inter-involvement with other corporeities. He has, he notes, accorded prominence to the theory of evolution to "give this depth to the human body, this archaeology, this natal past, his phylogenetic reference."[70] This means, of course, giving phylogenetic depth to dimensions of human life such as memory, imagination, the oneiric dimension, or symbolism and culture, and thus marking their place in animal life.[71] If nonetheless Merleau-Ponty's direct engagement with evolutionary theory remains critical rather than reconstructive, it thereby restricts itself to a function that is properly philosophical, rather than seeking to usurp the territory of the specialist.

The Role of Expression

Whereas Merleau-Ponty's engagement with the "embryology of behavior" and with *Umwelt* theory enabled him to envisage the animal as a non-positive totality that differentially and expressively realizes itself, his further studies of directiveness (as a teleological orientation that cannot be reduced to a mere utilitarian finality),[72] of mimicry, and of animal appearance and the nature of instinct allow him to extend and radicalize his recognition of non-positivity. To begin with, he extends it from the organism as a totality to the species, in that he observes that the notion of species acquires genuine "ontological value" (in contrast to a merely

nominalist status) through the way animals show themselves to one another and are thus able to see themselves, in de Witte's words, "in the
mirror of the other," or by virtue of an expressive intervisibility.[73]

However, in the reciprocity, still horizonal in the nature lectures,
between Portmann's late preoccupation with "unaddressed appearances"
as what de Witte calls "optical sendings into the void," and Merleau-
Ponty's own late understanding of an intrinsic in/visibility—a *Sichtbarkeit*
that will be integral to his ontology of flesh—non-positivity is no longer
limited to any sort of entities, such as animal life, but is thought as the
very core of manifestation. It constitutes now an empty radix or root from
which issues an unstilled expressive (and sometimes mendacious) proliferation of forms, activates, and behaviors, with their bearing on oneiric
themes, symbolism, and culture that Merleau-Ponty elaborates. Much
as, according to a working note to *The Visible and the Invisible,* "being requires creation of us so that we may experience it,"[74] the emptiness at
the core of manifestation continues to call for and sustain the creative
and expressive magic (mimetic or not) of appearances. Intervisibility as
the matrix of expression has therefore been transcended in the direction of the non-positive ontology that Merleau-Ponty also adumbrates in
his readings of Husserl[75] and in his engagement with painting and other
arts, as well as throughout the whole spectrum of his late thought, even
though the sudden truncation of his life did not allow him fully to articulate it. It should be evident, however, that his dialogue with the biological
sciences, in the wider context of rethinking the ontology of nature, is not
only integral to but indispensable for its inspiration.

Part 3

Expression in Merleau-Ponty's Ontology

The Role of Expression in Merleau-Ponty's Dialogue with the Rationalists

Subsequent thought will never again attain this harmony between philosophy and science, this ease of going beyond science without destroying it and limiting metaphysics without excluding it . . . There is an innocent way of thinking *on the basis of the infinite* which made major rationalism what it was, and which nothing will ever allow us to recapture. These words should not be taken to express nostalgia . . . What separates us from the seventeenth century is not a decline but a growth of consciousness and experience.

—Maurice Merleau-Ponty, "Everywhere and Nowhere," in
Signs, translated by Richard C. McCleary (1960)

Philosophy owes to Merleau-Ponty a rich, subtle, and insightful reading of Descartes who is, for him, the foremost partner in his sustained philosophical dialogue with the seventeenth-century rationalists. This dialogue, which has so far been barely touched upon in the Merleau-Ponty scholarship,[1] is pertinent here because expression is a key rationalist concept and is particularly central for Spinoza and Leibniz.

Merleau-Ponty's readings of Descartes can be traced all the way from *The Structure of Behavior* through *Phenomenology of Perception* on to "Eye and Mind," *The Visible and the Invisible,* and the late lecture courses, including "L'ontologie cartésienne et l'ontologie d'aujourd'hui" ("Cartesian Ontology and Ontology Today," one of the two courses interrupted by his death).[2] Furthermore, his readings of Descartes are particularly important for the courses on nature, since, as Robert Vallier emphasizes in his "Translator's Introduction," Merleau-Ponty sees in Descartes "the institution of a philosophical tradition of the concept of Nature" which has proved fateful and tenacious.[3] Searching reflections on Leibniz, focused generally on monadic expression, can be found in the first lecture course on nature (often in the context of reflections on Schelling), as well as in the working notes to *The Visible and the Invisible*.[4]

Merleau-Ponty tends, however, to be critical and rather dismissive of Spinoza, for whom the infinite attributes of God or Nature (only two of which are accessible to the human mind) are intrinsically infinite expressive orders of manifestation. In the first nature course, "The Concept of Nature" of 1956–57, Merleau-Ponty characterizes Spinoza's metaphysics as based on "a *one-way* relation" between an infinity of essence (God/Nature as *ens necessarium* and as *natura naturans*) and finite reality as *natura naturata*, which is already contained "eminently" (in the technical sense of *eminenter*) within the infinite and constitutes, when bodied forth, a mere "product" or "dead effect."[5] One should note, however, that Merleau-Ponty's use of *naturata* (without the subject term, *Natura*) is idiosyncratic, for Spinoza's *Natura naturata* is not finite. Similarly he speaks of a Spinozism that, in equating God and Nature, treats nature as "infinite positivity" and fails to realize that what is negative for intelligence is "positive for life."[6] The "positivism" with which Spinoza is charged is, of course, at odds with Merleau-Ponty's own insistence on what Robert Vallier calls "a dimension of negativity internal to Being," or integral to flesh as such.[7] In "The Concept of Nature," Merleau-Ponty is especially critical of Spinoza's concept of *conatus* (a notion that has a long philosophical history, going back to Roman thought) as the "actual essence" of a given thing, which constitutes a mode "whereby the attributes of God are expressed in a definite and determinate way," and which cannot, as such, contain anything that would annul it. It therefore involves, Spinoza points out, not finite but "indefinite time."[8] Merleau-Ponty understands this thought as one that treats negativity as sheer absence or lack (in contrast to the positivity of essence),[9] and he elaborates this criticism by referring to Spinoza's Letter XII, to Lodewijk Meyer, where Spinoza supposedly speaks of "the infinite power of existence or being."[10] The passage that, within the letter, most closely corresponds to this citation reads (in Samuel Shirley's translation): "It is to the existence of modes only that we can apply the term duration; the corresponding term for the existence of substance is eternity, that is, the infinite enjoyment of existence or—pardon the Latin—of being (*essendi*)."[11]

For "enjoyment" Merleau-Ponty (or perhaps the transcriber of the lecture notes) has substituted "power" which is, for Spinoza, equivalent to "essence," whereas the quotation focuses, not on *essentia*, but on being or *esse*.[12] Merleau-Ponty further chides Spinoza for a homogenization of Nature and for failing to recognize (in contrast to Descartes) a distinction (or even an "opposition") between "real extension and extension in thought."[13] The reference here seems to be to Spinoza's contention, in EIP13Cor that, since absolutely infinite substance is indivisible, indivisibility must equally be affirmed of it when considered under the attribute of extension. In Letter XII, he writes that the common human tendency to conceive of infinite substance (under the attribute of extension) as made of really distinct finite parts is due to a habit of thinking "abstractly and superficially," in keeping with imagination, rather than according to pure intellect.[14] Merleau-Ponty does not seem to recognize that Spinoza's equation of real or substantial extension to the way it is apprehended by pure intellect means that actual extended nature is not for him any sort of "product" but one of the infinite self-expressions of Nature or God. A product would, by its very nature, be finite.

It seems that Merleau-Ponty is ready, in general, to treat Spinoza's thought as a sort of radicalization of Cartesianism that is oblivious of Descartes's subtle strategies of limitation (or sometimes evasion) and that thereby becomes "positive." He disregards the fact that, as a transformation of Cartesian creationism into a metaphysics of expression, it offers an alternative to the "institution" of an ontology of nature that he traces to Descartes.

The Merleau-Pontyan criticisms of Spinoza just considered are echoed again in chapter 2 of *The Visible and The Invisible,* titled "Interrogation and Dialectic," where he writes that he himself has come not only to rehabilitate negative thought as an originary manner of thinking but that he has also negatively formulated the principle of causality, "without which there is no representation," and finally has come to conceive as negativity thought as such, which for Spinoza in contrast "was positivity itself."[15] However, in a working note of January 17, 1959, titled "Being and Infinity," he also criticizes "the Cartesians" for failing to realize that infinity, even if thought merely as a ground, is really the inexhaustibility of being; and he speculates that this realization resonates in Leibniz's notion of other possible worlds and perhaps also in Spinoza's recognition of the infinite attributes of substance.[16] When he goes on to claim that "their notion of infinity is positive," however, the referents are ambiguous (are "they" the Cartesians, or also Spinoza and Leibniz?);[17] and it seems that he is, after all, ready to lump the rationalists, as well as the Cartesians,[18] together as having "congealed" infinity by allowing thought to take possession of it, at least to the extent of being able to "prove" its reality.[19]

Certainly Spinoza cannot, as a thinker of his time, be credited with the realization with which Merleau-Ponty concludes the working note, namely that true infinity, as what outstrips (*dépasse*) us, must be a *negative* infinity and, as such, "*Offenheit*. . . sense or reason that are contingency."[20] Nonetheless, Spinozan substance expressing itself in infinite orders of manifestation is nothing positive that could be exhaustively represented; it does indeed in every way "outstrip us." It is true that his dynamically expressive understanding of substance raises the vexed problem of its unity. As Alan Donagan asks: "How can really distinct Attributes, which express really distinct essences, each infinite in its kind, constitute the essence of one and the same substance?[21] He considers that, in E2P7, Spinoza gives a clue as to how he might resolve the problem through the necessary identity, under each of the attributes, of the order and connection of modes (which may, as Donagan notes, entail the postulation of trans-attributive laws of nature).[22] Although the problem cannot be pursued in any detail here, a possible way of resolving it would be to call into question the "real distinction" between the attributes, given that Spinoza states in EIIP7Sch that "thinking substance and extended substance are one and the same substance," and that this is the reason why their modes must also constitute "one and the same thing expressed in two ways." A difference of expression is not a "real" distinction (between *res* and *res*). Furthermore, if substance is in no sense other than or prior to its infinite (thus non-totalizable) expressions, it cannot truly be considered as "positivity" in Merleau-Ponty's sense.

Spinoza's friend Baron Ehrenfried Walter von Tschirnhaus (who was responsible for communicating portions of a manuscript of the *Ethics* to Leibniz) was agitated by the questions why the human mind cannot know any of the attributes of substance (in which it would find itself to be expressed in infinite diversity) other than extension and thought, and of whether the modes of other attributes would be similarly restricted in their understanding.[23] In his replies to these queries, Spinoza points out that, since the power of a given thing is defined by its essence, and it is the essence of the human mind to be the idea of the actually existing (or living) human body, its power of understanding is finite and "extends only to those things which this idea of the body contains in itself or which follow from it." For this reason the human mind "neither involves nor expresses any other attribute of God than extension and thought"; and from these no further attribute can *in concreto* be inferred or even conceived.[24] He further explains that, even though each thing or finite mode is expressed in infinite ways in the infinite divine intellect, "these infinite ideas which express it cannot constitute one and the same mind of a singular thing" but must rather constitute infinitely many minds.[25]

There is thus, first, a clear sense in Spinoza's metaphysics and philosophy of mind in which the human mind is debarred (contrary to Merleau-Ponty) from any possession of infinity; and second, this nonpossession is due to its very nature as the complex idea of the complex human body in its living actuality. Neither in Descartes nor even in Leibniz does the human body similarly define the scope and nature of the mind's apprehension of reality (although Leibniz regards body as indissociable from the soul or mind). Furthermore, in discussing his rejection of psychophysical causality in EIIIP2Dem, Spinoza points out that "nobody has as yet determined the limits of the body's capabilities, that is, nobody has as yet learned from experience what the body can and cannot do." It is therefore surprising that Merleau-Ponty, as a thinker of embodiment, never interrogates Spinoza's understanding of the bodily conditions of thought—conditions which, to be sure, are not causal but expressive in nature. Even insofar as the mind forms adequate ideas and comes to understand things "under the aspect of eternity" (*sub specie aeternitatis*), it does so, in Spinoza's view, not by utterly transcending the body but rather by conceiving, not the present and actual existence of the body, but rather its essence as it follows eternally from God or Nature.[26]

This Spinozan understanding of the very nature of thought cannot, to be sure, be interpreted in Merleau-Ponty's terms of conceiving thought itself "as negativity" (a conception that would have been alien to a thinker of his time), but neither can it straightforwardly be dismissed as "the positive itself." What would be more fruitful is to undertake what Heidegger calls "the step back" from out of metaphysics into its essentiality (*Wesen*) which, as he notes, requires the freeing release (*Freilassung*) of the historical tradition of philosophy "into its still reserved essential past [*Gewesenes*]."[27] This freeing release can only be accomplished by the sort of patiently sustained questioning that Merleau-Ponty does devote to Descartes, but not to Spinoza. His failure to engage more searchingly with Spinoza is the more astonishing since not only Descartes, but also Spinoza and Leibniz, were working scientists whose thought is pertinent to the question of the relation of "classical science" to contemporary techno-science that Merleau-Ponty addresses in the opening section of "Eye and Mind"; and furthermore, Spinoza and Leibniz shared an interest and competence in optics that would also be relevant to "Eye and Mind's" discussion of Cartesian optics.[28]

In a working note to *The Visible and the Invisible* of February 1959 titled "Genealogy of Logic, History of Being, History of Meaning," Merleau-Ponty notes that he is clarifying his philosophical project "by recourse to Descartes and Leibniz," but that the chapters he envisages devoting to these thinkers are also intended to show "the historico-ontological and ontological implications of the being of science." With an echo of his critique of Spinoza, he characterizes these implications in terms of "objectified infinity," in contrast to "the *Offenheit* of the *Umwelt*."[29] One cannot, to be sure, anticipate in Descartes the thought of such openness, any more than of "the emergence of flesh as expression"[30] (a thought that Descartes's mechanistic physiology precludes from the outset); but Merleau-Ponty claims that Descartes had glimpsed in a flash the possibility of negative thinking and had, in his understanding of mind and of freedom as involving an unlimited power of negation, also anticipated philosophy's engagement with subjectivity and the negative.[31] Nonetheless, Descartes's position that the mind's innate idea of infinity is the precondition for its awareness of (its own) finitude resolutely forecloses any tarrying with the negative, for the divine infinity and perfection remains for him a positive ground.[32] Although Merleau-Ponty does not point this out, the innate idea of infinity is ultimately, for Descartes, even the precondition of the cogito, insofar as he apprehends the certainty of his own existence only for "as long as I am thinking," and as radically dependent on the divine infinity and perfection, which is to say, in its finitude and ontological fragility.[33] His glimpse of negative thinking is thus sustained from the outset by the thought of divine infinity and perfection understood as *plenum realitatis* or the fullness of reality and is thus mediated by what Merleau-Ponty would consider a positive understanding of infinity.

Although Merleau-Ponty highlights Descartes's engagement with negativity in *Signs,* in "Eye and Mind," where he focuses on the *Optics,* he finds that Descartes's discussion of the graphic representation of space (in the medium of copperplate engravings) opens upon "the absolute positivity of being."[34] Descartes, he points out, was justified in his constructivism and his bold deliverance of space from naive and reifying modalities of understanding; but his error lay in setting space up "as an entirely positive being, irrespective of any viewpoint and without latency, depth, or any true density."[35] Far from inviting absolutization, the perspectival representation of space constitutes, as Merleau-Ponty notes, a cultural or symbolic form in which "the moment of style" does not efface "the moment of who" (the *Wermoment*), or the expressive potentialities of perspectival construction in the hands of individual artists.[36] The "positivity" that he reproaches Descartes for is thus at least in part a disregard for expression.

Merleau-Ponty reflects, however, that Descartes would not have been who he was had he thought himself capable of "eliminating the enigma of vision." Yes, there is for him no vision apart from thought; but thought is nonetheless neither productive of nor in total command of vision; there remains rather at its heart "a mystery of passivity."[37] For Descartes, this passivity is not simply a delimited or localized phenomenon but derives from his ontology, namely his understanding of the duality of created substance (for Spinoza a contradiction in terms) as extension and thought, together with the "substantial union" that is constitutive of human existence.

In his "Replies" to the fifth set of "Objections" (by Pierre Gassendi), and in the "Appendix" to these "Replies," Descartes briefly addresses Gassendi's misgivings about the possibility of any interaction between, or of a union of, soul and body as set apart by a real or substantial distinction. He makes the points that the mind, though united to the entire body, is nonetheless in no way extended, that it need not make use of any "extended semblance" to understand extension, and finally that the real distinction between soul and body does not preclude their interaction.[38] He does not, however, address the problem posed by the substantial union with the requisite care and straightforwardness until challenged by Princess Elizabeth of Bohemia, to whom he confesses at last that the human mind (*l'esprit humain*) is incapable of simultaneously and distinctly conceiving *both* the real distinction between body and soul and their union, since doing so involves a manifest contradiction. He therefore advises her temporarily to suspend or to bracket her understanding of the real distinction, so as to "represent to herself the notion [which he considers to be a "primitive notion"] of their union, which everyone always experiences within himself without philosophizing."[39] He adds that what pertains to this union is known only obscurely by the pure intellect (*entendement*), or even by the intellect aided by imagination, but is known "very clearly by the senses." Hence the union of body and soul is best conceived extra-philosophically, "by resorting to ordinary life and conversation,"[40] and philosophy cannot, on this crucial issue, rejoin the experience of life.

Merleau-Ponty, who alludes to this letter in "Eye and Mind," argues that Descartes's recognition of the resistance that embodiment offers to thought remains nonetheless marginal to his philosophical project, since he considers a thought that remains bound to the body (as vision is on his analysis) to be by definition not genuine thought: "In truth, it is absurd [for Descartes] to submit to pure understanding the mixture of understanding and body. These supposed thoughts . . . are the indices of an order of existence—of existing man, the existing world—which we are not called upon to think."[41]

This order rests ultimately on the divine infinity which, Merleau-Ponty remarks, "is for us an abyss." For Descartes, to recognize this abyss *means only to delimit the scope of human knowledge;* to seek actually to plumb the abyss of divine infinity is "just as futile as to think the space of the soul and the depth of the visible."[42]

Descartes's strategy of neutralizing the threat that human embodi-

ment and the infinity of God pose to his scientific project and its philosophical basis by means of delimitation is pervasive. It bespeaks itself, for
instance, in his resolution, as a being "intermediate between God and
nothingness," to avoid error by constraining judgment (by an act of will)
within the limits of clear and distinct apprehension, or in his granting to
scientific explanation only the status of a model or *modus concipiendi,* as
well as by treating the correlation between sensory mechanism and perceived qualities as the inexplicable "institution of nature."[43]

Metaphysically speaking, Descartes's strategies of limitation com-
pensate for the thinker's finitude and precarious closeness to nonbeing,
which not only presuppose, as already discussed, a "positive" understanding of infinity, but also the created status of the thinker who, rather than
expressively participating in the divine self-understanding, remains radically external to God. Descartes is not a thinker of expression but rather
gives precedence to creative causal agency and the dependence of finite
reality on *creatio continua.* It seems that the "*one-way* relation" between infinity and finitude, with which Merleau-Ponty charges Spinoza, is instead
characteristic of Descartes.

With regard to the problem of thinking human embodiment, the
fact that he understands the human and animal body as a mechanism
or living machine creates further difficulties. First of all, his refusal to
recognize any sort of animal soul or sentience (so that the animal is reduced to a mere mechanism)[44] is obviously alien to and incompatible
with Merleau-Ponty's insistence on thinking human existence in its "*Ineinander* with animality and nature."[45] A metaphysics or philosophy of
nature that denies the expressivity of animal life not only cannot do justice to the phenomena but also cannot, in the end, aspire to an adequate
understanding of human embodiment.

In the first lecture course on nature, Merleau-Ponty points out that,
for Descartes, it is the soul that gives unity to the human body, so that
the animal body, being devoid of soul, can then not be genuinely unified, and that even the human body, lacking any unity intrinsic to it,
cannot enter into a genuine union with the soul.[46] The problem derives,
once again, from Descartes's metaphysics which considers only thinking substance to be genuinely individuated. Thus he states in *Principles,*
I, 60 that, since each person "regards himself as a thinking thing and is
capable, in thought, of excluding from himself every other substance,
whether thinking or extended, he is really distinct from every other
thinking substance."[47] Extended substance, however, is not intrinsically
individuated, so that, as Descartes explains in the "Synopsis" prefaced
to the *Meditations,* the human body is just "a configuration of limbs and
other accidents," whereas the human mind "is pure substance."[48] The

causal reasoning that underlies Descartes's postulation of a duality of created substances (each defined by its essential attribute) and of the substantial union, not only excludes meaningful expressive relations, but shows itself to be intractably problematic as a basis for a philosophy of nature and of life.

Merleau-Ponty, who discusses Leibniz chiefly in the working notes to *The Visible and the Invisible,* nowhere offers any specific textual references; but it is clear that the Leibniz who fascinates him is the late Leibniz, from "A New System of the Nature and Communication of Substances, and of the Union of the Soul and Body," of 1695 to the *Theodicy* of 1710 and the *Monadology* and *Principles of Nature and Grace,* both of 1714.[49] Merleau-Ponty refers to Leibniz's "system of monads"; and the notion of monad begins to make its appearance in Leibniz's writings in 1695.[50]

The relative scarcity of Merleau-Ponty's discussions of Leibniz, and their near-confinement to working notes, should not mislead one to underestimate the importance of this rationalist philosopher for the development of his own late thought. In the working note of December 1959, devoted entirely to Leibniz, he states explicitly that, in his own work in progress, "the relation of *In der Welt Sein* [being in the world] will take the place held, in Leibniz, by the relation of the reciprocal expression of perspectives taken upon the world, and thus [of] God as the unique author of these perspectives." In this context, he nonetheless also indicates that certain Leibnizian insights "are to be entirely retained."[51]

The first of these is that each of the monadic viewpoints upon the universe constitutes "a world apart," while yet (here the quotation marks are Merleau-Ponty's own) "what is peculiar to one would be public to all."[52] Although Leibniz, unlike Spinoza, does affirm divine creation (and indeed, he asserts that his monadic substances can begin to exist only by creation and end only by annihilation),[53] he does not elaborate the paradigm of creation causally (as does Descartes and, in his wake, occasionalism) but largely in terms of expression. The infinitely diverse created substances or monads, having the basic character of "souls," all express the entire universe "exactly and in [their] own ways" (although with varying degrees of distinctness), while yet the series of expressions or representations (the terms are equivalent in Leibniz) thus produced will naturally correspond "to the changes in the universe itself," in a harmony that is grounded in God.[54] As stated in the *Principles,* every monad "is a living mirror, or a mirror endowed with internal action," which represents the universe from its own point of view, yet is ordered in keeping with the order of the universe itself.[55] One hears here an echo of Spinoza's assertion in EIIP7Sch that God, "insofar as he consists of infinite attributes, is in fact the cause of things as they are in themselves."

Merleau-Ponty, who refers to this Leibnizian order as the *géométral*, affirms its basis in reciprocal and all-pervasive expression, together with the infinite diversity of monadic expressions; but he points out the need to relinquish Leibniz's "substantialist and ontotheological elaborations," so as to take his insights up anew "in uncultivated being" (*l'être brut*).[56]

Uncultivated being, as Merleau-Ponty understands it, repudiates the explanatory adequacy of both the causal and the subject-object relation,[57] yet it not only accommodates but *calls* for expression, provided that the very notion of expression is problematized and rethought. As Bernhard Waldenfels comments, in Merleau-Pontyan expression the expressive act must differentiate itself within itself and from itself, giving rise to "a play of multiple differences to which one can attribute definite movements of expression."[58] Waldenfels comments further that, for Merleau-Ponty, "creative expression becomes expression as response, not only by taking up again the proper possibilities that are offered, but in acquiescing in the exigencies of the other that provoke it" (acknowledging that this demand proceeds, for Merleau-Ponty, not in the first place from the person of the Other but rather from "something other" [*autre chose*]).[59] It is evident that these articulations of creative and responsive expression cannot be understood as constitutive of a Leibnizian *géométral*. The Leibnizian equation of expression with representation by monads that are "windowless" and thus closed in upon themselves (and which invariably falls short of the distinctness and perfection of the divine understanding) will have to be relinquished as part and parcel of his "onto-theological elaborations."

In the cited working note, Merleau-Ponty nonetheless includes the expressive interrelation of the monadic perspectives (each of which is distinctive or unique), both among themselves and with the world, among the Leibnizian insights that he proposes to retain.[60] He stresses, however, that "the expression of the universe within us" is not the harmonious mutual adjustment of monadic perspectives but is rather "what we register in perception, to be taken as it comes instead of being explained." He concludes the note with a striking statement: "It is the recovery of the theme of perception that transforms the import of the Leibnizian idea of expression."[61]

The Leibnizian monads do, of course, have perception, as well as "appetition," or a principle of action and change (and thus of impermanence). This is true even of the monads constitutive of inorganic nature (whereas conversely Leibniz is willing to attribute a certain materiality to beings conventionally considered to be discarnate, such as angels or spirits). As he writes to Queen Sophie Charlotte in 1702:

> I am inclined to think that all finite immaterial substances . . . are
> joined to organs and accompany matter. I am even inclined to think
> that souls or active forms are found everywhere. And in constituting a
> complete substance, matter cannot do without them, since form and
> action are found everywhere.[62]

Leibniz's late metaphysics, which is closely connected to his dynamics
(as articulated in the *Specimen Dynamicum* of 1693),[63] leads him to understand all of nature as alive, active, and sentient.

Although it could be said that, in Leibniz's understanding of perception, the seer is—as the late Merleau-Ponty likes to stress—included
within the seen (since every monad, though "windowless," represents the
entire universe and is therefore itself represented, however confusedly,
by the infinity of other monads), there is for him no genuine interaction,
reciprocity, or solicitation by the other involved in perception. As he explains in the autobiographical style of the "New System":

> Since I was forced to agree that it is not possible for the soul or any
> other true substance to receive something from without . . . I was led
> . . . to the view that God originally created the soul . . . in such a way
> that everything must arise for it from its own depths [*fonds*] through a
> perfect *spontaneity* relative to itself, and yet with a perfect *conformity* to
> external things . . . [The soul's] perceptions must arise because of its
> own original constitution . . .That is what makes every substance repre-
> sent the whole universe exactly and in its own way, from a certain point
> of view, and makes the perceptions or expressions of external things
> occur in the soul at a given time, in virtue of its own laws.[64]

Notwithstanding the soul's "perfect spontaneity," it is, in Leibniz's view,
in a passive condition insofar as its perceptions are indistinct and confused (and may not even rise to explicit consciousness), and conversely
it is said to act only insofar as it has distinct perceptions. Both action and
passion, however, arise from itself alone and are part and parcel of its
distinctive contribution to the preestablished harmony of the whole.[65]

It is evident that, in Merleau-Pontyan terms, perception is here not
only explained, rationalized, and systematized, rather than being taken
"such as it comes," but is also stripped of a genuine "worldliness" or belonging to the world. His working note of April 1960 is instructive on this
point. He writes that his description of the visible as invisible must lead
(in the third part of his book in progress) to a confrontation with Cartesian ontology (he exhorts himself to read Gueroult's works on Descartes

and Nicolas Malebranche, and to have recourse to Leibniz and Spinoza). The focus will be on "the *Weltlichkeit* of mind [*de l'esprit*]." In contrast to the Cartesian problem of "the communication of substances," and the proposed solutions of "occasionalism, harmony, parallelism" developed in its wake, his own rehabilitation of perception and of the perceived world will lead to a genuine *Weltlichkeit,* whereas the Leibnizian schema reveals an unawareness of "the wild or perceived world."[66]

Since Merleau-Ponty's philosophy of nature (including animality and human embodiment), as articulated in his late lecture courses, forms a pathway to the ontology partially developed in *The Visible and the Invisible,* it will be of interest to consider Leibniz's understanding of animality and of the human body, even though the nature courses do not address it explicitly.

Merleau-Ponty returns again and again to the impasse that Descartes encountered in seeking to explain the union of soul and body in the human being; but he tends to see this impasse positively as part and parcel of the recognition, on the part of "classical science," of its own limits, which kept it from self-absolutization.[67] Leibniz, however, states flatly that Descartes had just "given up the game at this point," opening the door to Malebranche's occasionalism which (perceiving perhaps not only a threat to religion but also mendaciousness in the Cartesian position) ascribed causal efficacity to God alone as though, in Leibniz's words, to a deus ex machina.[68] His own position is essentially that the soul *expresses* its own body, and through it everything else, and that the union of soul and body is grounded in the preestablished harmony: "It is this mutual relation, regulated in advance in each substance of the universe, which produces what we call their *communication,* and which alone brings about *the union of soul and body.*"[69]

This raises, of course, the question of Leibniz's understanding of body, which is vexed not only because this understanding went through several successive changes, but also because, from about 1703 on, he seems to have abandoned the view that matter or body have any autonomous reality, viewing material phenomena instead as arising purely from the interrelations of monads.[70] Since this study remains focused on Merleau-Ponty's thought in relation to Leibniz rather than on Leibniz in his own right, it will not take up the complexities and difficulties of his late understanding of body but will work instead with the model he offers in the *Principles of Nature and Grace,* which seems to be his prevalent late model. He writes there:

> Each distinct simple substance or monad, which makes up the center
> of a composite substance (an animal, for example), and is the principle

of its unity, is surrounded by a *mass* composed of an infinity of other monads, which constitute the *body belonging to* this central monad.[71]

Surprisingly, Merleau-Ponty not only fails to address Leibniz's radically expressive understanding of the body of a living being (plant, animal, or human) but also his challenging view that (as already indicated) there are no minds, souls, or monads that lack a body, since such a lack would deprive them of both sentience and agency, and indeed of what Merleau-Ponty terms *Weltlichkeit*. Thus Leibniz concludes the "Preface to the *New Essays*" of 1703–5 with the statement that "immaterial substances . . . have never existed naturally among created things."[72] If no minds are discarnate, however, neither can animals (nor even plants) be considered mere nonsentient mechanisms. Although, as Leibniz recounts in the "New System," he was, as a young man, "charmed by [the 'modern authors'] beautiful ways of explaining nature mechanically," he subsequently saw the need to introduce not only the notion of force into physics (whereas Cartesian mechanism had contented itself with extension and motion, to which some thinkers added impenetrability), but also to resist the degradation of animals to machines.[73] He became henceforth a tireless advocate of animal (and indeed universal) sentience (in agreement with Spinoza, but in sharp contrast to Descartes). He seems also to have derived from Spinoza's philosophy of organism the notion that "all bodies are in perpetual flux, like rivers, and parts enter into them and depart from them continually."[74]

The most striking inference that Leibniz draws from his analysis of substantial composites such as animals is that they are ungenerable and indestructible (except by divine agency), so that naturally there is, strictly speaking, no death. What is called death involves a protracted state of stupor or unconsciousness during which the living being is not annihilated but transformed, since "souls never entirely leave their body and do not pass from one body into another that is entirely new to them."[75] To give way for a moment to imagination (much maligned though it is by rationalism), the Paleolithic humans who painted the caves of Chauvet or Lascaux (Merleau-Ponty is fond of tracing art to the latter) would then not only be the remote ancestors of certain contemporary humans, in an unbroken line, but also would actually still continue to live, transformed into ourselves, while the animals with whom they were intimately interconnected would continue their own lives as contemporary animals (regardless of extinctions). The traditional sharp distinction between humans and animals has been retained here (even though "primitive" peoples recognized a fluidity that erased it) since Leibniz grants rational souls or minds, capable of apperception, and participation in the city of God, to humans alone.

The reader will have noticed that, in this context, Merleau-Ponty's voice has fallen silent. It is astonishing that, although he does acknowledge the importance of Leibniz for his own late thought, and specifically with a view to expression, his treatment of the philosopher remains— in contrast to his searching reflections on Descartes (and even Malebranche)—rather sketchy and casual. His sustained engagement with Husserl, author of the *Cartesian Meditations*,[76] is no doubt relevant to this state of affairs but does not explain it. The nature lectures treat both Aristotle (to whom Leibniz was indebted) and Descartes briefly, but Spinoza and Leibniz hardly at all (and only in the first course). Yet, as Catherine Wilson points out, Leibniz's thought had its eventual echo in Driesch's vitalism.[77] Furthermore, there also seems to be a still insufficiently explored connection in the history of ideas (passing perhaps through Immanuel Kant) between Uexküll's recognition of a vast diversity of animal worlds, interlinked like melodies in a symphonic ensemble, and the Leibnizian recognition of monadic perspectives, each of which is "a world apart" yet is harmoniously integrated within the cosmic whole.

In *Signs,* Merleau-Ponty concludes his essay "Everywhere and Nowhere" with a reference to the rationalists:

> Tomorrow philosophers will have no "anaclastic line," "monad," "conatus," "substance," "attribute," or "infinite mode." But they will continue to learn in Leibniz and Spinoza how happy centuries thought to tame the Sphinx, and in their own less figurative and more abrupt fashion, they will keep on giving answers to the many riddles she puts to them.[78]

Rather than appreciatively contemplating the philosophical thought systems of supposedly "happy centuries" (which really were not such, but were tormented by warfare, religious and intellectual intolerance, and a devastating plague epidemic), it would be more fruitful today to trace the living bond that interlinks a contemporary philosophy of nature, drawing upon the innovative biology of the mid-twentieth century, with the challenging intellectual creativity of rationalist thought, and with the Spinozan and Leibnizian understanding of life and of organism.

The Irreducibility of Expression: Merleau-Ponty's Ontology and Its Wider Implications

> Before it [language], a "mute" experience, and one that of itself calls for its "expression," but a "pure" expression, i.e., foundation and not product of language . . . This speech truly dimension or *Eröffnung* of an immense page spread *[feuillet]* of being, and across it of being itself speaking within us ("pure" expression).
>
> —Maurice Merleau-Ponty, *Notes de cours sur l'origine de la géométrie de Husserl* (1998)

In the "Second Sketch" of "Nature and Logos: The Human Body," which constitutes the third of Merleau-Ponty's lecture courses on nature, he writes that "there is always a language before language, which is perception."[1] The human body is "symbolism" in a nonconventional sense, which he characterizes as *expressive,* noting that perception and movement symbolize, and that their expressivity is equivalent to "their insertion in a non-conventional system of equivalences, in the cohesion of a body."[2]

Renaud Barbaras has noted that the task of thinking expression has oriented Merleau-Ponty's thought from the outset, even though, in *Phenomenology of Perception,* expression is not yet grasped "at a level that will allow him to integrate it with the phenomenon of truth," or to let it emerge as the body's originary signifying power, indissociable from ideality. He notes further that, for the early phenomenological analysis of perception to fulfill itself "as a philosophy of expression, articulated ontologically," it must be able to do justice to expression in its eminent form, which is linguistic.[3]

Merleau-Ponty is haunted by Husserl's remark in the *Cartesian Meditations* that the beginning for "the radically initiatory descriptive doctrine of consciousness" lies in "the pure and, so to speak, still mute experience that is now to be brought to the pure enunciation of its own sense."[4] Thus, in the chapter on "Interrogation and Intuition" in *The Visible and the Invisible,* addressing Husserlian eidetic intuition, Merleau-Ponty writes that the way to things in themselves must be traced through language. From the standpoint of the traditional conception of truth as an adequation of intellectual apprehension to reality, however, language is a power of distortion and error. The philosopher's speech then attests only to his or her weakness; ideally he or she should seek to coincide with things in their silence which he or she, nonetheless, persistently and absurdly strives to give voice to: "He [the philosopher] wrote so as to say his contact with Being; but he did not say it and could not have said it, since it is silence. So he recommences . . ."[5]

If, however, as Merleau-Ponty writes, it is "the patient and silent labor of desire" that brings motility, vision, or touch back to their source and initiates "the paradox of expression,"[6] that source cannot be a sheer primordial silence and self-containment. The paradox exhibits not only the formal structure outlined by Waldenfels (an infrangible originary silence could never come to word, whereas a still inchoate articulation could simply be left to explicate itself),[7] but, more concretely, it points to the fact that one cannot hope ever to experience things "all naked" (like Descartes's wax), or in sheer immediacy. Rather, my gaze, according to Merleau-Ponty, clothes things with its own flesh; and this interposed "thickness of flesh" (which is fundamentally expressive) is far from obstructing proximity. It is rather "profoundly in accord" and even "synonymous" with it, constituting the only means for reaching the very heart of things.[8]

Merleau-Ponty explores not only the "inspired exegesis" that allows the perceiver to interrogate the visible or the tangible in such a way as to solicit what it can optimally yield, and thus seemingly "according to its own wishes," or the way in which complex sensory, oneiric, or imaginative "participations" inform even the most elementary sensory quale, such as a patch of red—not to speak of the trans-personal memory that animates not only the sight of "the plane trees of Delphi," but may equally invest one's contemplation of a dwarf olive tree that, in northern latitudes, one may devotedly cultivate in a pot.[9] In all of these expressive investments that both veil and reveal things as genuinely themselves, the emphasis rests on perception; yet the late Merleau-Ponty places at least equal emphasis on language.

Among the texts in which he explicitly addresses language are both *The Visible and the Invisible,* and the third of the lecture courses on nature. One of his key concerns is to argue—against the model of language in structural linguistics, where the relation between signifier and signified is arbitrary—that language is rooted in the natural world; and that this rootedness is not representational but rather expressive in character. Language carries forward the expressivity of perception and motility, as well as of the symbolic articulation of the life world or surrounding world (all of which already characterize animal life) in the manner of what Merleau-Ponty likes to call a "surpassing in place." Conversely, therefore, ideality is not dissevered from this expressive continuum, but rather, as Hass points out:

> Below the abstract level of representation, language is a marvellous conjunction of a socio-cultural structure sustained by carnal life, but a structure which can be transformed and transcended by embodied acts of expression. In a phrase, carnal life and non-material linguistic structures are in a relationship of *reversibility*.[10]

This conjunction is at least an important part of the sense in which Merleau-Ponty, in his lecture course on Husserl's *The Origin of Geometry*, speaks of a "braiding together" (*Verflechtung*) of human being, world, and language.[11]

In the "First Sketch" of the third nature course, Merleau-Ponty notes that "there are no substantial differences between physical nature, life, and mind, and therefore also between "the perceptual silence and a language that always carries a thread of silence."[12] The differential structure (and thus the non-positivity) of linguistic articulation, which he accepts from Saussure, carries forward, for him, the differential structure of perception itself which constitutes a primary interrogation of the world. In the "Third Sketch," he not only reiterates that "there is a logos of the sensible world, a savage mind that animates language," and that "communication in the invisible" continues what is first instituted in the visible, but he also points to the sedimentation, within language, of an "invisible surplus."[13] Hass explains this sedimentation as the origin of constituted language:

> Instead of beginning with Saussure's dichotomy between *la langue* and *la parole,* Merleau-Ponty would say that we must understand language as an interwoven duality between constituted language and expressive language. That is, a movement between the culturally and historically sedimented field of the already spoken word and the expressive act which transcends and transforms it.[14]

Merleau-Ponty points forward, in the third nature course, to his project of studying, in *The Visible and the Invisible,* "systems of expression" which are to include not only language, but also painting and cinema, as well as "history and its architectonic."[15] The discussion of language in this fragmentary work takes up the themes already discussed; but it also returns the focus once again to the "paradox of expression" in its concrete form.

Here also Merleau-Ponty criticizes the positivism that treats language as a self-contained system of significations, together with the reduction of philosophy to linguistic analysis, for their failure to do justice to the mutability and historicity of linguistic articulation, to the spoken and written word's "halo of significations," and fundamentally to the expressive power of language. Language, he writes, is itself a being or a world, but one "raised to the second power," since it speaks of beings and the world and thus "redoubles their enigma, rather than making it disappear."[16]

Philosophy, Merleau-Ponty reflects, also interrogates what does not speak and what precedes reflection; but it does so to *say* it, which is possible only because language is itself "a power of anticipation and prepossession," expressing "an ontogenesis of which it is a part."[17]

He characterizes as "hyper-reflection" (*sur-réflexion*) a philosophical reflection that addresses "the transcendence of the world as transcendence" and that remains sensitive to the changes that it inevitably introduces into what it brings to articulation. To do so, however, it cannot speak in keeping with accepted linguistic significations but will need to engage in the difficult effort of making use of them "so as to express, beyond themselves, our silent contact with things, when they are not as yet things said."[18] Language indeed "lives only from silence"; but this silence is not mute coincidence. It is, rather, precisely in its incapacity of coinciding with things themselves that language is "the most valuable witness to Being."[19]

Merleau-Ponty concludes the chapter on "The Intertwining—the Chiasm" with the reflection that, on the one hand, philosophy consists in a restoration of the power to signify, through "an expression of experience by experience," clarifying in particular "the special domain of language," or its power to bring mute experience to the expression of its own sense. On the other hand, he complements this Husserlian thought with the claim, phrased in the words of Valéry, that language is the voice of no-one, but rather of the things themselves, such as "the waves and the forests." This reiterated paradox of expression bespeaks itself here as "reversibility," and hence as having no need for any elucidating synthesis.[20]

Reversibility is, for him, an ontological structure; and as he writes in a slightly different context, the paradox that has haunted him "is indeed a paradox of Being, not a paradox of man."[21] As he remarks in a working note of February 1959, it has become necessary for him to bring the results of *Phenomenology of Perception* to ontological explicitation;[22] and the role of expression will therefore have to be traced out in his late ontology of flesh.

Having described the living body as sentient/sensible, or as flesh that both (actively) incorporates and is (passively) incorporated by the flesh of the world, Merleau-Ponty writes that flesh is "this very anonymity inherent in myself."[23] Being neither *hypokeimenon* nor *substantia*, nor yet spirit or matter, it has so far lacked a name in the Western philosophical tradition. To designate it, Merleau-Ponty reflects: "One would need the old term 'element,' in the sense in which it was used to speak of water, of air, of earth, and of fire . . . a sort of incarnate principle that brings with it a style of Being wherever there is any particle of it. Flesh in this sense is an 'element' of Being."[24]

Emmanuel Alloa critically examines the not uncommon assimilation, based on Didier Franck's reading of Husserl, of the Husserlian notion of the lived body or *Leib* as flesh to Merleau-Ponty's understanding of flesh. He rejects the assimilation, chiefly on the grounds that the latter notion undercuts the very distinction between the proper and the mediational (*médialité*) that underlies Franck's interpretation, and that the idea of *Leib* as mediational can already be found in Merleau-Ponty's *Phenomenology of Perception*, whereas flesh only makes its appearance in the 1950s.[25] Rather than taking such a Husserlian approach, it may be more productive to take Merleau-Ponty at his literal word and consider the pre-Socratic understanding of what Aristotle (transmitter of many fragments of the *physiologoi*) termed "elements" (*stoicheia*), but what Empedocles—who offers perhaps the clearest articulation—called the four "roots" (*rhizomata*) out of which, under the agency of Love and Strife, and within the pattern of the cosmic cycle, all phenomena arise. Empedocles accorded to each of these elemental realities (to which he also gave the divine names of Zeus, Hera, Aidoneus, and Nestis) its own characteristic and perceptible style of being, so that, for instance, the solar brilliance and radiant heat contrasts with the chill and darkness of winter's rain.[26]

As concerns Merleau-Ponty, the important point is that each of these elements stands for a certain "style" of expression—style being inherently expressive—and furthermore, that these expressive registers are *carnal* in nature, making for the intricate articulations of intercorporeity or of the inter-animality, among which the human body, as *Leib*, constitutes "a remarkable variant."[27] Although this account of the elemental expressivity of flesh, and of flesh characterized as a "pregnancy of possibles,"[28] differs from Hass's in that Hass does not focus on the elemental, it does agree with his conclusion that flesh is an "expressive multiplicity," which makes it a matrix of possibilities.[29]

The expressive multiplicity of flesh is not, of course, limited to the archetypal elemental schema of the pre-Socratics but is rather a limitless proliferation of "styles," both natural and cultural, that are expressive in their own right. In contrast to the rationalists' disdain for qualitative phenomena as "secondary qualities," these styles are not only emphatically qualitative but are also genuinely apprehensible only in the manner of what Merleau-Ponty terms the "carnal essences"—idealities that are indisseverable from their carnal and sensuous modes of presencing. Among such idealities, attesting to "the bond between idea and flesh," he himself names light, sound, plasticity or relief, and bodily voluptuousness;[30] but one might just as well, and more concretely, invoke the myriad styles of natural existence—not only of animal life, but also of plants, minerals, or geological formations which, although they can be scientifically described, studied, classified, and technologically put to use, are apprehended in their modalities of being or in their inherent expressivity only "in transparency behind the sensible" or (as Merleau-Ponty also describes the carnal essences) as "negativity or absence circumscribed."[31] There is no access to the very style of being of, say, a jaguar in the rainforests or cloud forests of the Amazon, of a hummingbird or a luna moth, as a pure ideality, nor yet as mere empirical materiality. This thought calls to mind Heidegger's discussion of a block of granite as a "mere thing" (*blosses Ding*) in "The Origin of the Work of Art," and his reflection concerning it:

> Or should this very self-withdrawing of the mere thing, should this utter non-constrained-ness [*Zunichtsgedrängtsein*]—should precisely this pertain to the essential being [*Wesen*] of the thing? Must not then this off-putting strangeness [*jenes Befremdliche*] and being closed off in the thing's essentiality become precisely what is most familiar to a thinking that seeks to think the thing?[32]

As Heidegger goes on to reflect, the mere thing, such as the block of granite, is ultimately more akin to the work of art than is its seemingly close cousin, the thing of use [*Zeug*]; and the Merleau-Pontyan repercussions of this thought will eventually need to be pursued to reveal the deeper connections that expression establishes between ontology and aesthetics. For the moment, however, one can confine oneself to considering that the multiple expressivity of flesh helps to elucidate Merleau-Ponty's remark in a working note—a remark that also carries a Heideggerian echo—to the effect that: "*One cannot make a direct ontology. My "indirect" method (being in the beings) is alone in conformity with being.*"[33]

Flesh, however, is not simply a collective nor yet a generic concept, embracing and standing in for myriad styles. It has a structural unity of defining features, including intertwining (*entrelacement*), nondivision (*indivision*), reversibility, and divergence (*écart*), which will need to be further explored. In this sense, flesh is not only an expressive multiplicity but also a matrix of expression; and this may be one of the senses—beyond Merleau-Ponty's own characteristic invocation of psychoanalysis, or the interconnections with the *khora* of Plato's *Timaeus* explored by Vallier—in which Merleau-Ponty speaks of it as "the Mother."[34] In one sense, at least, a mother is a figure of pure donation, akin to the *es gibt,* bringing to birth with no claim to any lasting substantial bond.

Merleau-Ponty speaks of flesh not only as a "pregnancy of possibles," but also as a "mirror phenomenon," noting that the flesh of the world "is indivision of this sensible being that I am, and of all the rest that senses itself in me."[35] Superficial appearances notwithstanding, however, the relations that make for this indivision—relations such as reversibility and chiasmatic intercrossing—are not symmetrical. If they were, Merleau-Ponty would—as he emphatically does not—need to reaffirm a model of truth as coincidence, which would leave no meaningful place to expression. As Hass argues, certain critiques of Merleau-Ponty's notion of reversibility—critiques that also implicate chiasmatic intertwining and that construe reversibility as a symmetrical exchange that neutralizes alterity (he names Emmanuel Levinas and Luce Irigaray)—are insufficiently attentive to the relevant texts (Merleau-Ponty always requires a reading sensitive to his dialogical and metaphorical yet precise articulation). In fact, and contrary to any espousal of reversibility as a symmetrical exchange, he anticipates, as Hass points out, "the philosophical concern with difference that marks so much of subsequent and contemporary continental thought."[36] In the chapter on "The Intertwining—the Chiasm," and in the working notes to *The Visible and the Invisible,* one often hears an echo of—or perhaps rather a convergence with—Heidegger's near-contemporary texts on "The Principle of Identity" and "The Onto-Theo-Logical Constitution of Metaphysics."[37] In the latter text (which addresses Hegel's *Science of Logic*), in particular, Heidegger emphasizes that the same (*das Selbe*) is not the equal (*das Gleiche*), within which difference would disappear, and that for him (in contrast to Hegel) the very issue (*Sache*) for thinking is difference.[38]

For Merleau-Ponty, the reversal between seer and seen that situates vision within the visible, and that can also be traced out in other sensory modalities, as well as in phonation and hearing, and with respect to activity and passivity, is always disrupted, decentered, or deferred and falls short of coincidence. Although divergence or *écart* is thus indissociable from reversibility, it cannot be treated as just an innocuous other name for it but marks the primacy of difference. What Merleau-Ponty calls "the invisible" is therefore not simply the complementary reverse of the visible but, as he states somewhat enigmatically in a passage that Derrida takes special note of: "The visible is *there* without being object, it is pure transcendence without an ontic mask. And the 'visibles' themselves, on the last analysis, are themselves also just centered on a nucleus of absence."[39]

Merleau-Ponty rejects not only a symmetrical complementarity between the visible and the invisible but also explicitly denies that reversibility juxtaposes the self (or else the Sartrean for-itself) to the other, since none of these are positive entities. Reversibility thematizes instead their insubstantiality, and the constant "veering I-Other Other-I."[40] This means also that the relational structures that characterize flesh have priority over the relata rather than presupposing them. Thus Merleau-Ponty writes of a visibility or tangibility as such that does not belong either to the factual body or the factual world but has autonomy. He compares it to the series of images generated by two facing mirrors "which truly belong to neither of the two surfaces, since each one is only the rejoinder of the other, [and] which thus make up a couple, a couple more real than each of them."[41]

This autonomous visibility or sensibility makes for "the anonymity innate to myself" that is, Merleau-Ponty writes, what he terms flesh.[42] The mirror is here not a figure of an unproblematic symmetrical reflection or double, but of a visibility that undercuts the binary schemata of subject and object, self and other, and that allows a Narcissus, in the more profound sense of his infatuation with his own reflection, "to be seen by it, to exist in it, to emigrate into it, to be seduced, captivated, alienated by the phantasm,"[43] because the reciprocity between seer and seen effaces their assured self-identity; and allows alterity to permeate the self. As Merleau-Ponty reflects in a working note, "self-presence is presence to a differentiated world"; and (expanding on Heidegger's view that, rather than man's being the traditional *zōon logon ekhon*, it is language that has man), he notes further that it is the things that have us and not we who have the things, and that "it is being that speaks in us and not we who speak of being."[44] Even self-reflection is ultimately "*absence from oneself, contact with Self through divergence [l'écart] with respect to Self.*"[45]

Merleau-Ponty traces the figure of the chiasm as diacritical cohesion by divergence (*écart*) in the various forms of the relations between self and body, self and world, and self and other; and here again the terms are in no way prior to the relation. In particular the self—extolled by Western philosophy from Descartes's *fundamentum inconcussum* through Fichte's *Ich* and on to the Sartrean for-itself which opposes its own nothingness to being and is thus not caught up in the flesh of the world—is as elusive as "the tip [*la pointe*] of the stroboscopic spiral which is *who knows where,* which is 'nobody.' "[46] It is the chiasm, as the fundamental articulation of flesh, within which the seer is ultimately understood as "the world itself with a certain coherent deformation" that, in Merleau-Ponty's final reflection on Leibniz, constitutes "the truth of the pre-established harmony."[47]

Like the chiasm, the appearance of expression in what is ultimately the "vertical genesis" of different levels of ideality from out of and within flesh, is traced in its different aspects. There is, as already mentioned, the emergence of expression in "the patient and silent labor of desire" which effaces the binary distinctions between self and other, or inside and outside, in a consuming erotic fascination oblivious of the wider world that Merleau-Ponty describes hauntingly,[48] and which one could certainly supplement by the distinctively feminine experiences of pregnancy, parturition, and the care and nurture of the newborn. Although these experiences take on distinctively human forms, they are also shared in significant ways with animal life, so that the expressivity of animal behavior tends to communicate itself directly to humans (and in some cases the reverse may also be true).[49]

Together with this vital expressivity, Merleau-Ponty also traces, in the reversibility (without coincidence) of phonation and hearing "the point of the insertion of speaking and thinking in the world of silence," noting, however, that this point marks a manifest coming to appearance, and not the initiation of an empirical genesis.[50] He acknowledges that he will have much more work to do to follow out "the passage from the mute world to the speaking world" (work that, had he lived to do it, might well have included a study of animal vocalization and communication); but he does conclude:

> One cannot speak either of a destruction nor of a conservation of si-
> lence . . . [It is] the same fundamental phenomenon of reversibility that
> sustains mute perception no less than speech, and which manifests itself
> by an almost carnal existence of the idea as well as by a sublimation of
> flesh.[51]

The expressivity of flesh is "pure" because it is not only never reproductive, nor yet a matter of mere externalization, but also because it is not brought about by language but is rather "being speaking within us" in a primordial way. This is, of course, a point on which Merleau-Ponty differs from Heidegger, for whom language alone allows for the Clearing of manifestation.

Flesh is, for Merleau-Ponty, an ultimate ontological notion; but one may still question its relation to being in the sense of Heidegger's *Seyn,* as well as to the "savage" or untamed being (*l'être brut ou sauvage*) that Merleau-Ponty so frequently invokes. As Emmanuel de Saint Aubert notes at the outset of an important study of Merleau-Ponty's understanding of polymorphism in its different registers, ranging from child development and psychoanalysis to ontology, his characterizations or definitions of flesh are "not always easy to reconcile."[52] An important Merleau-Pontyan text on the polymorphism of wild being is a working note of May 1960, in which he starts out with a critique of construals of representation that involve an understanding of being as "In Itself," rather than as "what alone gives it meaning: distance, divergence, transcendence, the flesh."[53]

He goes on to affirm his own effort to restore a meaning of being "absolutely different from 'the represented' "—namely the "vertical" or "wild" being, which intercrosses the natural and cultural orders in its polymorphism.[54]

This "absolutely different" meaning cannot be fixated in any one conceptual or linguistic designation, all of which remain, and must remain, metaphoric given that, as Heidegger notes in "The Onto-Theo-Logical Constitution of Metaphysics," "our own occidental languages are, in ways [that are] different in each case, languages of metaphysical thinking."[55] For Merleau-Ponty, as Saint Aubert points out, "differentiation progresses by the very exercise of reversibility,"[56] leaving no metaphysical residue of sheer identity. Being, as Merleau-Ponty understands it, is "carnal, raw, natural, if not 'maternal,' is not above but below, [a] being of infrastructure and no longer of an overhang [*surplomb*]."[57]

This infrastructure which is also enveloping (and perhaps "maternal" in this sense) is flesh; and the metaphoric name highlights (in contrast with Heidegger) the need to think human existence in its phylogenetic bond with animal life, and to think the pervasive intercrossing of nature and culture, carnality and ideality. If flesh is also the "brute" or "wild" being, it is important to realize that these notions, for the late Merleau-Ponty, do not carry the sense of constituting any originary or foundational stratum of reality. Here also, Saint Aubert's comments are insightful. He writes that, since the ideas of a pure beginning or origin themselves derive from a phantasm or metaphysical illusion:

> Merleau-Ponty finally renounces any pretension to think the origin (notably his famous "origin of truth") and affirms that the originary bursts forth, divests itself of our grasp, for it is as inaccessible to us as the end or final limit and remains forever, like death, an "ultra-thing."[58]

It is because, according to Merleau-Ponty, "the originary bursts forth [*l'originaire éclate*]" so that philosophy must "accompany this breaking forth, this non-coincidence, this differentiation,"[59] that it is also true that "Being is *what requires creation from us* to experience it," and that philosophy, as "the expression of mute experience by itself, is creation."[60] In simpler words, the refusal of any identity, ground, center, or origin in Merleau-Ponty's ontology is what renders expression both ineluctable and pervasive.

In a working note of January 1959, Merleau-Ponty writes:

> The "amorphous" perceptual world that I spoke of in relation to painting—perpetual resource for the remaking of painting—which does not contain any one mode of expression and which nonetheless calls all of them forth—this perceptual world is at bottom Being in Heidegger's sense.[61]

The Heideggerian allusion is to the relation of being addressed and called upon to respond (*ansprechen, entsprechen*) that forms what Heidegger likes to call the "unbinding bond" between being and man, or being and mortals. Thus the note goes on to speak of the *logos endiathetos* that calls forth the *logos prophorikos;* and a later note speaks of the visual work of art as the trace of "a total movement of Speech which goes toward the whole of Being" and which involves complex registers of expression.[62]

It is important that, for Merleau-Ponty (in contrast to Heidegger), this solicitation of creative expression by being (as *ester,* translating Heidegger's *Wesen,* "to be understood verbally") proceeds from the perceptual world or the flesh of the world and does not privilege the arts of language, and further, that artistic creation in its historicity is subtended by the vast, intricate, and proto-artistic creativity of natural life (recalling here, for instance, Portmann's "unaddressed appearances").

If the multiple expressivity of flesh shows itself in a proliferation of "styles" of natural being, which are apprehended as such in the manner of the carnal essences, they require in their turn an expressive and creative mode of being figured forth and communicated. Although expressivity and creativity are traditionally considered to be the special province of art, the equally traditional opposition of art to science on this score needs today to be problematized. There are, for instance, techniques of scientific imaging of biological specimens that tend to subvert it. Merleau-Ponty, however, prefers to leave this opposition intact; and therefore the "initiation" to the invisible "that inhabits this world, sustains it, and renders it visible"[63] will here be discussed within his privileged framework of aesthetics.

In "Eye and Mind," Merleau-Ponty speaks of "the carnal formula of their presence" that the sensible and sensuous phenomena of the world evoke within the artist's attuned sensitivity, and which, elusive though it may be, elicits in its turn "a visible of the second power, carnal essence or icon of the first."[64] In her reflections on the icon, Jenny Slatman characterizes it as "the image of the visible that bears its invisibility within it," and that inscribes the chiasma of seeing and being seen, and of the visible and the invisible.[65]

Although Merleau-Ponty tends, probably by personal predilection, to neglect the nonfigurative art that came into prominence in the middle decades of the twentieth century (and, unlike Heidegger, he makes no effort to understand the interrelation of calligraphy, painting, and poetry in classical Chinese aesthetics that dissociates painting *ab initio* from representation), it is, as he himself points out, irrelevant to his analysis whether or not painting and sculpture are figurative.[66] In the circuit that leads from the solicitation of the artist's sensibility by the sensuous presencing of the world and by its carnal essences to the icon as a created "equivalent" that, while sensuous and invested in materiality, also transcends these aspects, it is "impossible to say that here nature finishes and man, or expression, begins."[67] Expression has always already begun anonymously in phenomenalization, or in the flesh of the world. For this reason there is, as Stéphanie Ménasé argues in her book that relates Merleau-Ponty's thought to contemporary art, a "passivity of activity" that characterizes artistic creation and that dissociates it from the artist's subjectivity as traditionally conceived.[68]

Philosophy carries forward in its distinctive manner the creation that being requires of humans (and probably already of prehuman life, anterior to language). Barbaras points out that perception and expression appear as two modalities of flesh "insofar as it is institution," and that, even though "every perception is primordial expression, and the thing is a figurative sense," perception and expression cannot be fused or confused.[69] As creation, philosophy is not any sort of arbitrary fabrication but is rather, like art, a manner of establishing "contact with being precisely as creation."[70] Philosophy also carries to the limit the interrogation of the perceptual interrogation of the world that is involved in artistic practice, in particular, the visual interrogation of vision that fascinates Merleau-Ponty in painting. Of course, given the complex emotional, oneiric, and recollective "participations" that inform every fragment of the sensible for a person who is genuinely open or receptive to it (rather than contenting himself or herself with a perception that only identifies the thing or labels it as desirable or undesirable), an understanding of painting as a visual interrogation of visuality in no way reduces it to mere opticality. The visible, as Barbaras writes, "is not then the negation of the invisible, but the element of its manifestation."[71]

If painting is then, at least in some of its aspects, the "secret science" as which Merleau-Ponty likes to characterize it, philosophy is for him "the science of pre-science, as the expression of what is before expression *and sustains it from behind*."[72] Thus the paradox of expression, considered in its logical or abstract form, resolves itself: the expression of what is before expression is itself, as *expression,* a responsive but free creation that could never be accomplished by the pre-reflective silence left to itself, while this silence, being already expressive, is not infrangible and is not disrupted, but rather figured forth in difference by expressive articulation. Since philosophical reflection needs to become hyper-reflection, interrogating its own idealizations and the changes they introduce into the primary perceptual presencing, it must also in the end, as Merleau-Ponty writes in the same working note, achieve "an elucidation of philosophical expression itself."[73]

Strictly speaking, however, one can ultimately no longer recognize, in Merleau-Ponty's last thought, what is "before expression," since natural being is expressive through and through. Much as, in *Phenomenology of Perception,* Merleau-Ponty writes that what the Husserlian phenomenological reduction reveals in the end is the impossibility of a complete reduction, given the irrecusable upsurge of the perceptual world,[74] so also the search for what is before expression reveals the irreducibility of expression. This irrecusable expressive "dehiscence" which erodes any positivity does not allow philosophy to exercise the "total and active grasp" of intellectual possession, "since what is there to be grasped is a dispossession"; and furthermore its ideality is not absolute, since it "shows by words" and is thus, like literature, immersed in language.[75] The sensible, Barbaras notes, gives rise expressively out of its non-positivity to "other modes of the presentation of the invisible; it makes itself speech."[76] Merleau-Ponty concludes the cited note—one of his last—by considering that, even though there is really no absolute difference between what Heidegger called the ontic and the ontological, which means also that there is "no absolutely pure philosophical word," philosophy does not, for all that, simply become nonphilosophy, precisely because it vigilantly exposes, criticizes, and rejects the positivism (and thus the disregard for expression) prevalent in "nonphilosophy," and especially in the quest for "a pure political [so-called] philosophy" (the spectrum of "nonphilosophies" cloaked by the mantle of philosophy could probably be expanded today). This quest threatens to "reduce history to the visible, depriving it precisely of its depth, under the pretext of more closely adhering to it," in keeping with the models of "irrationalism, *Lebensphilos-ophie,* fascism, and communism."[77] In eroding the philosophical tenabil-ity of any sort of positivism, whether blatant or subtle, the irreducibility of expression shows itself to be significant not only for humanity's inter-relation with nature, but also for human interrelations and thus (though not without the requisite further elaboration) for the ethical import that Merleau-Ponty himself discerns in the phenomenon of expression.[78]

Concluding Thoughts

> What if seeing the world's beauty—and that of human works
> and bodies—would merely consist in removing the waste of ap-
> propriation? . . . I wish for and practice the dispossession of the
> world . . . Ecstatic, fervent, rare . . . dispossession admires lucidly
> and protects efficiently.
> —Michel Serres, *Malfeasance* (2010)

The trajectory of Merleau-Ponty's thought, with its complex philosophical
and interdisciplinary engagements, which are at least partially interconnected by the thematic of expression, is oriented toward re-visioning
ontology. Although his late ontology is phenomenologically inspired, it
moves beyond phenomenology in seeking to divest itself of any traces of a
philosophy of consciousness and in taking up the late twentieth-century
problematic of difference. Much like Heidegger, he holds that an ontology must be articulated "in the beings." Hence his sustained and searching meditations on the visual and literary arts, his effort to formulate a
philosophy of nature in dialogue with the history of philosophy as well
as with scientific research (ranging from physics to zoology, evolutionary
theory, and psychology), and finally his challenging readings of thinkers
who were his contemporaries or near-contemporaries, including Husserl, Bergson, Sartre, and Whitehead.

The fundamental importance of ontology, or of seeking to articulate the parameters of an understanding of reality, manifestation, or phenomenalization cannot intelligently be disputed. Nonetheless, for many
contemporary readers of Merleau-Ponty, ontology has not retained a
comparable primacy, especially since his aesthetics, philosophy of embodiment and of nature, or his dialogues with other thinkers are rich
resources in their own right (as is also true of his political thought which
has not been addressed in this study). In conclusion, then, it may be fit-
ting to reflect on the bearing that his thought, centered on expression,
may have on more "ontic" areas of inquiry, singling out here environ-

mental ethics and environmental aesthetics. This concluding reflection takes up Merleau-Ponty's own tantalizing remark that expression is capable of yielding not only a metaphysics but also "the principle of an ethics."[1]

The dispossession of the world that Serres considers to be imminent, since "after exhausting the number of its occurrences, acts of appropriation [in the globalized world] will inevitably lead to the end of property,"[2] may prove to be salutary and even necessary to enable one to see and treasure "the world's beauty," but it may not in itself be sufficient. Leaving aside the complex question of how, in the context of aesthetics, to think beauty and its relevance today, the very experience (or "seeing") of beauty is also what has long lighted the fires of the lust for possession (even though possession may then be established, as Serres thinks, by acts of defilement, such as dirtying or polluting).

There is certainly no question today as to the need to rethink, in a philosophically sophisticated manner, the ethical interrelations of humans with nature (an interrelation that the Western ethical tradition has, for all its brilliance, distressingly neglected). This rethinking cannot meaningfully be done on a purely empirical or pragmatic basis (important though pragmatic thought and "hands-on" work continue to be); but it must ultimately issue from deeper intellectual wellsprings.

Merleau-Ponty's philosophy of expression, as articulated in the contexts of aesthetics, the study of nature, and ultimately ontology is promising for environmental thought for a plurality of reasons. Most obviously, Merleau-Ponty seeks philosophically to expose the phylogenetic bond of humanity with animality and ultimately with all of nature. He interlinks carnality and ideality and, in treating expression as fundamentally equal to phenomenalization, he allows it to encompass animal appearance and behavior (including embryonic maturation), and animal pre-culture, as well as, on the human and historical level, institution, reinstitution, the creation of symbolic forms, and the passage to culture.

It is striking that Merleau-Ponty's privileged interlocutors, the rationalists, and in particular Spinoza and Leibniz, seem to be insensitive to the ethical implications of their own expressive understanding of nature. Hans Jonas succinctly characterizes Spinoza's understanding of the organismic individual as

> the sustained sequence of states of a unified plurality, with only the form of its union enduring, while the parts come and go. Substantial identity is thus replaced by formal identity, and the relation of parts to

whole, so crucial for the nature of organism, is the converse of what it is in the mechanistic [Cartesian and occasionalist] view.[3]

The organism's differentiated complexity of organization makes for its degree of discriminatory sensitivity which, as Jonas stresses, involves both the active aspect of conative self-assertion and the passive aspect of a perceptual openness to the world (which may, to be sure, be extremely inchoate but is nonetheless irreducible). Spinoza, however, limits ethicality to human interrelation and asserts outright, in E4P37Sch1, that animal sentience or animal interests in no way constrain man's liberty to make use of animals and deal with them as he pleases. Similarly, in E4App.#26 he states that legitimate regard for their own advantage licenses humans "to preserve or destroy external Nature" as they deem to be useful to themselves. Animals, he emphasizes in E4P37Sch1, "do not agree with us in nature"; and difference thus becomes (in contrast to its role for thinkers such as Emmanuel Levinas and Jacques Derrida) the criterion for ethical irrelevance.

Even Leibniz, who recognizes infinite degrees of sentience among monads, considers only rational souls or minds to be mirrors, not only of the universe, but of divinity, so that they alone are capable of entering "into a kind of society with God."[4] Their doing so does not seem to depend in any way on their ethical relationships with nonhuman nature.

The point of rethinking the rationalist philosophy of nature and of organism is not, of course, to dwell on its omissions, insensitivities, or blind spots, but to understand and further develop its crucial insights and their implications. Merleau-Ponty's dialogue with rationalism, focused as it is on expression, provides a framework for doing so in a manner that promises to be fruitful for environmental ethics.

Merleau-Ponty's aesthetics is, in form, a philosophy of art rather than an aesthetics of nature; but his focus on perception, expression, and wild being serve to open it to a pervasive engagement with nature. Somewhat surprisingly, his philosophy of biology tends to ignore the aesthetic dimension (which is more prominent in Portmann).

One of the challenges posed by his legacy is perhaps to bring art and nature into closer and more explicit interrelation.

As concerns the still emerging field of environmental aesthetics, Merleau-Ponty's thought spans the divide between a "cognitive" approach, which considers scientific knowledge indispensable for a meaningful aesthetic appreciation of nature, and an "engaged" approach, which rejects any form of Kantian aesthetic distancing (Kant himself nonetheless valued the beauty of nature over that of art). Furthermore, his grounding in psychology and psychoanalysis enables him to thematize the imaginative, oneiric, or sometimes traumatic investments of natural as well as humanly created environments. The issues here are complex, but the basic point is that Merleau-Ponty's philosophical voice can contribute importantly to philosophical concerns that are contemporary and that he therefore does not address as such. This is, of course, entirely in keeping with his own emphasis on institution, and more basically on natality.

Abbreviations

This list comprises only the titles of the works of Merleau-Ponty that are most frequently cited. For a more comprehensive listing of Merleau-Ponty's works and for full bibliographical references, see the bibliography.

"EM" "Eye and Mind." Translated by Michael B. Smith, reprinted in *The Merleau-Ponty Reader*, ed. Leonard Lawlor and Ted Toadvine (Evanston, Ill.: Northwestern University Press, 2007). Originally published as *L'œil et l'esprit* (Paris: Gallimard, 1964).

"ILVS" "Indirect Language and the Voices of Silence." Translated by Richard McCleary, in *Signs*, by M. Merleau-Ponty (Evanston, Ill.: Northwestern University Press, 1964).

IP *L'institution, la passivité: Notes de cours au Collège de France (1954–1955)* (Paris: Editions Belin, 2003). Published in English as *Institution and Passivity: Course Notes from the Collège de France*. Translated by Leonard Lawlor and Heath Massey (Evanston, Ill.: Northwestern University Press, 2010).

N *Nature; Course Notes from the Collège de France*. Translated by Robert Vallier. (Evanston, Ill.: Northwestern University Press, 2003). Originally published as *La Nature: Notes, cours du Collège de France* (Paris: Éditions du Seuil, 1995).

OE *L'œil et l'esprit* (Paris: Gallimard, 1964).

PhP *Phenomenology of Perception*. Translated by Colin Smith (London: Routledge, 1962). Originally published as *Phénoménologie de la perception* (Paris: Gallimard, 1945).

S *Signs*. Translated by Richard C. McCleary (Evanston, Ill.: Northwestern University Press, 1964). Originally published as *Signes* (Paris: Gallimard, 1960).

SNS *Sense and Non-Sense*. Translated by Hubert L. Dreyfus and Patricia Allen Dreyfus (Evanston, Ill.: Northwestern University Press, 1991). Originally published as *Sens et non-sens*, 3rd rev. ed. (Paris: Nagel, 1961).

VI *The Visible and the Invisible*. Translated by Alphonso Lingis (Evanston, Ill.: Northwestern University Press, 1968). Originally published as *Le visible et l'invisible*, edited by Claude Lefort (Paris: Gallimard, 1964).

Notes

Introduction

1. Maurice Merleau-Ponty, *The Prose of the World,* ed. Claude Lefort, trans. John O'Neill (Evanston, Ill.: Northwestern University Press, 1973). Merleau-Ponty abandoned this manuscript but extracted from it the chapter "Indirect Language and the Voices of Silence," now published in M. Merleau-Ponty, *Signs,* trans. Richard McCleary (Evanston, Ill.: Northwestern University Press, 1964), 39–83. *L'origine de la vérité* was the original title for what became *Le visible et l'invisible,* ed. Claude Lefort (Paris: Gallimard, 1964). English translation by Alphonso Lingis, *The Visible and the Invisible* (Evanston, Ill.: Northwestern University Press, 1968). The book was left a fragment at Merleau-Ponty's death. It will be referred to as *VI,* with the French pagination preceding the English. In quoting from it, I have sometimes modified Lingis's translation. See also M. Merleau-Ponty, *Phénoménologie de la perception* (Paris: Gallimard, 1945), and *The Structure of Behavior,* trans. Alden Fisher (Pittsburgh: Duquesne University Press, 2008).

2. M. Merleau-Ponty, "An Unpublished Text by Maurice Merleau-Ponty: A Prospectus of His Work," chapter 14 in *The Merleau-Ponty Reader,* ed. Leonard Lawlor and Ted Toadvine (Evanston, Ill.: Northwestern University Press, 2007), 283–90.

3. Claude Lefort, "Préface" to Maurice Merleau-Ponty, *L'institution, la passivité: Notes de cours au Collège de France (1954–55)* (Paris: Editions Belin, 2003), 5–28 (13).

4. Ibid.

5. M. Merleau-Ponty, *La nature: Notes, cours du Collège de France* (Paris: Editions du Seuil, 1995). English translation by Robert Vallier, *Nature: Course Notes from the Collège de France* (Evanston, Ill.: Northwestern University Press, 2003). This work will be referred to as *N.*

6. Robert Vallier, "Translator's Introduction," *N,* xvi, and *N,* 4.

7. Renaud Barbaras, *The Being of the Phenomenon,* trans. Ted Toadvine and Leonard Lawlor (Bloomington: Indiana University Press, 2004), 98.

8. Ibid., 44.

9. Ibid., 65.

10. Lawrence Hass, *Merleau-Ponty's Philosophy* (Bloomington: Indiana University Press, 2008).

11. M. Merleau-Ponty, *L'œil et l'esprit* (Paris: Gallimard, 1964), 67. English

translation by Michael B. Smith, "Eye and Mind," reprinted in *The Merleau-Ponty Reader*, ed. Leonard Lawlor and Ted Toadvine (Evanston, Ill.: Northwestern University Press, 2007), 351–78 (370).

12. M. Merleau-Ponty, "Cézanne's Doubt," in *Sense and Non-Sense*, trans. Hubert L. Dreyfus and Patricia Allen Dreyfus (Evanston, Ill.: Northwestern University Press, 1964), 9–25. The essay was first published in 1945.

13. M. Merleau-Ponty, "Prospectus," 7. M. Merleau-Ponty, "Metaphysics and the Novel," in *Sense and Non-Sense*, 26–40.

14. Merleau-Ponty, *Phénoménologie de la perception*, part 3, chapter 3.

15. See note 3.

16. Michel Haar, "Peinture, perception, affectivité," in *Phénoménologie et experiences*, ed. Marc Richir and Etienne Tassin (Grenoble, Fr.: Jérôme Millon, 2008), 101–22.

17. See, in particular, Jakob von Uexküll, *Umwelt und Innenwelt der Tiere* (Berlin: Springer Verlag, 1909), and *Streifzüge durch die Umwelten von Tieren und Menschen: Ein Bilderbuch unsichtbarer Welten* (Berlin: Springer Verlag, 1934).

18. Martin Heidegger, *Die Grundbegriffe der Metaphysik: Welt—Endlichkeit—Einsamkeit*, in *Heidegger Gesamtausgabe*, 29–30 (Frankfurt, Ger.: Klostermann, 1983). English translation by William O'Neill, *The Fundamental Concepts of Metaphysics: World, Finitude, Solitude* (Bloomington: Indiana University Press, 1995).

19. Edward S. Russell, *The Directiveness of Organic Activities* (Cambridge: Cambridge University Press, 1946).

20. *VI*, 282 and following, 229.

21. Merleau-Ponty relies mostly on a text that is a popularization of Lorenz's work: Konrad Lorenz, *Les animaux, les inconnus* (Paris: Éditions de Minuit, 1953).

22. Hass, "Prelude: Scenes from the Cartesian Theater," in *Merleau-Ponty's Philosophy*.

23. Barbaras, *The Being of the Phenomenon*, 234.

24. *N*, 219.

25. *VI*, 203 and following, 135. Merleau-Ponty acknowledges the poetic phrase as Valéry's.

26. *VI*, 319 and following, 266.

Chapter 1

1. *PhP*, 345–97. "Cézanne's Doubt" ("La doute de Cézanne") was first published in 1945, the year of the publication of *PhP*, but was then incorporated by Merleau-Ponty into *Sens et non-sens*, a collection of essays first published in 1948.

2. *PhP*, 347. Spinoza's *facies totius universi* (the make of the whole universe) is the infinite and eternal mode that corresponds, under the attribute of extension, to the eternal and infinite mode that is the *Idea Dei* (Idea of God) under the attribute of thought.

3. *PhP*, 368.

4. See *PhP*, 368, 373. Merleau-Ponty's references are to Émile Bernard, "La méthode de Cézanne," which appeared in 1920 in *Mércure de France,* and to Joachim Gasquet, *Cézanne* (Paris: Bernheim-Jeune, 1926). Bernard and Gasquet will here respectively be cited from *Conversations with Cézanne,* ed. Michael Doran, trans. Julie Lawrence Cochran (Berkeley: University of California Press, 2001). See also Joachim Gasquet, *Cézanne: A Memoir with Conversations,* trans. Christopher Pemberton (New York: Thames and Hudson, 1991). Gasquet (who is, however, not the most factual of reporters) writes that Cézanne asked him about the scent of his painting of a landscape and, correcting his answer, noted that "the total blue odor of the pines . . . must marry the green odor of the fields . . . with the odor of the stones" (*Conversations,* 112). The implications of synesthesia are interesting.

5. *PhP*, 369.

6. *PhP*, 373.

7. Galen A. Johnson offers the following information: "Cézanne's conversations with Bernard are recorded in *Souvenirs sur Paul Cézanne* (Paris, 1912). *The Merleau-Ponty Aesthetics Reader,* ed. Galen A. Johnson, trans. and ed. Michael B. Smith (Evanston, Ill.: Northwestern University Press, 1993), 386, n1. A closely similar quotation is given by Léo Languier, in "Cézanne Speaks . . . ," in *Conversations,* 17.

8. *PhP*, 372.

9. *PhP*, 376.

10. *PhP*, 385.

11. Barbaras, *The Being of the Phenomenon,* 7.

12. *PhP*, 380 and following. Merleau-Ponty does not identify the work in question. One possible candidate is the watercolor *The Green Jug,* which dates from 1885–87 (Louvre), and another is *Still Life with Apples* (1893–94, private collection). Both paintings were included in the 1996 exhibition *Cézanne* at the Philadelphia Museum of Art (and other venues). For discussion, see the exhibition catalog, *Cézanne* (Philadelphia: Philadelphia Museum of Art, 1996), 288, and as to the watercolor, Lawrence Gowing, "Cézanne: The Logic of Organized Sensations," in *Conversations with Cézanne,* 180–212 (187–88).

13. M. Merleau-Ponty, "La Liberté," in *PhP*, 496–520.

14. See M. Merleau-Ponty, "Le roman et la métaphysique," in *Sens et non-sens* (Paris: Gallimard, 1996). English translation, "Metaphysics and the Novel," in *Sense and Non-Sense,* trans. Dreyfus and Dreyfus, 25, 34–52 (26–40). I give my own translations and cite the French pagination, followed by the English in parentheses. See Simone de Beauvoir, *L'invitée* (Paris: Gallimard, 1943). English translation (anonymous), *She Came to Stay* (New York: Norton, 1954).

15. M. Merleau-Ponty, "Un auteur scandaleux," in *SNS*, 53–60 (41–47).

16. *SNS*, 36 and following (28).

17. Ibid., 47 (36).

18. Ibid., 52 (40).

19. Ibid., 15 (10 and following).

20. Ibid.

21. Ibid., 15 (11).

22. Paul Valéry, *Introduction to the Method of Leonardo da Vinci*, trans. Thomas McGreevy (London: J. Rodker, 1929).

23. *SNS*, 28 (22).

24. Sigmund Freud, "Eine Kindheitserinnerung des Leonardo da Vinci," in *Gesammelte Werke* (London: Imago, 1940–95), 8:128–211. For discussion, see Paul Ricoeur, *Freud & Philosophy: An Essay on Interpretation*, trans. Dennis Savage (New Haven, Conn.: Yale University Press, 1970), especially 170–76.

25. Jean-Claude Frère, *Leonardo: Painter, Inventor, Visionary, Mathematician, Philosopher, Engineer* (Paris: Terrail, 1995), 35.

26. *SNS*, 23 (17).

27. Gowing, "Cézanne: The Logic of Organized Sensations," 198.

28. See *SNS*, 25 and 15 (19, 11).

29. Ibid., 27 (20).

30. Ibid., 33 (25).

31. Ibid., 26 (20).

32. "Eye and mind" (or "eye and brain") is a Cézannian phrase, which has become familiar as the title of Merleau-Ponty's last essay on painting. For Cézanne's use of it, see, for instance, the fifth of his "opinions," supposedly voiced in 1904 and reported by Bernard: "In the painter, there are two things: the eye and the brain; they must serve each other. The artist must work at developing them mutually: the eye for the vision of nature, and the brain for the logic of organized sensations, which provide the means of expression (*Conversations*, 38).

33. *SNS*, 18 (13).

34. Jack Flam, "Bathers but Not Beauties: Cézanne's Nude Figures in a Landscape Are Meant to Disturb Rather Than Delight Us," *Art News* (May 2012): 96–99 (96).

35. *SNS*, 19, 22 (14, 16).

36. See Joachim Gasquet, *Cézanne: A Memoir with Conversations;* and Lawrence Gowing, "Cézanne: The Logic of Organized Sensations," in *Conversations with Cézanne*, 198.

37. Gowing, "Cézanne: The Logic of Organized Sensations," 204.

38. Yve-Alain Bois, "L'écart: Théorie et pratique cézanniennes," in *Cézanne aujourd'hui*, eds. Françoise Cachin, Henri Loyrette, and Stéphane Guégan (Paris: Réunion des Musées Nationaux, 1997), 87–108 (01).

39. "Expressing what exists is an endless task," Merleau-Ponty writes at *SNS*, 21 (15).

40. Flam, "Bathers but Not Beauties," 99.

41. The quotation is from Merleau-Ponty's discussion of Schelling in the first nature course, *N*, 41.

42. *SNS*, 18 (13).

43. See Bernard, "Memories of Paul Cézanne," in *Conversations*, 72.

44. *SNS*, 16 (11 and following).

45. Ibid., 17 (12).

46. Bois, "L'écart," 94. Cézanne himself used the vulgarism "une couillarde"

("something ballsy") to characterize his early works, in particular the portrait of his uncle Dominique as a Dominican monk, which is in the Annenberg Collection at the Metropolitan Museum of Art. The characterization refers to facture, not subject matter.

47. Examples abound, but the 1998–99 exhibition *Impressionists in Winter* is particularly instructive in this regard. See the catalog, *Impressionists in Winter: Effects de Neige* (Washington: Phillips Gallery, 1998).

48. Bernard, "Memories of Paul Cézanne," 62.

49. Gowing, "Cézanne: The Logic of Organized Sensations," 181.

50. *SNS*, 17–20 (12–14).

51. Theodore Reff, "Cézanne et Chardin," Jean-François Allain, trans., in *Cézanne aujourd'hui*, 11–28 (22).

52. *SNS*, 19 and following (14).

53. *SNS*, 18, 20 (13f).

54. *SNS*, 20 and following (15).

55. *SNS*, 18 (14).

56. Bois, "L'écart," 88. The reference is to Cézanne to Bernard, April 15, 1904 (Letter 1), in *Conversations*, 29.

57. Bois, "L'écart," 88.

58. *SNS*, 22 (16).

59. His reference is to Rosalind Krauss, "The Motivation of the Sign," *Picasso and Braque: A Symposium*, ed. William Rubin and Lynn Zelevansky (New York: Museum of Modern Art, n.d.), 267–70.

60. Bois, "L'écart," 89.

61. It is interesting to compare the Giacometti sculptures with Auguste Rodin's *Walking Man* of 1907. For a discussion of the latter, see Galen A. Johnson, *The Retrieval of the Beautiful: Thinking Through Merleau-Ponty's Aesthetics* (Evanston, Ill.: Northwestern University Press, 2010), 75 and following.

62. Johnson, *The Retrieval of the Beautiful*, 75 and following.

63. Bois, "L'écart," 91.

64. Ibid.

65. See Cézanne to Bernard, October 23, 1905 (Letter 8), in *Conversations*, 48.

66. *SNS*, 21 (15). Merleau-Ponty emphasizes "existe."

67. Bois, "L'écart," 91.

68. See *SNS*, 32 (25).

69. Cézanne to Bernard, July 25, 1904 (Letter 5), in *Conversations*, 46.

Chapter 2

1. The essay was first published in *Les Temps Modernes* in 1952, then revised again for publication in *Signs* (1960). The fragment *The Prose of the World* was written in 1951 and edited posthumously by Claude Lefort as *La prose du monde* (Paris: Gallimard, 1969); English translation by John O'Neill, *The Prose of the World* (Evanston, Ill.: Northwestern University Press, 1973).

2. Galen A. Johnson, "Merleau-Ponty's Essays on Painting," in *The Merleau-Ponty Aesthetics Reader,* ed. Galen A. Johnson, trans. and ed. Michael B. Smith, 22.

3. This text was first published as "Un inédit de Merleau-Ponty," in *Revue de Métaphysique et de Morale* 4 (1962): 401–9. An English translation by Arleen Dallery appears in *PhP,* 3–11. For the citations, see *PhP,* 9 and 11.

4. André Malraux, *Psychologie de l'art* (Geneva, Switz.: Skira, 1947–50). This volume combines three separate volumes available to Merleau-Ponty (*Le musée imaginaire* [1947], *La création esthétique* [1948], and *La monnaie de l'absolu* [1949]). See also Malraux, *Les voix du silence* (Paris: Pleïade, 1951); English translation by Stuart Gilbert, *The Voices of Silence* (Princeton, N.J.: Princeton University Press, 1978); Jean-Paul Sartre, *Literature and Existentialism,* trans. Bernard Frechtman (Secaucus, N.J.: Citadel, 1980); and Michel Contat and Michel Rybalka, eds., *Selected Prose: The Writings of Jean-Paul Sartre,* trans. Richard McCleary (Evanston, Ill.: Northwestern University Press, 1974). See also J.-P. Sartre, "What Is Literature?" in *What Is Literature, and Other Essays* (Cambridge, Mass.: Harvard University Press, 1988), reprinted in R. Kearney and D. Rasmussen, eds., *Continental Aesthetics: Romanticism to Postmodernism* (Malden, Mass.: Blackwell, 2000), 276–87.

5. Merleau-Ponty criticizes Malraux for invoking a Reason unifying the history of (Western) painting; see "ILVS," 102. This text is cited by the pagination in *The Merleau-Ponty Aesthetics Reader,* and thus in the translation revised by Michael B. Smith.

6. "ILVS," 78.

7. Merleau-Ponty will make a similar claim, as to the immanence of the whole in the parts, in his discussion of embryological development in the second of his nature courses.

8. See "ILVS," 80–85.

9. Merleau-Ponty, *Le visible et l'invisible;* English translation by Alphonso Lingis, *The Visible and the Invisible.*

10. Merleau-Ponty, *L'œil et l'esprit;* "Eye and Mind," in *The Merleau-Ponty Aesthetics Reader,* 221–49. See chapter 4.

11. "ILVS," 86.

12. See M. Merleau-Ponty, "The Philosopher and His Shadow," trans. Richard McCleary, in *Signs* (Evanston, Ill.: Northwestern University Press, 1964), 159–81; and M. Merleau-Ponty, *Notes de cours sur l'origine de la géométrie de Husserl, suivi par recherches sur la phénoménologie de Merleau-Ponty* (Paris: Presses Universitaires de France, 1998). For a translation of the lecture course, see Leonard Lawlor and Bettina Bergo, eds., *Husserl at the Limits of Phenomenology* (Evanston, Ill.: Northwestern University Press, 2002).

13. "ILVS," 90.

14. Ibid., 92.

15. Ibid., 91–93.

16. Ibid., 93. The somewhat incongruous mention of odor interestingly recalls Merleau-Ponty's claim, in "Cézanne's Doubt," that a painting must convey even the odor of a landscape. See chapter 1 for discussion.

17. For an indication of the distinction between the material and primor-

dial elements, see my *Epochal Discordance: Hölderlin's Philosophy of Tragedy* (Albany: State University of New York Press, 2006), chapter 2. Edward S. Casey offers an inspired discussion of how abstract painting, earth works, and even conceptual art engage in a creative and transformative way with the elements (particularly the earth) in his *Earth-Mapping: Artists Reshaping Landscape* (Minneapolis: University of Minnesota Press, 2005). Michael Kimmelman, in *The Accidental Masterpiece: On the Art of Life and Vice Versa* (New York: Penguin, 2005), devotes a chapter ("The Art of Pilgrimage") to works that, for the most part, engage with the elements, such as Walter de Maria's *Lightning Field,* Robert Smithson's *Spiral Jetty* (also, and more extensively, discussed by Casey), Nancy Holt's *Sun Tunnels,* or the work of James Turrell and Michael Heizer.

18. "ILVS," 99 and following. The identity of museums has, of course, changed quite dramatically since Merleau-Ponty's writing, so that today these institutions face other challenges.

19. Ibid., 97.

20. Ibid., 104. It is interesting to compare here the discussion between the physicist Arthur Zajonc, the neuroscientist Bob Livingston, and His Holiness the Dalai Lama concerning the relativity of perception to the perceiver in Arthur Zajonc, ed., *The New Physics and Cosmology: Dialogues with the Dalai Lama* (Oxford: Oxford University Press, 2004), 141–45.

21. "ILVS," 106 and following.

22. Ibid., 106.

23. Ibid., 105.

24. See here the prolonged exchange between Thomas McEvilley, William Rubin, and Kirk Varnedoe concerning the exhibition *"Primitivism" in Twentieth Century Art: Affinity of the Tribal and the Modern,* held at the Museum of Modern Art in 1984, reprinted in Bill Beckley and David Shapiro, eds., *Uncontrollable Beauty* (New York: Allworth, 1998), 149–258.

25. "ILVS," 97.

26. "ILVS," 194.

27. See Charles Merewether, "From Inscription to Dissolution: An Essay on Expenditure in the Work of Ana Mendieta," in *Ana Mendieta,* ed. Gloria Moure (Barcelona, Sp.: Ediciones Polígrafa, 1996), 83–131. On Mendieta's *Silueta* series, see Mary Sabbatino, "Ana Mendieta: Identity and the *Silueta* Series," in the same volume, 135–65.

28. The latter concerns inform his work from the workshop Art and Environment, sponsored jointly by the Goethe Institute and by Silpakorn University in 1991, and in the art project Klima Global: Arte Amazones in Brasil of 1992, sponsored likewise by the Goethe Institute.

29. "ILVS," 101.

30. Ibid., 100.

31. Briony Fer, *On Abstract Art* (New Haven, Conn.: Yale University Press, 1997), 127.

32. This narrative is based on my memory of conversations with Karen Kosasa during my stay at the University of Hawaii at Manoa in 1987.

33. Compare "ILVS," 112.

34. Ibid., 107.

35. Ibid., 109.

36. Ibid., 110. The reference is to Hegel's *Principles of the Philosophy of Right*.

37. Lydia Goehr comments on this passage in her "Understanding the Engaged Philosopher: On Politics, Philosophy, and Art," in *The Cambridge Companion to Merleau-Ponty*, ed. Taylor Carman and Mark B. N. Hansen (Cambridge: Cambridge University Press, 2005), 318–51. Strangely, she situates Merleau-Ponty's essay (with triple repetition) "at the end of his life" (346 and following). She argues that the philosopher stands between painter and politician, and that Merleau-Ponty here "finally finds his connection between philosophical engagement and political commitment" through the techniques of indirection he gleans from the artist (348). Quite apart from questions of interpretation, the actual place of the text in the chronology of Merleau-Ponty's work calls her reading into question.

38. "ILVS," 110–13.

39. Ibid., 114 and following.

40. Ibid.

41. Ibid., 119 and following.

42. Ibid., 116.

43. Ibid., 117.

44. Holland Cotter, "Miró, Serial Murderer of Artistic Conventions," *New York Times*, October 3, 2008, C21 and C30. The exhibition being reviewed is *Joan Miró: Painting and Anti-Painting*, held at New York City's Museum of Modern Art.

45. For an insightful rethinking of the relationship of Merleau-Ponty's thought to the Chinese tradition of painting, see Jacques Taminiaux, "On the Fundamentals of Painting: Chinese Counterpoint," in *Merleau-Ponty and the Possibilities of Philosophy*, ed. B. Flynn, W. J. Froman, and R. Vallier (Albany: State University of New York Press, 2009), 221–35.

46. "ILVS," 117.

47. Ibid.

48. Ibid., 119.

49. Claude Lefort, "Préface" to M. Merleau-Ponty, *L'institution dans l'histoire personnelle et publique: Le problème de la passivité, le sommeil, l'inconscient, la mémoire (Notes de cours au Collège de France, 1954–1955)*, eds. D. Darmaillacq, C. Lefort, and S. Ménasé (Paris: Editions Belin, 2003). This volume will be referred to as *IP*.

50. Working note of July 1959, titled "Dualism—Philosophy," *VI*, 253, 200.

51. Renaud Barbaras, "Le tournant de l'expérience: Merleau-Ponty et Bergson," in *Le tournant de l'expérience: Recherches sur la philosophie de Merleau-Ponty* (Paris: Vrin, 2004), 44. My translation.

52. Claude Lefort, "Préface," *IP*, 13.

53. *IP*, 35.

54. Ibid., 37; on time, see ibid., 38 and following.

55. See ibid., 82–84.

56. Ibid., 78.

57. Claude Lefort, "Préface," *IP*, 16.

58. Ibid., 23 and following.

59. *IP,* 38.

60. *N,* 227.

61. *IP,* 38.

62. Ibid., 76. On Merleau-Ponty and Proust, see Leonard Lawlor's fine study, "Benign Sexual Variation: An Essay on the Late Thought of Merleau-Ponty," *Chiasmi International* 10 (2008): 47–57.

63. *IP,* 77.

64. Ibid., 41.

65. Ibid.

66. Ibid., 43. In this lack of a name in the philosophical tradition, Merleau-Ponty's "institution" is analogous to his "flesh."

67. See ibid., 104, for the schema of the three aspects of personal/intersubjective history and the fourth moment of history as such.

68. See Ibid., 47.

69. Ibid., 70; see also 72 and 74.

70. Ibid., 78.

71. Ibid., 90.

72. Ibid., 103.

73. Ibid., 104.

74. Erwin Panofsky, *La perspective comme forme symbolique,* trans. G. Ballengé (Paris: Editions de Minuit, 1981). See *IP,* 79–86.

75. Liliane Guerry, *Cézanne et l'expression de l'espace* (Paris: Flammarion, 1950). See *IP,* 86–88.

76. Guerry, *Cézanne et l'expression de l'espace,* as quoted by the editors of *IP,* 142.

77. Merleau-Ponty, "Cézanne's Doubt," 62.

Chapter 3

1. The text was first published as an essay in the inaugural volume of *Art de France,* in 1961, then brought out as a short monograph by Gallimard in 1964.

2. See Galen A. Johnson's discussion of the "Text and Context" of "Eye and Mind" in *The Merleau-Ponty Aesthetics Reader,* 36–39, as well as his detailed discussion of the genesis and importance of the essay in *The Retrieval of the Beautiful,* 15.

3. Martin Heidegger, "Die Frage nach der Technik," in *Vorträge und Aufsätze,* I, 3rd ed. (Pfullingen, Ger.: Neske, 1967), 5–36 (27). This essay will be referred to as "FT." Translations from the German are my own.

4. *OE,* 9; "EM," 121.

5. On the latter topic, see Descartes's 1643 correspondence with Princess Elizabeth of Bohemia. Two key letters of his can be found, in Anthony Kenny's translation, in *The Philosophical Writings of Descartes,* vol. 3, trans. and ed. John Cottingham, Robert Stoothoff, and Dugald Murdoch (Cambridge: Cambridge University Press, 1991), 217–20, and 226–29. This work will be abbreviated as *PWD.*

6. *OE*, 11; "EM," 122.

7. "FT," 17.

8. *OE*, 12; "EM," 122.

9. "FT," 32.

10. Ibid., 34.

11. Ibid., 35.

12. *OE*, 13; "EM," 123.

13. Ibid.

14. See Galen A. Johnson's thoughtful reflection on Merleau-Ponty's relation to music in *Retrieving Beauty*, 114–16, and 123 and following. Johnson interprets Merleau-Ponty's characterization of music in part 1 of "Eye and Mind" (as being *trop en deça du monde*) to place it on the side of subjectivity, which is where Malraux places abstract painting.

15. Edouard Pontremoli, "Description fragmentaire d'un désastre: Sur Merleau-Ponty et Claude Simon," in *Merleau-Ponty: Phénoménologie et expériences*, eds. Richir and Tassin, 139–59 (140). For M Merleau-Ponty, "Five Notes on Claude Simon," trans. Hugh J. Silverman, see H. J. Silverman and J. Barry, eds., *Merleau-Ponty: Texts and Dialogues* (Atlantic Highlands, N.J.: Humanities Press, 1992), 140–43. The "Notes" date from 1960; the translator details their original French publication.

16. "Five Notes," 140–43.

17. "Five Notes," 141.

18. Pontremoli, "Description fragmentaire," 142 and following; "Five Notes," 142.

19. *OE*, 13; "EM," 122.

20. *OE*, 13; "EM," 123.

21. *OE*, 21; "EM," 125.

22. See *OE*, 17; "EM," 124.

23. For discussion, see Christia Mercer and R. C. Sleigh, Jr., "The Early Period to the *Discourse on Metaphysics*," and Donald Rutherford, "Metaphysics: The Late Period," in *The Cambridge Companion to Leibniz*, ed. Nicholas Jolley (Cambridge: Cambridge University Press, 67–123, and 124–75.

24. *OE*, 21; "EM," 125.

25. *OE*, 22; "EM," 126. The "carnal essences" are discussed more extensively in *VI*, chapter 4.

26. *OE*, 24; "EM," 126.

27. *OE*, 28; "EM," 128.

28. *OE*, 33; "EM," 129. The theme of the mirror is also repeatedly taken up in the lecture courses on nature, particularly in the third course.

29. *OE*, 34; "EM," 130.

30. *SNS*, 18.

31. *OE*, 35; "EM," 130.

32. *OE*, 29; "EM," 127.

33. *OE*, 29; "EM," 128.

34. *OE*, 32; "EM," 129. Kwok-Ying Lau, in his detailed study "La folie de la vision: Le peintre comme phénoménologue chez Merleau-Ponty," *Chiasmi Inter-*

national 10 (2008): 163–80, similarly notes that Merleau-Ponty's late analysis of pictorial vision endeavors "to see the invisible across the visible" (173); but limits the sense of the invisible to what one might call the preconditions of the auto-constitution of visuality, such as space, light, or line.

35. *OE,* 32; "EM," 129.

36. The complete text of René Descartes, "La dioptrique," first published in 1637 as one of the three scientific treatises appended to the *Discours de la méthode,* can be found in Ferdinand Alquié, ed., *Œuvres de Descartes* (Paris: Galli-mard, 1970), 180–229. The English translation in *PWD,* vol. 1, 152–75, is partial but includes the discourses on vision. Merleau-Ponty divorces the discussion of vision from its Cartesian context, which includes the physics of light, mechanis-tic physiology, and the manufacture of optical instruments intended to "perfect vision." I have analyzed Descartes's constructivist account of vision in "Mecha-nism, Reasoning, and the Institution of Nature," which forms chapter 3 of my *Vision's Invisibles: Philosophical Explorations* (Albany: State University of New York Press, 2003).

37. Thus, in the First Discourse of the *Optics,* he states that there is no need for him to explain the true nature of light, but that it will be sufficient to offer "two or three comparisons [*comparaisons*]" that constitute a suitable model, ca-pable of explaining light's known properties and allowing for the deduction of others "not as easily noticed" (*Œuvres,* 181). See also *PWD,* vol. 1, 152.

38. *OE,* 41; "EM," 132.

39. *OE,* 38 and following; "EM," 131 and following.

40. *OE,* 43; "EM," 133. On color in the *Optics,* see *Œuvres,* 219, 228; *PWD,* vol. 1, 168, 174.

41. *OE,* 47; "EM," 134.

42. *OE,* 53; "EM," 136.

43. *OE,* 56; "EM," 137.

44. *OE,* 58; "EM," 138.

45. Jacques Garelli, "Voir ceci et voir selon," in *Phénoménologie et expériences,* 79–100 (87).

46. *VI,* 27; 218.

47. Garelli, "Voir ceci et voir selon," 97.

48. Haar, "Peinture, perception, affectivité," in *Phénoménologie et expériences,* 103–22 (105).

49. Haar, "Peinture, perception, affectivité," 118. Haar is referring to "In-direct Language and the Voices of Silence."

50. Martin Heidegger, "Der Ursprung des Kunstwerkes," in *Holzwege,* 4th ed. (Frankfurt, Ger.: Klostermann, 1963), 7–68 (29 and following).

51. *OE,* 62 and following; "EM," 139.

52. See the discussion in chapter 2. Michel Haar, "Peinture, perception, affectivité," 107, observes trenchantly that artists have never seconded the con-demnation of the museum on the part of certain intellectuals. To the painter, the museum is a place of revelation and reflection, and a resource for learning and inspiration.

53. OE, 64 and following; "EM," 140. An interesting comparison can be

made between Merleau-Ponty's discussion of depth and Heidegger's late essay or small monograph, *Die Kunst und der Raum / L'art et l'espace,* dedicated to the sculptor Eduardo Chillida (St. Gallen, Switz.: Erker Verlag, 1983). The essay dates from 1969 and is thus posterior to Merleau-Ponty's writing.

54. *OE,* 69; "EM," 141. Merleau-Ponty puts the expressions "autofigurative," and "spectacle of nothing" into quotation marks since he refers them to Ch. P. Bru, *Esthétique de l'abstraction* (Paris, 1959).

55. *OE,* 73; "EM," 142.

56. *OE,* 70 and following; "EM," 142.

57. *OE,* 70 and following; "EM," 142.

58. *OE,* 71; "EM," 142.

59. *OE,* 68; "EM," 141.

60. See Françoise Cachin's discussion "Portraits of Vallier," in the Philadelphia Museum of Art's exhibition catalog *Cézanne,* 512–15.

61. Haar, "Peinture, perception, affectivité," 118.

62. Ibid.

63. *OE,* 72–74; "EM," 142–44.

64. *OE,* 74; "EM," 143.

65. See Wen C. Fong, "Chinese Calligraphy as Presenting the Self," in *Chinese Calligraphy,* ed. Wang Youfen, (New Haven, Conn.: Yale University Press, 2008), 1–31.

66. See Wen C. Fong's discussion in "Wang Hui and Repossessing the Past," in *Landscapes Clear and Radiant: The Art of Wang Hui (1632–1717),* ed. Maxwell Hearn (New York: Metropolitan Museum of Art, 2008), 3–47 (see particularly 36–40).

67. Reproductions can be seen in C. H. Picón et al., *Art of the Classical World in the Metropolitan Museum of Art* (New Haven, Conn.: Yale University Press, 2007), 122.

68. *OE,* 76 and following; "EM," 144.

69. *OE,* 78; "EM," 144. Merleau-Ponty refers to Duchamp's work only as "The Bride"; possibly Duchamp's *Nude Descending a Staircase* would have served his point better.

70. *OE,* 79; "EM," 145.

71. *OE,* 81; "EM," 145.

72. A reproduction appears in *Chinese Calligraphy,* 12.

73. Compare Wolfgang Kersten, ed., *Paul Klee, Tagebücher, 1898–1918* (Bern, Switz.: Paul Klee Stiftung, 1988), and Galen A. Johnson's discussion *The Retrieval of the Beautiful,* 129–32.

74. Johnson, *The Retrieval of the Beautiful,* 130. See Paul Klee, *Journal,* trans. Pierre Klossowski (Paris: Bernard Grasset, 1959), 354.

75. Johnson, *The Retrieval,* 131.

76. *OE,* 83, 85; "EM," 146 and following.

77. In a working note of January 1960, Merleau-Ponty speaks of the invisible as "being there, without being object," and as "pure transcendence without an ontic mask." See *VI,* 282 and following; 229. "Transcendence" does not, of

course, carry here the metaphysical meaning that, as noted, Merleau-Ponty repudiates. Jacques Derrida quotes this passage and comments on it in his *Memoirs of the Blind: The Self-Portrait and Other Ruins*, trans. Pascale-Anne Brault and Michael Naas (Chicago: University of Chicago Press, 1990), 52.

78. *OE*, 94; "EM," 149.

79. *OE*, 89; "EM," 148.

80. *OE*, 88; "EM," 148.

81. *OE*, 91; "EM," 148.

82. *OE*, 88, 90; "EM," 148 and following.

83. See *N*. The three courses on nature date from 1956 to 1960.

84. *OE*, 90; "EM," 148 and following.

85. *OE*, 92; "EM," 149. On the important notion of lack, see Leonard Lawlor, "Foreword; *Verflechtung:* The Triple Significance of Merleau-Ponty's Course Notes on Husserl's 'The Origin of Geometry,' " in *Husserl at the Limits of Phenomenology*, ed. Lawlor and Bergo, ix–xxxvi. These course notes date from 1959 to 1960.

Chapter 4

1. M. Merleau-Ponty, *La nature: Notes, cours du Collège de France: Suivi de résumés de cours correspondants de Merleau-Ponty*, ed. and anno. Dominique Séglard (Paris: Éditions du Seuil, 1995). English translation by Robert Vallier, *Nature: Course Notes from the Collège de France* (Evanston, Ill.: Northwestern University Press, 2003). Hereafter referred to as *N*.

2. The second course, "The Concept of Nature: Animality, the Human Body, and the Passage to Culture," was offered in 1957–58. There was a year's gap between the second and the third course, given in 1959–60, since Merleau-Ponty was granted a reduction of his teaching responsibilities to pursue his research. See also M. Merleau-Ponty, *The Structure of Behavior*, trans. Alden L. Fisher, 9th ed. (Pittsburgh: Duquesne University Press, 2008). A look at the bibliography of this first major work shows, interestingly, that Merleau-Ponty had already read extensively in the biological sciences, particularly zoology. An engagement with these sciences thus shows itself to be a constant in his work.

3. The question of the interpretation of evolutionary theory runs throughout Merleau-Ponty's reflections on animality and on the human body in the nature lectures, as well as throughout much of the thought of the biologists he engages with. However, he actually addresses the question only in the form of "Sketches" in the third course, and of equally sketchy scattered comments. The question is both too complex and too specialized to be treated here; but it will at least be commented on in "A Note on Evolutionary Theory" in chapter 5.

4. *N*, 9–20. The quotation is from page 10. Compare Descartes's correspondence with Princess Elizabeth of Bohemia of 1643 concerning the union of body and soul in *The Philosophical Writings of Descartes*, vol. 3, 217 and 226. As to the auto-functioning of laws, the reference is presumably to Descartes's *The*

World (*Le monde, ou Traité de la lumière*), which Descartes decided to leave unpublished in 1634, after hearing of Galileo's condemnation.

5. Robert Vallier, "Translator's Introduction," *N*, xiv. I will at times refer the assertions or questionings in the first two courses to Merleau-Ponty, so as to avoid the extensive use of cumbersome locutions such as "as stated in the lecture notes;" but the reader should remain mindful of the status of the texts.

6. *N*, 204. These words from the third course are Merleau-Ponty's own.

7. G. E. Coghill, *Anatomy and the Problem of Behavior* (Cambridge: Cambridge University Press, 1929).

8. See Coghill, *Anatomy*, 2 and 17.

9. *N*, 140.

10. Coghill, *Anatomy*, 87.

11. *N*, 144.

12. Coghill, *Anatomy*, 88.

13. Coghill, *Anatomy*, 22, and *N*, 142. The auditor gives no evidence of firsthand familiarity with the texts that Merleau-Ponty comments on; thus, for instance, he or she misspells the name of the psychologist Pierre Janet (already extensively referenced in *Phenomenology of Perception*) as "Janey." The echo of the simile thus seems to attest to the auditor's close attention to Merleau-Ponty, who probably quoted from memory.

14. Coghill, *Anatomy*, 91.

15. Ibid., 84.

16. *N*, 143.

17. Coghill, *Anatomy*, 80 and 85 and following.

18. *N*, 143.

19. Ibid., 145. Merleau-Ponty already took up this question in "ILVS."

20. Arnold Gesell and Catherine S. Amatruda, *The Embryology of Behavior: The Beginnings of the Human Mind*, 9th ed. (Westport, Conn.: Greenwood, 1971).

21. See Coghill, *Anatomy*, 94 and 110.

22. Gesell and Amatruda, *The Embryology*, 162–65; *N*, 148 and following.

23. See, for instance, *VI*, 200; 153.

24. The weaving technique that would best illustrate Merleau-Ponty's comparison is that of *ikat*, in which the warp or weft threads, or both, are intricately resist-dyed prior to weaving, allowing complex designs to emerge in the weaving process.

25. Gesell and Amatruda, *The Embryology*, 188 and following.

26. *N*, 146.

27. Ibid.

28. See Gesell and Amatruda, *The Embryology*, chapter 12.

29. *N*, 147–49.

30. The notion of a field already makes its appearance in Coghill who writes that "the apparently particular elements in consciousness emerge from a general field and exist only in relation to that field" (*Anatomy*, 87). It is not known when Merleau-Ponty first read Coghill and Gesell and Amatruda.

31. *N*, 150. The notion of the "electrical field" probably refers to Gesell

and Amatruda's discussion of the zygote which, though only "a minute globule of protoplasm," contains a nucleus and genes within chromosomes, the simplest of genes being probably single protein molecules whose atoms are each "a system of positive and negative units of electricity" (Gesell and Amatruda, *The Embryology*, 19).

32. Zajonc, ed., *The New Physics*, 66–69. The comparison to "state logic" is made by Alan Wallace, another contributor to the symposium.

33. *N*, 150, 155.

34. Ibid., 153.

35. Ibid., 154.

36. Ibid., 156. Earlier (151) Merleau-Ponty had noted that the organism sketches out its milieu or *Umwelt*, using the term for environing world (derived from Jakob von Uexküll) that will soon come into focus.

37. *N*, 157.

38. For a well-researched and comprehensive study of Uexküll and his influences on philosophy (with a particular orientation toward Deleuze), see Brett Buchanan, *Onto-Ethologies: The Animal Environments of Uexküll, Heidegger, Merleau-Ponty, and Deleuze* (Albany: State University of New York Press, 2008). See 191, n.1 for an enumeration of philosophers influenced by Uexküll.

39. Giorgio Agamben, *The Open: Man and Animal*, trans. Kevin Attell (Stanford, Calif.: Stanford University Press, 2004), 39 and following.

40. Jakob von Uexküll, *Umwelt und Innenwelt der Tiere* (Berlin: Julius Springer Verlag, 1909); and Jakob von Uexküll with G. Kriszat, *Streifzüge durch die Umwelten von Tieren und Menschen: Ein Bilderbuch unsichtbarer Welten* (Berlin: Julius Springer Verlag, 1934). Kriszat provides the numerous illustrations of this *Bilderbuch* (picture book). For available English translations, see the bibliography. All translations of Uexküll given here are my own.

41. Uexküll, *Umwelt*, 7.

42. Ibid., 248.

43. Ibid., 249 and following.

44. Ibid., 248.

45. Ibid., 7.

46. Ibid., 6.

47. *Umwelt*, 39.

48. Ibid., 197. The question whether the earthworm may possess the remarkable ability to distinguish leaves by shape, which is brought up at *Umwelt*, 162 and following, is answered in the negative in *Streifzüge* on the basis of further research. See Uexküll and Kriszat, *Streifzüge*, 45.

49. Uexküll, *Umwelt*, 195.

50. Ibid., 197–99.

51. Ibid., 200 and following.

52. Ibid., 252.

53. Uexküll and Kriszat, *Streifzüge*, 11.

54. Ibid., 99–102.

55. Ibid., 91–99.

56. Rudolf Langthaler, *Organismus und Umwelt: Die biologische Umweltslehre im Spiegel traditioneller Naturphilosophie* (Hildesheim, Ger.: Georg Olms Verlag, 1992), 117.

57. Uexküll and Kriszat, *Streifzüge,* 5 and following.

58. Ibid., 51.

59. Ibid., 36.

60. Ibid., 91.

61. *N,* 174. Agamben, *The Open,* devotes a chapter to "Tick."

62. Uexküll and Kriszat, *Streifzüge,* 8.

63. Ibid., 38.

64. Ibid., 55.

65. Martin Heidegger, *Die Grundbegriffe der Metaphysik: Welt—Endlichkeit—Einsamkeit,* in *Gesamtausgabe* 29–30 (Frankfurt, Ger.: Klostermann, 1983). English translation by W. McNeill and N. Walker, *The Fundamental Concepts of Metaphysics: World, Finitude, Solitude* (Bloomington: Indiana University Press, 1995). My references are to the German text; and translations are my own.

66. For a fuller discussion of Heidegger than can be given here, see Buchanan, *Onto-Ethologies,* chapters 3 and 4.

67. Heidegger, *Grundbegriffe,* 380–82.

68. Ibid., 315, 383.

69. Ibid., 382.

70. Ibid., 383.

71. M. Heidegger, *Sein und Zeit* (1927), *GA* 2, sections 14–24.

72. Theodore Kisiel, *The Genesis of Being and Time* (Berkeley: University of California Press, 1993), 506. See also the discussion under n.49, 524 and following.

73. Heidegger, *Grundbegriffe,* 293.

74. Ibid., 287.

75. Jacques Derrida, *De l'esprit: Heidegger et la question* (Paris: Galilée, 1987), 87–90. My translation.

76. Heidegger, *Grundbegriffe,* 327, 329.

77. Ibid., 342.

78. See ibid., 347. Heidegger here draws on the senses and verbal derivatives of *treiben* (to drive) and *der Treib* (the drive).

79. Heidegger, *Grundbegriffe,* 350–58.

80. Ibid., 360. See the discussion of the "as-structure" (*als-Struktur*) of understanding in *Being and Time,* sections 31 through 34.

81. Heidegger, *Grundbegriffe,* 360.

82. Ibid., 361, 371.

83. Ibid., 372.

84. Ibid., 375.

85. Derrida, *De l'esprit,* 89 and following.

86. Heidegger, *Grundbegriffe,* 292.

87. *N,* 171.

88. Ibid., 167.

89. "La vision du peintre est une naissance continuée," OE, 31; "EM," 129.

90. Heidegger, 387 and following.

91. *N*, 170.

92. Ibid., 171.

93. Ibid., 171 and following.

94. Ibid., 173.

95. For a detailed discussion of Uexküll's idea of the music of life, see Buchanan, *Onto-Ethologies*, 26 and following.

96. Compare here Merleau-Ponty's discussion of the violinist and the sonata in *VI*, x; 151. See also Elizabeth A. Behnke, "At the Service of the Sonata: Music Lessons with Merleau-Ponty," in *Merleau-Ponty: Critical Essays*, ed. Henry Pietersma (Washington: University Press of America, 1990), 23–29.

97. *N*, 174.

98. See ibid., 178.

99. Ibid., 175.

100. Ibid., 176.

101. Ibid., 177.

102. Ibid., 176.

103. Ibid., 178.

104. Ibid., 154.

Chapter 5

1. Russell, *The Directiveness of Organic Activities*.

2. Ibid., 7.

3. I quote Edwin Curley's translation in *Benedict de Spinoza: The Ethics and Other Works* (Princeton, N.J.: Princeton University Press, 1994). For Russell's quotation (in Latin and English), see 191 of the cited work.

4. Russell, *Directiveness*, 178.

5. The transcriber of the lecture course refers to it as a worm, but the predatory behavior described is not characteristic of worms. Russell does not give the full scientific name of the organism; but he calls it a "worm" only once in quotation marks. *Microstoma* is a genus of fishes. My conjecture is that Russell is speaking of *Microstoma microstoma* which, due to its very slender body shape, has indeed a wormlike appearance.

6. *N*, 234/179.

7. Ibid., 238/182.

8. Ibid.

9. Ibid., 233/178.

10. Ibid., 240/183.

11. Ibid., 241/184.

12. Pierre Hardouin, *Le mimétisme animal* (Paris: Presses Universitaires de France, 1946).

13. Adolf Portmann, *Die Tiergestalt: Studien über die Bedeutung der tierischen*

Erscheinung, 2nd rev. ed. (Basel, Switz.: Verlag Friedrich Reinhardt, 1960), 141. Italics added.

14. Harry W. Greene, *Snakes: The Appearance of Mystery in Nature,* with photographs by Michael Fogden and Patricia Fogden (Berkeley: University of California Press, 1997), 226–29.

15. See Katharina Schmidt-Loske, ed., *Maria Sibylla Merian, Insects of Surinam* (Cologne, Ger.: Taschen, n.d.), plates 34, 39, 47, and accompanying (trilingual) text. This book is based on Merian's *Metamorphosis Insectorum Surinamensium* of 1705.

16. *N,* 243/185.

17. Portmann, *Tiergestalt,* 135, 137; *N,* 242/184.

18. Portmann, *Tiergestalt,* 124.

19. *N,* 243/186.

20. Ibid.

21. Jacques de Witte, "L'interanimalité comme intercorporéité et intervisibilité: Merleau-Ponty lecteur de Portmann," in *Colloque sous la direction de Jean Gayon et P.-F.Moreau* (Dijon, Fr.: Université de Dijon, 1998), 89–119.

22. *N,* 188, 190.

23. As de Witte points out, Merleau-Ponty was familiar only with the 1948 first edition of *Die Tiergestalt;* but the second revised and expanded edition of 1960 (commented on here) radicalizes Portmann's thought of the primacy of visual appearance in animal life by introducing "unaddressed appearances" (see, for example, 233) that do not function in a context of reciprocal visibility. De Witte notes that, just as Merleau-Ponty did not know this radicalization of Portmann's thought, neither did Portmann, who was familiar with *The Structure of Behavior* and *Phenomenology of Perception,* have access to Merleau-Ponty's late writings. See de Witte, "L'interanimalité," 106–10.

24. Portmann, *Tiergestalt,* 18.

25. Ibid., 19–33.

26. Ibid., 37.

27. *N,* 245/187.

28. Portmann, *Tiergestalt,* 77.

29. Ibid., 99.

30. *N,* 244/187.

31. Spinoza, *Ethics,* part 2, proposition 13, Scholium.

32. See Hans Jonas, "Spinoza and the Theory of Organism," in *Spinoza: A Collection of Critical Essays,* ed. Marjorie Grene (Garden City: Doubleday/Anchor, 1973), 259–78.

33. *N,* 245/187.

34. Portmann, *Tiergestalt,* 113.

35. Ibid., 115 and following. On mollusks and their shells, see also M.-G. Harasewych and Fabio Moretzsohn, *The Book of Shells* (Chicago: University of Chicago Press, 2010).

36. Portmann, *Tiergestalt,* 123.

37. *N,* 245/188.

38. See Claire Nouvian, ed., *The Deep: The Extraordinary Creatures of the Abyss* (Chicago: University of Chicago Press, 2007).

39. *N*, 187.

40. Portmann, *Tiergestalt*, 162.

41. *N*, 246/188.

42. See here Peter Goodfellow, *Avian Architecture: How Birds Design, Engineer, and Build*, ed. Mike Haskell (Princeton, N.J.: Princeton University Press, 2011), chapter 11.

43. Heidegger, *Grundbegriffe*, 363 and following.

44. *N*, 247/189.

45. Portmann, *Tiergestalt*, 253. See note 23.

46. *N*, 248/190.

47. De Witte, "L'interanimalité," 107.

48. See note 23.

49. Portmann, *Tiergestalt*, 247–53.

50. De Witte, "L'interanimalité," 198.

51. Ted Toadvine, *Merleau-Ponty's Philosophy of Nature* (Evanston, Ill.: Northwestern University Press, 2009), 78.

52. *VI*, 282 and following /229. Jacques Derrida, in *Memoirs of the Blind: The Self-Portrait and Other Ruins*, trans. Pascale-Anne Brault and Michael Naas (Chicago: University of Chicago Press, 1993), stresses the importance of this "*absolute invisibility.*" See 52.

53. De Witte, "L'interanimalité," especially 99.

54. Konrad Lorenz, *Les animaux, les inconnus* (Paris: Editions de Minuit, 1953); and Konrad Lorenz, *Studies on Animal and Human Behavior*, trans. R. Martin, 2 vols. (London: Methuen, 1970–71).

55. Konrad Lorenz, "Vergleichende Verhaltungsforschung," in *Antriebe menschlichen und tierischen Verhaltens*, by Konrad Lorenz and Paul Leyhausen (Munich: R. Piper, 1968), 15–47. English translation by B. A. Tonkin, *Motivation of Human and Animal Behavior: An Ethological View* (London: Methuen, 1973). I cite the German, referenced as "VV," in my own translation.

56. "VV," 26; *N*, 251/192.

57. Ibid., 42.

58. Ibid., 32 and following.

59. *N*, 251/192.

60. Ibid., 250 and following /191 and following.

61. Ibid., 252/193.

62. Ibid., 255/195.

63. Ibid., 256/196.

64. Ibid., 257/197.

65. Ibid., 258 and following /198 and following.

66. See here Buchanan's discussion, *Onto-Ethologies*, 9–21.

67. *N*, 251/193.

68. G. G. Simpson, *Tempo and Mode in Evolution* (New York: Columbia University Press, 1944).

69. *N*, 258.

70. Ibid., 273.

71. It is interesting that these depth strata or marginal areas of consciousness are the ones that rationalism, with which Merleau-Ponty carries on a sustained dialogue (see chapter 6) strenuously marginalizes or denies any reality to. See, for instance, Spinoza's correspondence with Pieter Balling in Letter 17, and with Hugo Boxel (who pressed him concerning the reality of ghosts) in Letters 52, 54, and 56. These can be found in Michael L. Morgan, ed., *Spinoza: Complete Works*, with translations by Samuel Shirley (Indianapolis: Hackett, 2002).

72. De Witte criticizes Merleau-Ponty for assimilating teleology to utility and points to the need for rethinking teleology ("L'interanimalité," 101).

73. See here de Witte's discussion, "L'interanimalité," 102–7.

74. Working note on "Philosophy and Literature" (undated, probably June 1959), *VI*, 251/197.

75. De Witte illuminatingly stresses the importance of Husserl as "an intermediary link" (particularly with respect to "the *Beilage* XXIII on the biology of the *Crisis*") for the development of Merleau-Ponty's own biological thought ("L'interanimalité," 92). See here *Husserl at the Limits of Phenomenology*, ed. Lawlor and Bergo.

Chapter 6

1. Lawrence Hass, in *Merleau-Ponty's Philosophy*, offers a "Prelude to the Cartesian Theater."

2. The documentation of this course consists of eight pages of notes by A. Métraux, published in German in *M. Merleau-Ponty, Vorlesungen*, ed. A. Métraux (Berlin: de Gruyter, 1973), 229–36.

3. *N*, xvi.

4. See *N*, 11, 40 and following, 43, and in particular the working note to *VI* of December 1959, titled "Leibniz;" *VI*, 276/22 and following.

5. *N*, 37 and following.

6. *N*, 13, 16.

7. Robert Vallier, "The Elemental Flesh: Nature, Life, and Difference in Merleau-Ponty and Plato's *Timaeus*," in *Merleau-Ponty and the Possibilities of Philosophy*, ed. Flynn et al., 129–53 (132).

8. B. Spinoza, *Ethics*, part 3, propositions 4 through 7. References will be given in standard abbreviated form and are based on Michael J. Morgan, ed., *Spinoza: Complete Works*, with the translations of Samuel Shirley (Indianapolis: Hackett, 2002), to be referred to as *CW*. The transcript of Merleau-Ponty's course cites only E3P4; and Vallier indicates that Merleau-Ponty seems to have used his own translations, which are what he translates in turn. See Vallier's notes 14 and 17 on page 287 of *N*. It seems, in fact, that Merleau-Ponty may sometimes have cited Spinoza from memory.

9. Essence is also, for Spinoza, by E1P34, "God's power by which he and all things are and act."

10. *N,* 14.

11. Spinoza, Letter 12, *CW,* 797–81.

12. Compare EIVDef8, where Spinoza equates virtue with power and both of these, as related to man, to man's very essence, insofar as he is able to bring about what follows solely from the laws of his own nature. Spinoza inserts a reference to EIIIP7, which characterizes *conatus* as a thing's actual essence; but since *conatus* characterizes finite modes rather than substance, Merleau-Ponty's reference to Letter XII does not seem to be connected with his animadversions to *conatus.*

13. *N,* 15.

14. Letter XII, *CW,* 789.

15. *VI,* 133/98.

16. *VI,* 223/169.

17. Ibid. The text reads: "La profondeur de l'être . . . l'ont-ils vraiment vue? Leur notion de l'infini est positive . . . (The depth of being . . . have they really seen it? Their notion of infinity is positive).

18. Spinoza was, in fact, after the publication of the *Theologico-Political Treatise,* maligned by the Cartesians who sought to dissociate themselves from the author of this supposedly "impious" and "most pestilential" work.

19. *VI,* 223/169. I have somewhat modified Lingis's translation.

20. Ibid. Spinoza, of course, denies the reality of contingency.

21. Alan Donagan, "Spinoza's Theology," in *The Cambridge Companion to Spinoza,* ed. Don Garrett (Cambridge: Cambridge University Press, 1996), 343–82 (351 and following).

22. Ibid. E2P7 claims that "the order and connection of ideas is the same as the order and connection of things." This proposition is crucial to Spinoza's articulation of his metaphysical system.

23. See Letter 63, from Schuller to Spinoza on behalf of Tschirnhaus, July 25, 1675, and Letter 65, Tschirnhaus to Spinoza, August 12, 1675, *CW,* 916 and following, 920. These letters are also translated, in part, by Edwin Curley and included in E. Curley, ed., *A Spinoza Reader* (Princeton, N.J.: Princeton University Press, 1994), 269 and following, 272.

24. See Letter 64, from Spinoza to Schuller for him and Tschirnhaus, July 29, 1675, and Letter 66, from Spinoza to Tschirnhaus, August 18, 1675, *CW,* 918 and following, 921; Curley, *Spinoza Reader,* 270–73. On the mind as the idea of the actually existing body, see E2P11–13.

25. Letter 65, *CW,* 920; *Spinoza Reader,* 270.

26. See E5P29. It is interesting to consider, in this connection, that Spinoza's personal library, inventoried after his death, contained the works of Aristotle in Latin translation, but not those of Plato (who, as is well known, likened *soma* to *sema,* or body to tomb). See here W. N. A. Klever, "Spinoza's Life and Works," in *The Cambridge Companion to Spinoza,* 13–60 (51).

27. Martin Heidegger, "Die onto-theo-logische Verfassung der Metaphysik," in M. Heidegger, *Identity and Difference* (Chicago: University of Chicago Press, 1999), 107–146 (117). The volume includes an English translation by Joan Stambaugh, "The Onto-Theo-Logical Constitution of Metaphysics," 42–76 (51). It is interest-

ing that Heidegger, who generally neglects Spinoza, does discuss him here, in relation to Hegel (see 113–14; 47–48).

28. See Letters 45 and 46, *CW,* 45 and following.

29. *VI,* 230–32/176 and following.

30. Ibid., 189/144.

31. M. Merleau-Ponty, "Everywhere and Nowhere," in *Signs,* 149.

32. Ibid. The reference is to the a posteriori theistic argument of the Third Meditation.

33. See *PWD,* vol. 2, 18, 24 and following. Vol. 3, devoted to Descartes's correspondence, includes translations by Anthony Kenny and will hence be referred to as *PWD3.*

34. *OE,* 48, "EM," 364.

35. *OE,* 47, "EM," 364.

36. *OE,* 48, "EM," 364.

37. *OE,* 51 and following, "EM," 365.

38. *PWD,* vol. 2, 266, 275.

39. Descartes to Elizabeth, June 28, 1643, *PWD,* vol. 3, 226–29. For the French text, see André Bridoux, ed., *Descartes: Œuvres et lettres* (Paris: Gallimard, 1973), 1157–61. This text also contains La dioptrique in its entirety.

40. Descartes to Elizabeth, *PWD,* vol. 3, 226–29.

41. *OE,* 55; "EM," 366.

42. *OE,* 55; "EM," 366.

43. On error, see "Meditation Four," *PWD,* vol. 2, 38. Modeling is pervasive in Descartes's scientific work. In the *Optics,* for instance, he considers it unnecessary to explain "the true nature" of light but offers "two or three comparisons" suitable for explaining light's observed properties and for deducing others "that we cannot observe so easily" (*PWD,* vol. 1, 152). See here Peter Galison, "Descartes' Comparisons: From the Invisible to the Visible," *Isis* 75 (1984): 311–26. Similarly, section 204 of part 4 of the *Principles of Philosophy* states, "With regard to the things which cannot be perceived by the senses, it is enough to explain their possible nature, although their actual nature may be different" (*PWD,* vol. 1, 289). I discuss the "institution of nature" in the *Optics* in chapter 3, "Mechanism, Reasoning, and the Institution of Nature," of my *Vision's Invisibles.*

44. Daniel Garber, in "Descartes' Physics," in *The Cambridge Companion to Descartes,* ed. J. Cottingham (Cambridge: Cambridge University Press, 1992), 286–334, points out that Descartes, when challenged by Henry More, admitted that he could not prove the impossibility of animal souls (303). The letter referred to, Descartes to More, February 5, 1649 (*PWD,* vol. 3, 360–67) is interesting. Notwithstanding the common "preconceived opinion" that animals think (in the inclusive sense of *penser*), he writes, we cannot prove their sentience, but neither can we disprove it, since "the human mind does not reach into their hearts." It is nonetheless more probable that they function like machines or in a manner similar to automata. The clinching point, in his view, is that animals lack language (this point is, of course, more questionable today than it was in Descartes's time). Descartes does not, he stresses, deny life to animals, "nor even

bodily sensation, insofar as it depends on a bodily organ"; but since they have no soul, one need have no "Pythagorean superstitions" or qualms about killing or eating them (365 and following). That the practitioner of methodological doubt considers probability sufficient to determine man's ethical relation to animals is astonishing.

45. *N,* 208.

46. Ibid., 20.

47. *PWD,* vol. 1, 213.

48. *PWD,* vol. 2, 10.

49. These can be found in Roger Ariew and Daniel Garber, eds. And trans., *G. W. Leibniz: Philosophical Essays* (Indianapolis: Hackett, 1989), 138–45, 213–25, 206–13. This work will henceforth be referred to as *PE.*

50. Working note of December 1959, "Leibniz," *VI,* 276/222 and following. As to the term "monad," see Donald Rutherford, "Metaphysics: The Late Period," in *The Cambridge Companion to Leibniz,* ed. Nicholas Jolley, 124–75 (see 126, n. 24).

51. *VI,* 276/222 and following.

52. Ibid.

53. See, for instance, G. W. Leibniz, *Monadology,* article 6, *PE,* 213.

54. G. W. Leibniz, "The New System," *PE,* 143 and following.

55. G. W. Leibniz, *Principles of Nature and Grace,* in *PE,* 207.

56. *VI,* 223/276.

57. Ibid., 276/222.

58. Bernhard Waldenfels, "Le paradoxe de l'expression," trans. from the German by Alain Pernet, in *Merleau-Ponty: Notes de cours sur l'origine de la géométrie de Husserl,* ed. R. Barbaras (Paris: Presses Universitaires de France, 1998), 330–48 (340); my translation.

59. Renaud Barbaras, ed., *Notes de cours,* 346 and following.

60. *VI,* 276/22 and following.

61. Ibid.

62. Leibniz to Queen Sophie Charlotte of Prussia, 1702, *PE,* 186–93 (192).

63. See G. W. Leibniz, "A Specimen of Dynamics," *PE,* 119–38. See also Daniel Garber, "Leibniz: Physics and Philosophy," in *The Cambridge Companion to Leibniz,* ed. Jolley, 270–352.

64. Leibniz, "New System ," *PE,* 143.

65. See here Leibniz, *Monadology,* article 49, *PE,* 219.

66. Working note of April 1960 titled "The Visible and the Invisible," *VI,* 295 and following/242 and following. The note includes, in the context of *Weltlichkeit,* a reference to a Husserlian text translated into French as "L'esprit collectif." See also Merleau-Ponty's working note of January 1960, *VI,* 281 and following/228, in which he criticizes Leibniz's understanding of possibility and actuality with reference to Husserl.

67. *OE,* 9 and following; "EM," 351.

68. Leibniz, "New System," *PE,* 143. For Leibniz's critical response to occasionalism, see also his "On Nature Itself" ("De ipsa natura") of 1696, which engages with the occasionalism of J. C. Sturm. For discussion, see Catherine Wilson,

Leibniz's Metaphysics: A Historical and Comparative Study (Princeton, N.J.: Princeton University Press, 1989), chapter 3 and 196 and following.

69. Leibniz, "New System," *PE*, 144.

70. See Leibniz to Volder, August 20, 1703, *PE*, 178. See also Wilson's discussion, *Leibniz's Metaphysics*, 190–96.

71. Leibniz, *Principles of Nature and Grace*, in *PE*, 207. Monads do not have extension; so it is difficult to understand how they can form a "mass."

72. *PE*, 306. The "Preface" (*PE*, 291–306) was to introduce Leibniz's response to John Locke in his *New Essays on the Understanding;* but Leibniz abandoned plans for publication when Locke died in 1704.

73. Leibniz, "New System," *PE*, 139.

74. Leibniz, *Monadology*, section 71, *PE*, 222. See Spinoza, Ethics 2 Proposition 13 with its axioms, lemmata, correlate, postulates, and scholia.

75. Leibniz, *Principles of Nature and Grace*, in *PE*, 209. Similar passages are numerous.

76. Edmund Husserl, *Cartesianische Meditationen, und Pariser Vorträge*, ed. S. Strasser (The Hague, Neth.: Nijhoff, 1950).

77. Wilson, *Leibniz's Metaphysics*, 175. Her analysis is also valuable for showing the connection of some of Leibniz's theories (including the recognition of unconscious or subconscious perceptions) to the Cambridge Platonists, especially Ralph Cudworth (whose daughter, Lady Masham, was Leibniz's correspondent).

78. *S*, 158.

Chapter 7

1. *N*, 219. The third course consists of Merleau-Ponty's own (characteristically condensed or sparse) preparatory notes, rather than of an auditor's transcript.

2. *N*, 219.

3. Barbaras, *The Being of the Phenomenon*, 42–44, 48.

4. Husserl, *Cartesianische Meditationen*, section 16, 77 (my translation).

5. *VI*, 125/166 and following.

6. *VI*, 189/144.

7. Bernhard Waldenfels, "Le paradoxe de l'expression," trans. from the German by Alain Pernet, in *Merleau-Ponty: Notes de cours sur l'origine de la géométrie de Husserl*, ed. R. Barbaras, 286–99.

8. *VI*, 173, 178/131, 134.

9. *VI*, 176/133, 173–75/131–33, 164/123.

10. Hass, *Merleau-Ponty's Philosophy*, 190.

11. Lawlor and Bergo, eds., *Husserl at the Limits*, 22. Lawlor emphasizes the theme of *Verflechtung* in his "Foreword." See also Merleau-Ponty, "The Philosopher and his Shadow," in *S*, 177.

12. *N*, 211 and following.

13. Ibid., 227.

14. Hass, *Merleau-Ponty's Philosophy*, 191.

15. Ibid.

16. *VI*, 131 and following /96 and following.

17. Ibid., 188 and following /102.

18. Ibid., 61/38.

19. Ibid., 167/126.

20. Ibid., 203/155.

21. Ibid., 180/136.

22. Working note of February 1959, *VI*, 235/183.

23. *VI*, 183/139.

24. Ibid., 184/139.

25. Emmanuel Alloa, "La chair comme diacritique incarnée," *Chiasmi International* 11 (2009): 249–62. See Didier Franck, *Chair et corps: Sur la phénoménologie de Husserl* (Paris: Editions de Minuit, 1981). See also Mauro Carbone, "Flesh: Toward the History of a Misunderstanding," *Chiasmi International* 4 (2002): 49–62.

26. See Empedocles, Fragment 21 (Diels-Kranz numbering). Nestis, "who with her tears moistens mortal springs," is thought to have been a Sicilian form of Persephone.

27. *VI*, 179/136.

28. M. Merleau-Ponty, working note of May 1969 titled "Flesh of the World—Flesh of the Body—Being," *VI*, 304/250.

29. See Hass, *Merleau-Ponty's Philosophy*, 141. See also Hass's very helpful "Appendix" to this book listing "The Multiple Meanings of Flesh in Merleau-Ponty's Writings," 201–3.

30. *VI*, 196/149.

31. Ibid., 197, 199/150 and following.

32. Martin Heidegger, "Der Ursprung des Kunstwerkes," in *Holzwege*, 4th ed. (Frankfurt, Ger.: Klostermann, 1963), 21. My translation.

33. M. Merleau-Ponty, working note of February 1959, "Genealogy of Logic, History of Being, History of Meaning," *VI*, 233/179.

34. M. Merleau-Ponty, working note of November 1960, "Nature," *VI*, 321/267. Merleau-Ponty writes: "To do a psychoanalysis of Nature: it is the flesh, the mother." See R. Vallier, "The Elemental Flesh."

35. Merleau-Ponty, working note of May 1960, "Flesh of the World—Flesh of the Body—Being," *VI*, 309/255.

36. Hass, *Merleau-Ponty's Philosophy*, 133 and following.

37. See Martin Heidegger, *Identity and Difference*. As before, I cite the German of this bilingual text, giving my own English translation.

38. Ibid., 111, 113.

39. M. Merleau-Ponty, working note of January 1960, "Problematic of the Visible and the Invisible," *VI*, 282 and following /229. See Jacques Derrida, *Memoirs of the Blind*, trans. Pascale-Anne Brault and Michael Naas (Chicago: University of Chicago Press, 1990), 32 and following.

40. M. Merleau-Ponty, working note of November 16, 1960, "Chiasm—Reversibility," *VI*, 317/263.

41. *VI*, 183/139.

42. Ibid.

43. Ibid.

44. M. Merleau-Ponty, working note of May 1959, "Husserl, *Zeitbewusstsein*," *VI*, 245/191; and working note of May 20, 1959, "(Bergson) Transcendence—Forgetting—Time," *VI*, 247/194.

45. Continuation, "on the same page," of a working note of May 1959, but with its own title: "Thought, Consciousness," *VI*, 246/192. The English translation by A. Lingis contains an error here: it reads: "a Self-presence that is not an *absence* from *oneself*," whereas the French reads: "d'une présence à Soi qui est *absence* de soi." The passage is one that requires the reader to sort out Merleau-Ponty's critique of Husserl's "idea of the time of *Empfindung*" from his own assertions.

46. M. Merleau-Ponty, working note of November 16, 1960, "Myself—the World, Myself—the Other," *VI*, 317/264.

47. M. Merleau-Ponty, working note of November 1960, "Seer—Visible," 315/262. The English translation reverses the terms of the title.

48. *VI*, 189/144.

49. It is, of course, not the case that the birth and subsequent nurture of the young are the province of the female in all species. The sea horse, for instance, is a notable exception.

50. *VI*, 190 and following /144 and following.

51. *VI*, 202 and following /154 and following.

52. Emmanuel de Saint Aubert, "Les 'différenciations d'une seule et massive adhérence à l'être qui est la chair': Etude de la notion de polymorphisme chez Merleau-Ponty," *Chiasmi International* 11 (2009): 185–200. The title contains a quotation from a working note by Merleau-Ponty of December 1960, "Body and Flesh—Eros—Philosophy of Freudianism," *VI*, 323 and following /269 and following.

53. M. Merleau-Ponty, working note of May 1960, " 'Visual Picture'—'Representation of the World' *Todo y Nada*," *VI*, 306 and following /252 and following.

54. Ibid.

55. Heidegger, *Identity and Difference*, 142. It remains to be seen, in this time of international Merleau-Ponty scholarship, whether this difficulty or obstacle, as Heidegger describes it, can be surmounted in non-Indo-Germanic languages, such as Chinese, Japanese, Korean, or Turkish.

56. Heidegger, *Identity and Difference*, 190. My translation.

57. Ibid., 194.

58. Ibid., 189.

59. *VI*, chapter 3, 165/124.

60. M. Merleau-Ponty, undated working note, "Philosophy and Literature," *VI*, 260 and following /197.

61. M. Merleau-Ponty, working note of January 1959, *VI*, 223 and following /170.

62. M. Merleau-Ponty, working note of Sunday, October 10, 1959, *VI*, 264 and following /211 and following.

63. *VI*, 198/151.

64. *OE*, 22; "EM," 355.

65. Jenny Slatman, "Phenomenology of the Icon," in *Merleau-Ponty and the Possibilities of Philosophy*, ed. Flynn et al., 197–219. Slatman's study contains an interesting comparison of Merleau-Ponty's and Jean-Luc Marion's understanding of the icon.

66. See *OE*, 87; "EM," 376.

67. *OE*, 87; "EM," 376.

68. Stéphanie Ménasé, *Passivité et création: Merleau-Ponty et l'art moderne* (Paris: Presses Universitaires de France, 2003).

69. Barbaras, *The Being of the Phenomenon*, 302 and following.

70. M. Merleau-Ponty, undated working note (probably June 1959), *VI*, 250 and following /197.

71. Barbaras, *The Being of the Phenomenon*, 235.

72. M. Merleau-Ponty, working note of January 1959, "Origin of Truth," *VI*, 120 and following /167.

73. Ibid. For a discussion of hyper-reflection, see *VI*, 61/38, 71/46.

74. Merleau-Ponty, *Phénoménologie de la perception*, viii.

75. M. Merleau-Ponty, working note of November 1960, "Politics—Philosophy—Literature," *VI*, 31 and following /266.

76. Barbaras, *The Being of the Phenomenon*, 237.

77. Ibid., 237. It is true, of course, that ideologies such as fascism also have their repercussions in art, depriving art of the pure power of saving that Heidegger wants to accord to it. This problem is not explicitly considered by Merleau-Ponty who tends, like Heidegger, to a certain idealization of art; but it is one that deserves further and vigilant study.

78. See the epigraph to the "Introduction" in this volume.

Concluding Thoughts

1. See the epigraph to the "Introduction" in this volume, taken from "An Unpublished Text by Merleau-Ponty."

2. Michel Serres, *Malfeasance*, trans. Anne-Marie Feenberg-Dibon (Stanford, Calif.: Stanford University Press, 2010), 79.

3. Hans Jonas, "Spinoza and the Theory of Organism," *Journal of the History of Philosophy* 3 (1965): 43–58. Note the emphasis on the relationship between parts and whole, which Merleau-Ponty also considers to be of central importance.

4. See his *Principles of Nature and of Grace*, and *Monadology*, 83–87, in *PE*, 211 and following and 223 and following.

Selected Bibliography

Works and Editions of Works by Merleau-Ponty

Consciousness and the Acquisition of Language. Translated by Hugh J. Silverman. Evanston, Ill.: Northwestern University Press, 1973.

Husserl at the Limits of Phenomenology, Including Texts by Edmund Husserl. Edited by Leonard Lawlor with Bettina Bergo. Evanston, Ill.: Northwestern University Press, 2002.

In Praise of Philosophy, and Other Essays. Translated by John O'Neill. Evanston, Ill.: Northwestern University Press, 1988.

L'institution dans l'histoire personelle et politique; Le problème de la passiveté, le sommeil; L'inconscient, la mémoire. Notes de cours au Collège de France. Paris: Editions Belin, *2003.*

Merleau-Ponty: Texts and Dialogues. Edited by Hugh J. Silverman and James Barry, Jr. Atlantic Highlands, N.J.: Humanities Press, 1992.

The Merleau-Ponty Aesthetics Reader: Philosophy and Painting. Edited by Galen A. Johnson and Michael B. Smith. Evanston, Ill.: Northwestern University Press, 1993.

The Merleau-Ponty Reader. Edited by Ted Toadvine and Leonard Lawlor. Evanston, Ill.: Northwestern University Press, 2007.

La nature: Notes de cours du Collège de France. Paris: Seuil, 1995. *Nature: Course Notes from the Collège de France.* Translated by Robert Vallier. Compiled and with notes by Dominique Séglard. Evanston, Ill.: Northwestern University Press, 2003.

Notes de cours sur l'origine de la géométrie de Husserl, suivi de recherches sur la phénoménologie de Merleau-Ponty. Edited by Renaud Barbaras. Paris: Presses Universitaires de France, 1998.

L'œil et l'esprit. Paris: Gallimard, 1964.

Phénoménologie de la perception. Paris: Gallimard, 1945. *Phenomenology of Perception.* Translated by Colin Smith. London: Routledge, 1962. Translation revised by Forrest Williams. Reprinted Routledge, 2002.

Le primat de la perception et ses conséquences philosophiques. Grenoble, Fr.: Cynara, 1989. *The Primacy of Perception.* Edited by and translated by James M. Edie. Evanston, Ill.: Northwestern University Press, 1964.

The Prose of the World. Edited by Claude Lefort, translated by John O'Neill. Evanston, Ill.: Northwestern University Press, 1991.

Sens et non-sens. 3rd rev. ed. Paris: Nagel, 1961. *Sense and Non-Sense.* Translated by
Hubert L. Dreyfus and Patricia Allen Dreyfus. Evanston, Ill.: Northwest-
ern University Press, 1991.
Signs. Translated by Richard C. McCleary. Evanston, Ill.: Northwestern University
Press, 1964.
The Structure of Behavior. Translated by Alden L. Fisher. Pittsburgh: Duquesne Uni-
versity Press, 2008.
L'union de l'âme et du corps chez Malebranche, Biran, et Bergson. Paris: Vrin, 1968.
Le visible et l'invisible, suivi de notes de travail. Edited by Claude Lefort. Paris: Galli-
mard, 1964. *The Visible and the Invisible.* Translated by Alphonso Lingis.
Evanston, Ill.: Northwestern University Press, 1968.

Works or Collections of Works on Merleau-Ponty

Barbaras, Renaud. *The Being of the Phenomenon: Merleau-Ponty's Ontology.* Translated
by Ted Toadvine and Leonard Lawlor. Bloomington: Indiana University
Press, 2004.
———. *Le tournant de l'expérience: Recherches sur la philosophie de Merleau-Ponty.*
Paris: Vrin, 1998.
Carbone, Mauro. *The Thinking of the Sensible: Merleau-Ponty's A-Philosophy.* Evanston,
Ill.: Northwestern University Press, 2004.
Carman, Taylor, and Mark B. N. Hansen, eds. *The Cambridge Companion to Merleau-
Ponty.* Cambridge: Cambridge University Press, 2005.
Dastur, Françoise. *Chair et langage: Essais sur Merleau-Ponty.* Fougères, Fr.: Encre
Marine, 2001.
Dillon, Martin C. *Merleau-Ponty's Ontology.* Bloomington: Indiana University Press,
1988. 2nd ed. Evanston, Ill.: Northwestern University Press, 1997.
Evans, Fred, and Leonard Lawlor, eds. *Chiasms:* Albany: State University of New
York Press, 2000.
Flynn, Bernard, Wayne J. Froman, and Robert Vallier, eds. *Merleau-Ponty and
the Possibilities of Philosophy.* Albany: State University of New York Press,
2007.
Fóti, Véronique M., ed. *Merleau-Ponty: Difference, Materiality, Painting.* Atlantic
Highlands, N.J.: Humanities Press, 1996.
Hass, Lawrence. *Merleau-Ponty's Philosophy.* Bloomington: Indiana University
Press, 2008.
Johnson, Galen A. *The Retrieval of the Beautiful: Thinking Through Merleau-Ponty's
Aesthetics.* Evanston, Ill.: Northwestern University Press, 2010.
Johnson, Galen A., and Michael B. Smith, eds. *Ontology and Alterity in Merleau-Ponty.*
Evanston, Ill.: Northwestern University Press, 1990.
Kaushik, Rajiv. *Art and Institution: Aesthetics in the Late Work of Merleau-Ponty.* Lon-
don: Continuum, 2011.
Lefort, Claude. *Sur une colonne absente: Écrits autour de Merleau-Ponty.* Paris: Galli-
mard, 1978.

Mazis, Glen A. "Merleau-Ponty's Concept of Nature: Passage, the Oneiric, and Interanimality," *Chiasmi International* 2, new series: 223–47.

Ménasé, Stéphanie. *Passivité et création: Merleau-Ponty et l'art moderne.* Paris: Presses Universitaires de France, 2003.

Pietersma, Henry, ed. *Merleau-Ponty: Critical Essays.* Washington: University Press of America, 1999.

Richir, Marc, ed. *Phénoménologie et expériences.* Grenoble, Fr.: Jérôme Millon, 2008.

Toadvine, Ted. *Merleau-Ponty's Philosophy of Nature.* Evanston, Ill.: Northwestern University Press, 2009.

Vallier, Robert. "The Indiscernible Joining: Structure, Signification, and Animality in Merleau-Ponty's *La Nature.*" *Chiasmi International* 3 (2001): 187–212.

Waldenfels, Bernhard. "Le paradoxe de l'expression," trans. from the German by Alain Pernet, in *Merleau-Ponty: Notes de cours sur l'origine de la géométrie de Husserl,* ed. Renaud Barbaras (Paris: Presses Universitaires de France, 1998), 331–48.

Journals

Chiasmi International: Trilingual Studies Concerning the Thought of Merleau-Ponty. Paris: Vrin, with Mimesis and Pennsylvania State University (formerly University of Memphis), 1999–.

Note: Articles published in *Chiasmi International* are for the most part referenced only in the notes.

Other Philosophical Works

Agamben, Giorgio. *The Open: Man and Animal.* Translated by Kevin A. Hall. Stanford, Calif.: Stanford University Press, 2004.

Benso, Silvia, and Brian Schroeder, eds. *Contemporary Italian Philosophy: Crossing the Borders of Ethics, Politics, and Religion.* Translated by Silvia Benso. Albany: State University of New York Press, 2009.

Derrida, Jacques. *De l'esprit: Heidegger et la question.* Paris: Galilée, 1987. *Of Spirit: Heidegger and the Question.* Translated by Geoff Bennington. Chicago: University of Chicago Press, 1987.

———. *Memoirs of the Blind: The Self-Portrait and Other Ruins.* Translated by Pascale-Anne Brault and Michael Naas. Chicago: University of Chicago Press, 1998.

Fóti, Véronique M. *Vision's Invisibles: Philosophical Explorations.* Albany: State University of New York Press, 2003.

Gadamer, Hans-Georg. *The Relevance of the Beautiful, and Other Essays.* Translated by Robert Bernasconi. Cambridge: Cambridge University Press, 1986.

Heidegger, Martin. *Die Grundbegriffe der Metaphysik: Welt—Endlichkeit—Einsamkeit. Gesamtausgabe* 29–30. Frankfurt, Ger.: Klostermann, 1983.

———. *Holzwege. Gesamtausgabe* 5. Edited by Friedrich Wilhelm von Hermann. Frankfurt, Ger.: Klostermann, 1977.

———. *Identität und Differenz.* Pfullingen, Ger.: Neske, 1962. *Identity and Difference.* Translated by Joan Stambaugh. Chicago: University of Chicago Press, 1969.

———. *Sein und Zeit. Gesamtausgabe* 2. Edited by Friedrich Wilhelm von Herrmann. Frankfurt, Ger.: Klostermann, 1977.

———. *Vorträge und Aufsätze,* 3 vols. Pfullingen, Ger.: Neske, 1962.

Husserl, Edmund. *Cartesianische Meditationen und Pariser Vorträge.* The Hague, Neth.: Nijhoff, 1950.

———. *The Crisis of the European Sciences and Phenomenology. An Introduction to Phenomenological Philosophy.* Translated by David Carr. Evanston, Ill.: Northwestern University Press, 1979.

Lawlor, Leonard. *Early Twentieth-Century Continental Philosophy.* Bloomington: Indiana University Press, 2012.

———. *Thinking Through French Philosophy: The Being of the Question.* Bloomington: Indiana University Press, 2003.

Mazis, Glen A. *Humans, Animals, Machines: Blurring Boundaries.* Albany: State University of New York Press, 2008.

Olkowski, Dorothea. *Gilles Deleuze and the Ruin of Representation.* Berkeley: University of California Press, 1999.

Richir, Marc. *Phénoménologie et institution symbolique.* Grenoble, Fr.: Jérôme Millon, 1998.

Sartre, Jean-Paul. *Literature and Existentialism.* Translated by Bernard Frechtmann. Secaucus, N.J.: Citadel Press, 1978.

———. *Qu'est que c'est la littérature?* Paris: Gallimard, 2001.

Schalow, Frank. *The Incarnality of Being: The Earth, Animals, and the Body in Heidegger's Thought.* Albany: State University of New York Press, 2007.

———. "Who Speaks for Animals? Heidegger and the Question of Animal Welfare." *Environmental Ethics* 22 (2000): 259–71.

Serres, Michel. *Malfeasance.* Translated by Anne-Marie Feenberg-Dibon. Stanford, Calif.: Stanford University Press, 2010.

Taminiaux, Jacques. *Dialectic and Difference: Finitude in Modern Thought.* Translated by Robert Crease and James T. Decker. Atlantic Highlands, N.J.: Humanities Press, 1985.

Weiss, Gail. *Body Images: Embodiment as Intercorporeality.* New York: Routledge, 1999.

Zajonc, Arthur, ed. *The New Physics and Cosmology: Dialogues with the Dalai Lama.* Oxford: Oxford University Press, 2004.

Works in Aesthetics and Art Theory

Beckley, Bill, and David Shapiro, eds. *Uncontrollable Beauty.* New York: Allworth, 1998.

Bryson, Norman. *Vision and Painting: The Logic of the Gaze.* New Haven, Conn.: Yale University Press, 1983.

Cachin, Françoise, Henri Loyrette, and Stéphane Guégan. *Cézanne aujourd'hui.* Paris: Réunion des Musées Nationaux, 1997.

Casey, Edward S. *Earth Mappings: Artists Reshaping Landscape.* Minneapolis: University of Minnesota Press, 2005.

Cheng, François. *Fünf Meditationen über die Schönheit.* Translated by Judith Klein. Munich: C. H. Beck, 2008.

———. *Vide et plein: Le langage pictural chinois.* Paris: Seuil, 1991.

Danto, Arthur C. *After the End of Art: Contemporary Art and the Pale of History.* Princeton, N.J.: Princeton University Press, 1997.

Doran, Michael, ed., *Conversations with Cézanne.* Translated by Julie Lawrence Cochran. Berkeley: University of California Press, 2001.

Escoubas, Eliane. *L'espace pictural.* La Versanne, Fr.: Encre Marine, 2000.

Fer, Briony. *On Abstract Art.* New Haven, Conn.: Yale University Press, 1997.

Frère, Jean-Claude. *Leonardo: Painter, Inventor, Visionary, Mathematician, Philosopher, Engineer.* Paris: Terrail, 1993.

Gasquet, Joachim. *Cézanne: A Memoir with Conversations.* Translated by Christopher Pemberton. New York: Thames and Hudson, 1991.

Guerry, Liliane. *Cézanne et l'expression de l'espace.* Paris: Flammarion, 1950.

Hacklin, Saara. *Divergencies of Perception: The Possibilities of Merleau-Pontian Phenomenology in Analyses of Contemporary Art.* Helsinki, Finland: University of Helsinki Press, 2012.

Hearn, Maxwell, ed. *Landscapes Clear and Radiant: The Art of Wang Hui (1632–1717).* New York: Metropolitan Museum of Art, 2008.

Kearney, Richard, and David Rasmussen, eds. *Continental Aesthetics: Romanticism to Postmodernism.* Malden, Mass.: Blackwell, 2000.

Kersten, Wolfgang, ed. *Paul Klee, Tagebücher, 1898–1918.* Bern, Switz.: Paul Klee Stiftung, 1988.

Kimmelman, Michael. The Accidental Masterpiece: On the Art of Life, and Vice Versa. New York: Penguin, 2005.

Lippard, Lucy. *Eva Hesse.* New York: De Capo, 1992.

Malraux, André. *Les voix du silence.* Paris: Pleïade, 1951.

Moure, Gloria, ed. *Ana Mendieta.* Barcelona: Ediciones Poligrafa, 1996.

Nancy, Jean-Luc. *The Muses.* Translated by Peggy Kamuf. Stanford, Calif.: Stanford University Press, 1996.

Panofsky, Edwin. *La perspective comme forme symbolique.* Translated by G. Ballengé. Paris: Éditions de Minuit, 1981.

Rubin, W., and L. Zelevansky, eds. *Picasso and Braque: A Symposium.* New York: Museum of Modern Art, n.d.

Sallis, John. *Shades—Of Painting at the Limit.* Bloomington: Indiana University Press, 2000.

Sidlauskas, Susan. *Cézanne's Other.* Berkeley: University of California Press, 2009.

Watkins, Jane, ed. *Cézanne.* Philadelphia: Philadelphia Museum of Art, 1996.

Youfen, Wang, ed. *Chinese Calligraphy*. New Haven, Conn.: Yale University Press, 2008.

Works in Biology and Philosophy of Biology

Atterton, Peter, and Matthew Calarco, eds. *Animal Philosophy: Ethics and Identity*. London: Continuum, 2004.
Brown, Charles, and Ted Toadvine, eds. *Eco-Phenomenology: Back to the Earth Itself*. Albany: State University of New York Press, 2003.
Buchanan, Brett. *Onto-Ethologies: The Animal Environments of Uexküll, Heidegger, Merleau-Ponty, and Deleuze*. New York: State University of New York Press, 2008.
Coghill, George E. *Anatomy and the Problem of Behavior*. Cambridge: Cambridge University Press, 1929.
De Witte, Jacques. "L'interanimalité comme intercorporéité et intervisibilité: Merleau-Ponty lecteur de Portmann." In *Colloque sous la direction de Jean Gayon et P.-F. Moreau*, 89–119. Dijon, Fr.: Université de Dijon, 1998.
Driesch, Hans. *The History and Theory of Vitalism*. Translated by C. H. Ogden. London: Macmillan, 1914.
Gesell, Arnold, and Catherine S. Amatruda. *The Embryology of Behavior: The Beginnings of the Human Mind*. Westport, Conn.: Greenwood, 1971.
Goldstein, Kurt. *The Organism: A Holistic Approach to Biology Derived from Pathological Data in Man*. New York: Zone Books, 1955.
Greene, Harry W. *Snakes: The Appearance of Mystery in Nature*. With photographs by Michael and Patricia Fogden. Berkeley: University of California Press, 1997.
Hardouin, Pierre. *Le mimétisme animal*. Paris: Presses Universitaires de France, 1946.
Jonas, Hans. *The Phenomenon of Life: Toward a New Biology*. New York: Harper and Row, 1982.
Langthaler, Rudolf. *Organismus und Umwelt: Die biologische Umweltslehre im Spiegel traditioneller Naturphilosophie*. Hildesheim, Ger.: Georg Olms Verlag, 1992.
Lorenz, Konrad. *Les animaux, les inconnus*. Paris: Éditions de Minuit, 1953.
———. *Studies on Animal and Human Behavior*. Translated by R. Martin. 2 vols. London: Methuen, 1970.
Lorenz, Konrad, and Paul Leyhausen. *Antriebe menschlichen und tierischen Verhaltens*. Munich: R. Piper, 1968.
Nouvian, Claire, ed. *The Deep: The Extraordinary Creatures of the Abyss*. Chicago: University of Chicago Press, 2007.
Portmann, Adolf. *Die Tiergestalt: Studien über die Bedeutung der tierischen Erscheinung*. 2nd rev. ed., with illustrations by Sabine Bousani-Baur. Basel, Switz.: Verlag Friedrich Reinhardt, 1960.
Russell, Edward S. *The Directiveness of Organic Activities*. Cambridge: Cambridge University Press, 1946.
Schmidt-Loske, Katharina, ed. *Maria Sibylla Merian: Insects of Surinam*. Cologne, Germany: Taschen, n.d.

Simpson, G. G. *Tempo and Mode in Evolution.* New York: Columbia University Press, 1944.

Uexküll, Jakob von. *Streifzüge durch die Umwelten von Tieren und Menschen: Ein Bilderbuch unsichtbarer Welten.* With illustrations by G. Kriszat. Berlin: Springer Verlag, 1934.

———. *Theoretische Biologie.* Berlin: Springer Verlag, 1929.

———. *Umwelt und Innenwelt der Tiere.* Berlin: Springer Verlag, 1909.

Continental Rationalism

Deleuze, Gilles. *Expressionism in Philosophy: Spinoza.* Translated by Martin Joughin. New York: Zone Books, 1992.

Descartes, René. *Œuvres et lettres,* edited by André Bridoux. Paris: Gallimard, 1953.

———. *The Philosophical Writings of Descartes.* Edited and translated by J. Cottingham, R. Stoothoff, and D. Murdoch, with translation of correspondence by Anthony Kenny. 3 vols. Cambridge: Cambridge University Press, 1985–91.

Garber, Daniel. *Descartes' Metaphysical Physics.* Chicago: University of Chicago Press, 1992.

Garrett, Don, ed. *The Cambridge Companion to Spinoza.* Cambridge: Cambridge University Press, 1996.

Gaukroger, Stephen, John Schuster, and John Sutton, eds. *Descartes' Natural Philosophy.* London: Routledge, 2000.

Grene, Marjorie, ed. *Spinoza: A Collection of Critical Essays.* Garden City, N.Y.: Doubleday Anchor, 1973.

Israel, Jonathan. *Radical Enlightenment.* Oxford: Oxford University Press, 2001.

Jolley, Nicholas, ed. *The Cambridge Companion to Leibniz.* Cambridge: Cambridge University Press, 1995.

Leibniz, Gottfried Wilhelm. *Philosophical Essays.* Edited by Roger Ariew and Daniel Garber. Indianapolis: Hackett, 1989.

Macdonald, Paul S. *Descartes and Husserl: The Philosophical Project of Radical Beginnings.* Albany: State University of New York Press, 2000.

Nader, Steven. *Spinoza: A Life.* Cambridge: Cambridge University Press, 1999.

Spinoza, Baruch (Benedict) de. *Complete Works.* Edited by Michael L. Morgan, translated by Samuel Shirley. Indianapolis: Hackett, 2002.

Wilson, Catherine. *Leibniz's Metaphysics.* Princeton, N.J.: Princeton University Press, 1989.

Woolhouse, R. S. *The Concept of Substance in Seventeenth Century Metaphysics: Descartes, Spinoza, Leibniz.* London: Routledge, 1993.

Index of Persons

Index of Topics

About the Author

Véronique M. Fóti is a professor of philosophy at the Pennsylvania State University who has written many articles on in European philosophy, continental rationalism, ancient Greek philosophy, and aesthetics. She is the author of *Epochal Discordance: Hölderlin's Philosophy of Tragedy* (2006), *Vision's Invisibles: Philosophical Explorations* (2003), and *Heidegger and the Poets: Poiēsis, Sophia, Technē* (1995); and the editor of *Merleau-Ponty: Difference, Materiality, Painting* (1996). She is also a painter, a member of the Philadelphia Society of Botanical Illustrators, and an affiliate artist at the Bellefonte Museum for Centre County in Pennsylvania.